Bad Fruits of the Civilized Tree

Indians of the Southeast

BAD FRUITS OF THE CIVILIZED TREE

ALCOHOL & THE SOVEREIGNTY OF THE CHEROKEE NATION

IZUMI ISHII

University of Nebraska Press ☙ Lincoln and London

Portions of chapters 1, 2, and 3 previously appeared in a different form as "Alcohol and Politics in the Cherokee Nation before Removal," *Ethnohistory* 50, no. 4 (Fall 2003): 671–95. Used with permission. A portion of chapter 6, "Cherokee Temperance, American Reform, and Oklahoma Statehood," previously appeared as "'Not A Wigwam Nor Blanket Nor Warwhoop': Cherokees and the Woman's Christian Temperance Union," *Journal of American and Canadian Studies* 18 (2000): 1–15. Used with permission.

Library of Congress Cataloging-in-publication Data

Ishii, Izumi, 1970–
Bad fruits of the civilized tree: alcohol and the sovereignty of the Cherokee nation / Izumi Ishii.
   p. cm.—(Indians of the Southeast)
Includes bibliographical references and index.
ISBN-13: 978-0-8032-2506-0 (cloth: alk. paper)
1. Cherokee Indians—Alcohol use—History. 2. Cherokee Indians—Rites and ceremonies. 3. Drinking of alcoholic beverages—Oklahoma—History.
4. Drinking of alcoholic beverages—Southern States—History. I. Title.
E99.C5175 2008
362.292004'970766—dc22
2007036540

Set in Adobe Caslon Pro.
Designed by A. Shahan.

For my parents, Jun and Keiko Ishii

CONTENTS

SERIES PREFACE

Bad Fruits of the Civilized Tree: Alcohol and the Sovereignty of the Cherokee Nation is a sophisticated study of political sovereignty and culture change. In this work Izumi Ishii historicizes alcohol. She examines the ways in which the Cherokees incorporated drinking into their culture in the eighteenth century, and she explores how the regulation of alcohol became a hotly contested issue in the nineteenth century. On the one hand, charges of drunkenness shaped an unflattering image of Indians and invited U.S. interference in Cherokee affairs. On the other hand, Cherokee temperance societies and laws governing the sale and consumption of alcohol presented an opportunity for Cherokees to demonstrate how "civilized" they were and to exercise their sovereign right to govern themselves. Ultimately temperance became the avenue by which Cherokee women, disenfranchised early in the nineteenth century, reentered the political arena only to be betrayed along with their nation by the movement that gave them a voice. Ishii has constructed a wonderful social and political history, but even more important, she subtly has challenged much of the conventional wisdom about Native Americans and alcohol. She avoids the trap of moral judgment about Native drinking and demonstrates that drinking patterns, attitudes about alcohol, and the effects of alcohol in Native communities are historical and change over time. Although a great deal has been written on Indians and alcohol, no one has ever done anything quite like this, and we welcome *Bad Fruits of the Civilized Tree* to the series Indians of the Southeast.

Theda Perdue
Michael D. Green
University of North Carolina

ACKNOWLEDGMENTS

I first encountered Cherokee history in my sophomore year at Sophia University, Tokyo, Japan. Since then, a number of professors, colleagues, and friends have both intellectually and personally assisted me in my efforts to contribute to our understanding of that history. Without their immeasurable support and encouragement, I would not have completed this work. First and foremost I would like to thank my graduate school mentors Theda Perdue and Michael D. Green, for faithfully directing my academic work. Consistently expressing genuine interest in my work, Green guided me with fatherly support and encouragement as well as insightful and invaluable advice. Perdue urged me to work hard and accomplish my goal with her loving "carrot-and-stick approach" (as she calls it) and great patience. Her motherly love and giggles have saved me on numerous occasions from reaching a dead end in my graduate life and even after. I am greatly indebted to both of them. They have constantly cultivated and reinforced my self-confidence, and they continue to inspire me. I will carry with me the lessons I have learned from them throughout my academic career.

I also wish to thank the scholars who served on my doctoral committee. Ronald D. Eller, Kathi Kern, Armando J. Prats, Tom Appleton, and Richard W. Jefferies kindly read the whole manuscript of the original dissertation and offered me instructive suggestions and comments that enabled me to turn the dissertation into a book. I also appreciate the guidance of Professor Kazuyuki Matsuo at Sophia University, whose classes introduced me to the history of the Cherokee Indians, and of Professor Randall M. Miller, who, while I was studying as an exchange student at St. Joseph's University, Philadelphia, recommended that I pursue graduate work with Perdue and Green.

I would like to express my gratitude to the Rotary Foundation and the P.E.O. Sisterhood for supporting my graduate education at the University of Kentucky. A grant from the Phillips Fund for Native American Research from the American Philosophical Society and grants from the Department of History and the Graduate School at the University of Kentucky generously financed archival research outside the Lexington area. I deeply appreciate the assistance of the staff in the Department of Special Collections at the University of Tulsa; the Oklahoma Historical Society; the Western History Collections at the University of Oklahoma; the Gilcrease Institute of American History and Art, Tulsa; the Frances E. Willard Memorial Library, Evanston, Illinois; the Houghton Library of Harvard University; and Wider Church Ministries of the United Church of Christ. Throughout the years of my graduate studies at the University of Kentucky I received friendly and supportive assistance from librarians in the M. I. King and the newly constructed William T. Young libraries. Among those to whom I am especially indebted are Brad Carrington and Danice Nutter.

I am grateful to my fellow graduate students who welcomed me to a vibrant intellectual community. Special words of appreciation go to James Taylor Carson, Greg O'Brien, David A. Nichols, Tim Garrison, Karl Davis, Caroline E. Light, Rose Stremlau, Malinda Maynor Lowery, and Cary Miller. I also wish to thank Ginny Carney, who, particularly at the earliest stage of the writing process, carefully and patiently read drafts and shared the stories of her people. I would like to express my gratitude also to my Japanese friends whom I encountered at Sophia University and at the University of Kentucky. Special thanks go to Shoko Manabe, Miya Sato, Megumi Aiuchi, Sei Obuse, Mami W. Hirota, and Chihoko Noma. I am grateful to my brother, Ken Ishii, as well.

Upon completion of my graduate studies at the University of Kentucky, the Japan Society for the Promotion of Science awarded me a postdoctoral fellowship that afforded me the time and space to continue to work with Perdue and Green as a visiting scholar at the University of North Carolina at Chapel Hill. Back in Japan, the Institute of American and Canadian Studies at Sophia University, the Kansai Forum for Japan–United States Intellectual Exchange in Osaka, and my colleagues in the Institute for Language and Culture at Doshisha University, Kyoto, provided me with opportunities to present portions of this project. I would also like to express my appreciation to both the editorial staff at the University of Nebraska Press, who always dealt graciously with the difficulties posed by having an author on the other side of the Pacific, and the anonymous reviewers for the press.

My deepest appreciation goes to my parents, Jun and Keiko Ishii. Without their genuine support, faith, and love, I would not have been so motivated and enthusiastic about the Cherokee Indians and pursuing a graduate degree in the United States. I am proud of my parents, and I feel truly honored to be their daughter. I owe them so much that I cannot express my full gratitude to them, but I would like to dedicate this work to my parents as a token. Along with the Indian spirits, which have led me to the old Cherokee world, my parents have offered me the inspiration and ways to live my lifelong dream wherever I am and wherever I go.

Bad Fruits of the Civilized Tree

Introduction

Before European contact, Native people of North America, with a few exceptions, had virtually no knowledge of alcohol.[1] Early European accounts of Indian drinking, however, suggest that once Indians acquired a taste for liquor, it functioned as an agent of European conquest. Through the gift and trade of liquor, Europeans disrupted Native societies and threatened to destroy them. Simultaneously, Indians' inebriation appalled European observers, who quickly incorporated alcohol into their myths about Native behavior. By prohibiting the sale and consumption of alcohol among Indians in the early nineteenth century, the U.S. government politicized this image, gave it "official recognition," and helped perpetuate it.[2] The image of drunken Indians has had a powerful influence on the lives of Native people. Furthermore, this deep-rooted notion of Indian drunkenness has overwhelmed scholars who study Native Americans and has prevented them from making an objective analysis of alcohol in Indian societies and cultures.[3] Although Indian historians all agree that "ardent spirits," a product of the European encounter, have posed a threat to Native American societies for centuries, none of them has explored specifically the issues of alcohol — its use, abuse, and control — among a particular Native people. This study traces the history of alcohol among the Cherokees from the colonial period to Oklahoma statehood in 1907 and examines the ways in which the Cherokees integrated alcohol into their society and used it both culturally and strategically. Although this book does not directly address the stereotype of drunken Indians, the study reveals the complexity of Indian drinking and presents an alternative framework for examining Indians and alcohol.

Anthropologists have attempted to refute the "firewater myths" that Indians inordinately crave alcohol and, when drunk, exhibit various deviant behaviors that are racially explicable. Edwin M. Lemert's intensive fieldwork in the early 1950s resulted in a widely accepted work on drinking among Northwest Coast Indians. Lemert argued that heavy drinking was a form of protest by Indians along the coast. When Native people faced Anglo-Americans' attacks on their traditions and tribal institutions in the mid-nineteenth century, they retaliated by abusively drinking alcohol, which helped them validate their social status and revitalize old leadership patterns and rituals.[4] Lemert also observed: "The number of coastal Indians whose drinking is sufficiently prolonged and excessive enough to be called pathological is decidedly small."[5] Although they were aware of the ruinous effects of alcohol on their societies, the coastal Indians never internalized the Anglo-American concept of the evil of drunkenness and the desirability of temperance. Less acculturated Indians drank alcohol to excess largely to fight back against missionaries who condemned their "heathenism" as well as intemperance, and many regarded drinking as a positive experience and did not consider it to be morally wrong.[6]

To many anthropologists, the question of *why* Indians drink seems to have been of more scholarly importance than the question of *how* Indians drink.[7] A popular theory among these scholars emphasizes the presence of "anomie," that is, social instability and cultural loss, in Native societies. Massive culture change and cultural disorientation caused frustration and a decline in prestige, particularly, of the male members of the tribe and led many to drink. Inebriation, as the theory ran, provided a temporary respite from the fear of deculturation. Anthropologist John H. Hamer, for example, argued that acculturation deprived Potawatomi men of all traditional, socially acceptable means of expressing aggression and retaining authority. In a society in which women increasingly enjoyed enhanced status and openly showed resentment toward men, only inebriation seemed to promise men the position they once had enjoyed over women.[8] Noting the adaptability of the Potawatomi men, however, Hamer concluded that the people in the community regarded this adaptive aspect of frequent heavy drinking as "outweighing the social costs."[9] Anthropologist Edward P. Dozier also used the anomie theory to examine excessive drinking patterns among Native Americans, but he observed that Indians were aware of alcohol-related problems and that they attempted to solve drinking problems themselves.[10] Contending that Indians were "primarily a social entity rather than a biological unit," Dozier made an important contribution to the study of alcohol among Native Americans that helped rectify the prevailing notion that Indians were racially susceptible to heavy drinking.[11]

While the concepts of anomie and escapism captivated many anthropologists, Craig MacAndrew and Robert B. Edgerton published, in 1969, a groundbreaking work, *Drunken Comportment*. Examining the ways in which Indians acted under the influence of alcohol, this psychologist-anthropologist team argued that Indians observed the "drunken changes-for-the-worse" behavior of Euro-American traders, trappers, and intruders and then incorporated into their societies not only liquor but also the drunken actions of those people who introduced alcohol to them. Furthermore, the purveyors of liquor demonstrated how to excuse such acts by blaming alcohol. Native people culturally patterned their drunken comportment after the non-Indians they knew on the frontier, and within these culturally defined limits, they behaved "disorderly" without transgressing widely acknowledged parameters.[12]

Two years later, anthropologist Nancy Oestreich Lurie presented a provocative discussion of Native American alcohol use. Lurie regarded Indian drinking as a politically oriented act and called it "The World's Oldest On-Going Protest Demonstration."[13] Lurie suggested that Native Americans had internalized the image, though negative, of the drunken Indians to assert and validate Indianness in an Anglo-American-dominated society. Discrediting the anomie or dependency theory, Lurie argued that Native Americans used alcohol as an effective weapon to unite themselves and appear to the American public as a culturally recognizable ethnic group. Whether or not this protestation reinforced the negative image of their people, Lurie contended, the exhibition of drunkenness "remains a very Indian thing to do when all else fails to maintain the Indian-white boundary."[14]

In 1974, Jerrold E. Levy and Stephen J. Kunitz joined the MacAndrew-Edgerton camp. Examining Navajo drinking patterns as well as those of the Hopis and White Mountain Apaches, the anthropologist-physician pair observed that the drunken comportment of Indians was considered "deviant" because "moral entrepreneurs" labeled it as such and that they quickly diagnosed those inebriated Indians who behaved disorderly as alcoholics.[15] Challenging the anomie theory, Levy and Kunitz maintained that an escapist response to frustration caused by acculturation pressure failed to explain Indian drunkenness.[16] Reinforcing MacAndrew and Edgerton's "within-limits clause," they concluded that drinking behaviors of Indians reflected culturally valued traditional forms, not social disorientation, and that Native people, even when they appeared to be disorderly to outsiders, drank in culturally acceptable ways.[17] Recognizing differences in drinking patterns among the tribes under study, Levy and Kunitz noted that the hunting-and-gathering societies—the Navajos and Apaches—valued individual prowess and that they rarely controlled individual aggressiveness and self-assertion. Consequently, they tolerated excessive drinking better than the Hopis. Furthermore, their belief in supernatural power gave a positive meaning to alcohol, which seemed to induce an ecstatic state.[18]

While MacAndrew and Edgerton analyzed the "drunken comportment" paradigm, anthropologist Joy Leland examined the "craving" motif that, along with the Indians' "drunk and disorderly" image, composed the firewater myths. By surveying the ethnographic literature on Native American drinking, which increasingly advocated that "alcohol addiction is actually rare in the Indian groups they have studied," Leland argued against the widely held belief in Indians' genetic susceptibility to alcoholism.[19] As Leland observed, lack of agreement on the definition of alcohol addiction and alcoholism further exacerbated the perpetuation of the firewater myths.[20] She recognized that refutation of the "craving" motif would not lead to the total demise of the myths, and she herself acknowledged that problem drinking existed among Native people.[21] Nevertheless, Leland's extensive review of the secondary literature revealed rather uniform views of scholars on Indian drinking.[22]

By the early 1980s, anthropologists had largely reached a consensus on Indian alcohol use. When Indians drink, they behave "disorderly" within their own cultural framework, and, therefore, heavy drinking is a culturally accepted form among Indian tribes. Rather than alleviating frustration that many Indians suffer because of acculturation and social disorientation, alcohol substitutes for traditional aspects of Native culture that they can no longer enjoy. Alcohol addiction and alcoholism are uncommon among Indians.

In 1984, sociologist Robin Room criticized these anthropologists for their tendency to "minimize the seriousness of drinking problems in the tribal and village cultures under discussion." With contention that "the patterns they observed did not fit North American or European disease concepts of alcoholism," Room insisted, the unwillingness of these anthropologists to fully appreciate alcohol problems in Indian societies caused a huge gap "between the ethnographic and other alcohol literatures."[23] As psychoneurologist Jacek Moskalewicz of Poland noted, however, "problem deflation" had resulted primarily from the disparate intellectual contexts in which anthropologists and scholars in other disciplines examined Indian drinking. Anthropologists did not necessarily underestimate problem drinking of Native people. They merely attempted to understand Indian drinking and alcohol use from the Natives' perspectives.[24] Anthropologist Jack O. Waddell demonstrated, for example, that such scholarly endeavors required balanced assessment of historical documents that often reflected the ethnocentric views and biases of the observers. Through his work Waddell revealed that the quantitative data that Francois Victor Malhiot, a Northwest Company fur trader, recorded in his journal of 1804–1805 among the Lac du Flambeau Chippewa did not support Malhiot's claim that Native people inordinately craved alcohol and abusively consumed it.[25]

Historians gradually have entered the debate. As the authority on colonial Indian-European encounters, James Axtell, has pointed out, the introduction of alcohol into Indian societies did not lead to their immediate demise and detribalization. Axtell described the Montagnais on the north shore of the St. Lawrence River who received biscuits and wine from the French: "The natives were appalled that these people 'drank blood and ate wood' and promptly threw the tasteless biscuits into the river."[26]

Although alcohol did not necessarily seduce Indians at first, it became a valuable commodity when Europeans began to trade with them. Presenting the first book-length attempt by a historian to examine the effects of alcohol on Indian societies in colonial America, Peter C. Mancall described how British traders and officials strategically employed alcohol in Indian country. He argued that in the latter half of the seventeenth century, colonial traders began providing rum to Native people in order to profit from the fur and deerskin trade. As Mancall has observed, Native Americans were not "passive victims" of European traders, and they eagerly sought alcohol. Although British officials gradually recognized the ruinous effects of alcohol on Native societies, they never agreed on an entire prohibition against its flow. Because they regarded Indians as faithful subjects of the empire and major participants in a trans-Atlantic commercial economy, British authorities did not know how to eliminate alcohol from the Indian trade. Colonial officials, moreover, felt compelled to maintain the allegiance of their Native allies. They encouraged alcohol gift giving to counteract French influence among the Indians, while the traders sold vast quantities of rum to them.[27]

The deerskin trade with South Carolinians in the early eighteenth century brought alcohol into Cherokee country. John Phillip Reid and Tom Hatley, who study colonial

Cherokee society, have observed, in Hatley's words, that "the full negative impact of alcohol consumption on the Cherokees and other large interior tribes appears to have come later."[28] Hatley, moreover, took a further step and argued that "drunkenness was a political statement" particularly among young Cherokee men. Cherokee warriors "distinctively connected" alcohol and body painting "to the missions of young manhood," he contended, and they prepared themselves for war with alcohol. The young men drank to excess because "Drinking was a way of not socializing, of removing oneself from control." Drunken Cherokees also learned to excuse their disorderly behaviors by blaming a third party.[29] The Cherokees in colonial America, therefore, found positive meanings in alcohol. In this book, I have further explored the connection of manliness and alcohol by examining how Cherokees incorporated alcohol into their culture as well as the ways in which they obtained and consumed alcohol.

Between the Revolutionary and early republic eras, the Cherokees found their lives increasingly threatened by Euro-American rivalry. When wars with Europeans finally ended in 1794, they faced the devastating loss of their people, hunting grounds, homes, farmlands, and lucrative deerskin trade. Although the newly established U.S. government encouraged Cherokee men to become farmers by exchanging their bows and arrows for hoes and plows, it was a bitter pill for them to swallow. William G. McLoughlin defined these difficult years from 1794 to 1810 as ones of "Cherokee anomie" and argued that distressed Cherokee men drank heavily, with many engaging in horse stealing, to ease their anger and frustration as well as replicate the feelings they had enjoyed as hunters and warriors.[30] McLoughlin contended that these years of confusion at the turn of the nineteenth century "were critical in every Native American tribe." While the Senecas spiritually revitalized themselves under the direction of a visionary prophet, Handsome Lake, the Cherokees underwent secular and, particularly, political revitalization.[31] The Senecas' loss of confidence in their traditional lifestyles led to the rise of Handsome Lake, who condemned alcohol; the Cherokees' inability to recover their traditional ways of life resulted in their political, economic, and social revitalization.[32] Unlike Richard White's Choctaw Nation, which by the end of the eighteenth century had become increasingly dependent on Euro-Americans and alcohol, many Cherokees, under the guidance of federal agents and missionaries, gradually accepted, in their own ways, the Anglo-American ideology and lifestyle.[33] McLoughlin calls this process the "Cherokee renascence."[34] Sequoyah's invention of the Cherokee syllabary in the early 1820s and its enthusiastic adoption by his countrymen made the Cherokees a literate people. In 1828, they began to publish a bilingual weekly newspaper, the *Cherokee Phoenix*. In mission schools, Cherokee children learned reading, writing, and American lifestyles and customs. Some converted to Christianity, and Christian religious values spread over the Nation. Many accepted the American farming system, and some even acquired African American slaves as southern planters were doing.[35] The Cherokees established a central government and became a republic with a written constitution.

During these prosperous decades of the early nineteenth century, the Cherokees also confronted a variety of social problems caused by excessive drinking. "Poisoned by the bad fruits of the Civilized tree," the Cherokees embraced temperance, and the Cherokees' temperance movement became an integral part of the "Cherokee renascence."[36] The Cherokees' early attempts to regulate alcohol began with the elimination of noncitizens from the tribal alcohol market in

1819. Well before the Cherokees became aware of the disruptive consequences of alcohol abuse to their society, the federal government had attempted to control the liquor trade in Indian country. As Francis Paul Prucha's study of federal Indian policy demonstrated, the U.S. government could never entirely prohibit the flow of alcohol among Indians.[37] The more intense the pressure of the federal and neighboring state governments, the more the Cherokees felt compelled to demonstrate that they, as a "civilized" and sovereign nation, could solve their drinking problems themselves.

Indian removal exacerbated alcohol-related problems when states extended their laws, which did not regulate alcohol, over the Cherokee Nation. Alcohol accompanied the Cherokees on the Trail of Tears and contributed to the factional strife of 1839 to 1846 in the new country. The Cherokees during this period sought to attain political unity and social harmony through temperance. Grant Foreman, in *The Five Civilized Tribes*, discussed the Cherokees' reforming efforts in the trans-Mississippi West and described the participation of Cherokee children in the Cold Water Army, but he considered temperance to be merely a social phenomenon during the idyllic decade of the 1850s.[38] In his classic study of Cherokee political history between 1839 and 1907, moreover, Morris L. Wardell concluded: "The temperance societies that flourished before the Civil War seem never to have been revived."[39]

The Cherokees' temperance movement, however, did not die out with the American Civil War. Their efforts were still inextricably intertwined with their exercise of sovereignty. McLoughlin explicitly characterized the years between 1839 and 1880 as *"the Cherokees' struggle for sovereignty,"* but he failed to discuss the temperance movement, which continued to function as a vital tactic for preserving the integrity of the Cherokee people.[40] The Cherokees' temperance efforts in the postbellum period document the incorporation of the movement into the broader national crusade of the late nineteenth century and the role prohibition played in the demise of the Cherokee Nation. This book examines the Cherokees' adoption of alcohol and their embrace of the temperance movement from a number of perspectives: cultural accommodation and persistence, federal Indian policy, philanthropic goals, Cherokee sovereignty, national reform movements, and the changing roles of women. It demonstrates that the history of alcohol among the Cherokees was not simply a narrative of the conquest and destruction of Native society. The role of alcohol was far more complicated than that.

1

Alcohol Arrives

The Cherokees had no tradition of alcohol consumption, so the history of alcohol among the Cherokees begins with its introduction by Europeans. To the purveyors of spirits, the Indians' consumption of alcohol appeared to support the Europeans' view of Native Americans as profligate and irrational. In the mid-eighteenth century, for example, John Gerar William De Brahm, surveyor general for the southern department, wrote about Native people's "love [of] strong Liquors, especially Rum or Brandy, at all times, which they prefer to anything in the World."[1] A closer look at the ways in which the Cherokees incorporated alcohol into their tribal life, however, reveals a range of responses that suggest more than simple addiction. If some Cherokees used liquor only to get drunk, others sought in it the power and prestige they associated with the exotic goods supplied by European traders. Alcohol found niches in Cherokee culture that the Europeans neither expected nor understood. These uses can tell us much about cultural persistence and change.

The deerskin trade and diplomacy were the conduit by which alcohol was first introduced to the Cherokees. The Cherokees initially regarded alcohol, like other items received from colonial officials and traders, to be an exotic good, and as such, it had spiritual power. Like other southern Indians, the Cherokees considered their towns to be sacred circles where kinship bound individuals together, rituals maintained spiritual harmony, and chiefs arbitrated between opposing forces by exercising spiritual power. The font of power lay in worlds beyond the sacred circle—in the upperworld, where the secrets of the past resided, and in the underworld, which controlled the future.[2] Similarly, in this world, the chaotic realm outside the reach of kin, ritual, or chiefly power represented a source of spiritual power, often in the form of exotic goods to which headmen attributed esoteric meaning.[3] Indigenous trade in the Southeast must be understood in this context. Foreign goods had value that Native people did not measure in solely material terms.

Cherokees may well have considered alcohol to be analogous to yaupon, a holly that grew outside their territory that they used to make a ceremonial beverage. Cherokees used this caffeinated, nonalcoholic beverage on various occasions, and they consumed it in highly ritualized ceremonial settings.[4] Since yaupon did not grow in Cherokee country, the Cherokees traditionally obtained it through trade with Indian groups on coastal areas.[5] The Cherokees had an indigenous exchange network through which they procured the sacred plant. The trade in yaupon as well as other Native goods meant that Cherokees had a well-established pattern of exchange into which they could fit the European traders who came into their country in increasing numbers in the eighteenth century and the goods, including alcohol, that these traders brought with them.

Cherokees do not seem to have consumed black drink, as the ceremonial beverage has come to be called, in the quantity that other southern Indians did, perhaps because yaupon did not grow within their mountainous territory.[6] Still, all public rituals demanded the consumption of spiritually purifying medicine, and in addition to black drink the Cherokees brewed medicine from other herbs.[7] Lt. Henry Timberlake, for example, observed the preparation of medicinal drink in the Cherokee country in the early 1760s: "Muttering something to herself," the beloved woman, a highly honored position, brewed the tea from "a shrub-like laurel." A group of Cherokee men invited Timberlake to join them in drinking what he described as "a spiritual medicine" to "wash away their sins."[8]

In Cherokee medicine making, evergreens almost certainly formed a key ingredient.[9] Cherokees considered evergreens anomalies of nature because they retained their leaves or needles in winter. Anomalies possessed spiritual power, and the Cherokees believed that evergreens were "greatest for medicine."[10] The purpose of taking medicine, therefore, was the acquisition of spiritual purity and power and not merely physical healing.

Native men in the Southeast consumed black drink and other spiritual medicines in ceremonial settings. In the council, Cherokee men took medicine and smoked tobacco to solidify friendship and peace and to obtain spiritual power. The preparation for male activities such as warfare and stickball, "the little brother of war," required spiritual and physical purity as well as the prowess attained through consumption of ritual decoctions.[11] The Green Corn Ceremony also demanded four days of purification with medicine immediately before the festivities.[12] Without ceremonial medicine, Native people would not go to war, play ball, or celebrate their annual Green Corn Ceremony.[13] Early use of alcohol among the Cherokees almost always took place in a similar ritual context, and liquor became a corollary to black drink and other spiritual medicines.[14] The terms for "alcohol" and "medicine" in colonial Cherokee society linguistically overlapped, and the word *nawohti*, meaning "medicine," came to signify alcohol as well.[15]

The gift of alcohol to chiefs by Europeans probably contributed to the Cherokees' conception of it as a powerful and sacred substance. Just as the South Carolina commissioners of the Indian trade in 1718 sent a gift of rum to Charitey Hagey in "Remembrance of Friendship," Indian headmen on diplomatic missions often received alcohol from British authorities as a token of hospitality.[16] James Adair, who traded among southeastern Indians from the 1730s to the late 1760s, described this practice as "a custom with the colony of South-Carolina towards those Indians who came on a friendly visit."[17] Legal historian John Phillip Reid has suggested that colonists interpreted the gifts of rum and other goods they gave to be "bribes offered to greedy beggars" and the presents they received as "marks of respect toward" the superior British authorities.[18] Cherokee headmen, on the other hand, probably interpreted the exchange of gifts in terms of reciprocity. Gift exchange expressed respect, confirmed alliances, and symbolized the equality that Indians believed existed between themselves and the English. Chiefs then redistributed the goods they received to others in the community as a demonstration of chiefly authority.[19] Rather than having a disruptive effect on Cherokee society, the redistribution of alcohol, particularly in a ceremonial context, helped headmen retain and solidify their power.

South Carolinians recognized that Native consumption of alcohol was not necessarily a good thing, and officials tried to limit its use to occasions of diplomacy. Drunken Indians could not hunt, and they were more likely to engage in random acts of violence along the frontier; the presence of alcohol also increased the likelihood that traders would cheat and abuse their Native customers, provoking complaints and retaliation. Consequently, in 1707 a regulatory act prohibited the sale of alcohol to Indians.[20] This regulation was one of a series of measures intended to ease relations between Native people and Carolina traders, which were extraordinarily tense in the early eighteenth century. Unscrupulous trading practices ultimately precipitated the Yamassee War of 1715–1716, which involved virtually all southern Indians except the Cherokees. The war brought the deerskin trade to a halt, claimed the lives of most European traders, and threatened the very survival of Carolina. Following the war, the South Carolina commissioners of the Indian trade struggled to reestablish commerce, and in 1716, they made the Indian trade a public monopoly.[21]

South Carolina traders had engaged in little direct trade with the Cherokees at this period, and so the 1707 regulation primarily affected Indian middlemen, such as the Catawbas, through whom the trade flowed. The Yamassee War largely destroyed this trade, and Carolinians sought to revitalize their economy by trading directly with the Cherokees.[22] Unsettled conditions in Indian country, however, rendered the transport of skins from Cherokee towns to Charlestown extremely dangerous. Although the Cherokees had not been directly involved in the war, packhorse trains bound to and from Cherokee country were vulnerable to attacks, especially from Creeks, with whom Cherokees had long been enemies. Consequently the South Carolina commissioners of the Indian trade, who managed to retain the public trade until 1721, decided that it was simply "too dangerous to send pack Horses to the Charikees."[23] Instead they proposed to employ Cherokee men as porters to carry packs of deerskins weighing forty to fifty pounds to Fort Moore in Savannah Town, six miles below present-day Augusta, Georgia, on the east bank of the Savannah River.[24] At first the Cherokees balked.

They were reluctant to expose themselves to Creek enemies and endanger their lives. To encourage the Cherokees, the commissioners promised to construct another trading factory with a garrison at the Congarees, a site closer to the Cherokees, if in the meantime they would bring skins to Fort Moore.[25] As an added incentive, the commissioners ruled that alcohol would be available only at Fort Moore.[26] The shift in policy on alcohol sales to Indians, according to John Phillip Reid, was intended to promote colonial security and economic gain rather than protect Indian welfare.[27]

Alcohol provided a powerful incentive. Cherokee factor Theophilus Hastings, who lived in the Cherokee country, notified the commissioners that Cherokee porters would not come to Savannah Town "except for Rum."[28] The rum they received at the end of their journey, "according to the Custom," was supposed to be "one third Part Water," but the local factor violated custom.[29] The Indians complained that there was "too much Water in the Rum," and the commissioners instructed their employee to use a more "convenient Proportion."[30] Hardly dupes of corrupt traders, Cherokee porters knew that the commissioners needed their transport as well as their skins, and so they used their favorable position to acquire the sort of rum they expected.

Even when distributed in the appropriate strength, however, alcohol did not, in the end, provide sufficient inducement. The Cherokees had only a limited demand for rum, which they consumed socially during their brief stay at Fort Moore or ritually when they returned to their towns. The restricted availability of alcohol, in fact, may have enhanced its ritual role more than if it had been sold widely in Cherokee towns. In any event, access to alcohol at Savannah Town failed to produce the number of porters the commissioners desired. As early as November 1717, Chief Assistant Factor

William Hatton expressed to the board his concern that the province would soon be unable to obtain Cherokee porters because they refused to come down the trading paths.[31] The burdener system virtually collapsed, and in June 1718, the commissioners began hiring local Carolinians to organize packhorse caravans to Indian country.[32]

The initial stage of regular commercial and diplomatic contact with Europeans did not automatically lead to a besotted Cherokee community. There was no strong Cherokee demand for alcohol, and it ultimately served as an unsatisfactory inducement to Cherokees to transport skins. The limited impact of rum stemmed in part from its association with chiefly power, confirmed in the gift of alcohol headmen received during diplomatic visits or negotiations. Furthermore, with alcohol primarily available at Fort Moore, its nonritualized consumption took place largely outside Cherokee country. When private trade entirely replaced the government monopoly in 1721, however, many "poor, loose and vagabond" traders entered Cherokee territory.[33] They brought rum with them, and alcohol began to threaten the internal harmony of the Cherokee community.

An act of 1723 stipulated that once a trader was issued a South Carolina license, he was free to start his business in the Cherokee country. By simply adding names on the back of his own license, the principal trader could employ two packhorsemen and send them, as his agents, to other towns. When he wished to hire more, he paid ten pounds for each and purchased licenses for the additional packhorsemen.[34] According to Col. George Chicken, commissioner of the Indian trade (1724–1731), these packhorsemen became "the Sole Means of Spoiling the Indians as well as the Trade." Within the boundaries of the Cherokee country in 1725, Chicken found "three times the Traders, the persons Inserted therein being on the same ffooting as the Principal."[35] The situation Chicken described in the 1720s worsened over the succeeding decades. In 1751, sixteen licensed traders of South Carolina were operating in the Cherokee country; after five years, the number rose to approximately one hundred and fifty traders and packhorsemen among the tribe.[36] Although provincial authorities considered many of these to be "Persons of neither Sense or Substance, nor Character," they did not take precautions against these reprobates and allowed them to remain unchecked among the southeastern Indian tribes.[37]

These traders and packhorsemen made alcohol more widely available to Cherokees in their own country, and they personally demonstrated how to consume casually vast quantities of alcohol. Eighteenth-century Europeans were not teetotalers, and excessive drinking by traders and packhorsemen in nonceremonial settings presented many Cherokees with a new model of behavior where alcohol was concerned.[38] Even John Stuart, the Indian superintendent for the Southern District of North America (1762–1779), did not serve as a good example for responsible drinking, at least in terms of modern sensibilities. The former French agent at Mobile, Chevalier Montaut de Monberaut, described Stuart's alcohol consumption: "Drinking had a peculiar effect on the Superintendent. He often drank all night. Usually he could hardly walk for the gout, but when the bacchic enthusiasm prevailed, he could dance long and violently to the music of instruments, and resembled a man bitten by a tarantula."[39] The Cherokees probably did not abandon old uses of alcohol, but following the example of Stuart and others, they grafted onto them casual drinking, prodigious consumption, and uninhibited behavior.[40]

Having witnessed excessive drinking in Indian country,

James Adair criticized traders who dispensed alcohol among Indians in the woods and hunting camps and lamented that Native people "sell even their wearing shirt[s] for inebriating liquors."[41] Adair observed that they "often transform[ed] themselves by liquor into the likeness of mad foaming bears," pulled off the "big ears" of one another in a drinking match, and, later when they became sober, sewed them together.[42] Adair recognized that such mindless actions on the part of some traders disgraced the reputations of their sober colleagues while disrupting Native societies. Nevertheless, in the spring of 1750, Adair himself, together with his "brave cheerful companion," Henry Foster, brought two kegs of rum into the Cherokee town of Keowee.[43] Trader David Dowey, who happened to meet with them on his way back home from the Overhill towns several months later, concluded that "Adair did no good there." Having lived in the Cherokee country for thirty-two years, Dowey could no longer bear to see traders "come in with Rum having neither License or Goods, and go from Town to Town selling their Rum, and spreading Lyes and bad News."[44]

The illicit liquor trade threatened to disrupt legitimate commerce. Many traders extended credit to Cherokee hunters and let them buy as many kinds of goods as they wanted. When rum sellers appeared in town, many men chose to exchange their mortgaged skins for rum rather than to settle their debts, and they found themselves even more deeply in debt when they obtained further credit to purchase goods. Many suffered from the vicious circle of soaring debts and alcohol abuse, and many hunters blamed unscrupulous traders for their plight. In the spring of 1745, Cherokee warrior Niconass appeared at a council in Charlestown and petitioned the colonial government to permit the Cherokees to regulate liquor sales by traders. Niconass complained that traders, "without a License," came into villages, sold rum, "snatche[d] the Skins away from us," and drove Cherokees into "jug Debts." Niconass did not "lay [*sic*] that we should be wholly without Rum," but he believed that his people should "have Liberty to seize" illicit liquor.[45] Governor of South Carolina James Glen (1743–1756) ignored the warrior's request. Ultimately the Cherokees' resentment against the traders flared into crisis in 1751.

Several separate incidents signaled the Indians' growing hostility toward traders. In March 1750, a group of Lower town Cherokees, in searching for a party of Chickasaws with whom they were at war, broke into William Clements's store on the Oconee River, burned it, and shot Clements's servant Jeremiah Swiney to death.[46] Then in the winter of 1750–1751, James Francis, justice of the peace at Saluda, refused to help a group of Cherokees who claimed that colonists had robbed them of three hundred deerskins; Francis believed that these Cherokees were lying in order to evade paying the leather they owed trader James Beamer.[47] Finally Cherokees at Sticoe raided Bernard Hughs's store in the spring of 1751, and tensions between South Carolina and the Cherokee country reached the breaking point.[48]

Although the Cherokees apologized for this last act, claiming "it was like Rum Drinking when their [Blood] was hot," and assured him that they would return to Hughs the goods they had stolen, Governor Glen convened the general assembly into an emergency session.[49] The headmen in the Lower towns petitioned the governor not to cut off the trade because "we don't know what to do" without it.[50] The council proposed military action, but the commons opposed such an expensive course and urged the governor to impose an embargo on the Cherokees instead. Ultimately South Carolina chose the economic sanctions that the headmen had feared over military operations and withdrew traders altogether from the Cherokee country.[51] Governor Glen distributed a letter of instructions among ranger captains to enforce the embargo.[52] Meanwhile, he sought to negotiate a settlement by persuading Lower town Cherokee headmen to deliver the miscreants to Charlestown for punishment within two months. The Cherokees refused, saying that exactly when they were about to leave, they heard that the Creeks, the Catawbas, and some Englishmen intended to waylay them.[53]

At the same time, Governor Glen had to confront complex intercolonial rivalries. Without the cooperation of its neighboring provinces, South Carolina could not successfully enforce the embargo against the Cherokees. Glen finally managed to persuade Georgia not to send goods or ammunition to the Cherokee country, but negotiations with Virginia failed.[54] In response to the embargo, the Overhill towns had sent a delegation to Williamsburg where they received "full Assurance that this Government would encourage any of His Majesty's Subjects to trade with them."[55] Accordingly, Virginia trader Richard Smith promised to secure goods at a lower price for the Cherokees.[56]

Virginia aimed to wrest the lucrative Cherokee trade from the control of South Carolina. This ambition forced South Carolina to lift the embargo within six months of its announcement. In November 1751, a headman named Tacit and several other chiefs led a delegation of 162 Cherokees to Charlestown, and Governor Glen agreed to restore all trade except rum in exchange for the Cherokees' promise to give satisfaction for all past incidents.[57]

Although he had ignored the traders' unscrupulous behavior, Glen had long held misgivings about the effect of the Indians' alcohol consumption on the trade. He had warned

Cherokees in April 1745 that alcohol served to "enervate you, so as to render you unfit either for War or Hunting" and urged them "to be sparing in the Use of Rum."[58] The governor, the council, and a special committee of the commons now formally discussed the prohibition of alcohol and inserted an article to that effect in an ordinance of December 3, 1751, for regulating the Cherokee trade. Until the expiration date of March 3, 1752, a licensed trader could legally seize illicit kegs of rum and destroy them in the presence of another licensed trader. The ordinance required them to report an incident to the Indian commissioner within three months so that they could receive legal assistance in case of trouble with smugglers.[59]

Trader Ludovic Grant praised this antiliquor provision and commented that he could not imagine "how glad the Indians, both Men and Women, are." Still, this veteran trader warned the governor to discipline the traders more strictly. He remained anxious about the conspiracy of "some self-interested Men without any Regard to the publick Wellfare" who advised some Cherokees to petition the governor for rum. Unless the traders scrupulously observed provincial laws, he wrote, the Cherokees would conclude that "the white Men, do not mind the Governour's Talk and why should the Indians."[60] Constantly reporting on the Cherokees' situation, Grant became Governor Glen's most reliable informant on Cherokee affairs.[61] He warned provincial authorities to watch the actions of the traders closely and to take seriously the alcohol-related problems within the Cherokee country. Grant's correspondence probably also enhanced public awareness in South Carolina of the harmful effects of the rum trade on Native societies.

South Carolina's initial attempt to control the liquor traffic among the Cherokees stemmed from retaliation for

Cherokee misconduct, not from any concern about the social welfare of the tribe. Although the ban on alcohol ended on March 3, 1752, a comprehensive Indian trade act passed on May 16 provided that "a Cherokee trader, . . . shall not carry any rum or other spirituous liquors to the [Cherokee] nation."[62] The embargo applied exclusively to the tribe, perhaps because of lingering ill will toward the Cherokees. Although they were somewhat concerned about the disastrous effects of drinking on the people, South Carolina officials blamed the Cherokees for the crisis of 1751 and insisted that they suffer for their actions. The limited prohibition clause of 1752, however, proved to be ineffective because traders ignored it. The remark of one Cherokee trader reflected the general view of the time: "A little Spirit is more necessary for [them] than the poor Traders."[63] Thus, South Carolina traders, by selling liquor to the tribe in defiance of provincial law, overwhelmed this supposedly alcohol-free Native society. Furthermore, traders from Georgia began to funnel rum into the Cherokee country.

Georgia traders directly challenged South Carolina's experiment with limiting the rum trade. Georgia had been a pioneer in alcohol regulations in the southern British colonies. In 1735, the province banned spirituous liquors entirely and prohibited both English colonists and Natives from purchasing them. The regulation was very strict, and a trader had to obtain a license even to sell beer or ale to Indian people.[64] The Georgia rum act of 1735, however, did not deter traders from smuggling liquor into the Cherokee country from Augusta. In February 1753, Grant wrote Governor Glen that a group of drunken Cherokees at Tuckasegee invaded Crawford's store and, after stabbing him repeatedly in the head, divided up the plundered goods among themselves. Recognizing the devastating effect of alcohol on the

Cherokees, Grant notified the governor "Again . . . [of] considerable Quantities of Rum imported by the Georgia Traders into this Nation." Although Cherokee headmen assured Grant that they would seize the kegs next time they discovered the "Rogues" from Augusta, such pronouncements did not discourage Georgians from trading rum to the Cherokees.[65] In early summer, trader Anthony L'antignac imported ten kegs of rum into the country from Georgia.[66]

In his 1755 plan for imperial control of the Indian tribes, Edmond Atkin pointed out the ineffectiveness of individual colonial attempts to regulate alcohol in Indian country. He explained that the provinces of South Carolina and Pennsylvania faced similar problems concerning the liquor trade; both failed to win the consent of adjacent colonies to rum prohibition clauses. South Carolina's antiliquor law, however, was far weaker than its northern counterpart as it was only a "partial Restraint upon the Cherokee Traders" rather than a provision that applied to all tribes. "The Restraint of carrying it," Atkin advised, "shou'd have been extended to all the Traders to every Nation."[67] Believing that "the present Disorders" in the Cherokee country were exacerbated "by so many Different Traders accountable to different Powers, under different Regulations, or none at all," Atkin suggested that the rum trade be placed solely under imperial control.[68]

Atkin described communities where traders waylaid Native hunters between hunting grounds and towns. "Unable to resist the Bait," he lamented, many Indians got drunk on their way home and, by thoughtlessly "parting with the fruit of three or four Months Toil," lost every means to support their family. In the end, rum traders exchanged their commodities in the woods for untrimmed or undressed skins, which worms soon destroyed and made unfit for sale in Charlestown, damaging the entire deerskin trade.[69]

Although Atkin sought penalties for Indians who bought and consumed alcohol, he also recognized the difficulty in "weaning the Indians intirely from Rum or other Spirits" and suggested gradual steps to control the flow among the Natives.[70] Under his plan, British authorities were to choose one reputable trader in each tribe, station him at or near the fort, issue him a liquor license, and entrust to him the entire rum trade with that tribe. This licensed trader was to have a good command of the Indian language, work as an interpreter, and under the supervision of the commanding officer, have liquor "temper'd . . . with a certain proportion of Water."[71] By placing Indian affairs entirely under imperial control, Atkin's scheme sought to rectify the evils of poor administration and eventually contributed to the establishment, in 1756, of the Indian superintendency system and the subsequent appointment of Atkin as southern superintendent of the Indians. With the intention of implementing his plan and conducting relations between the British and the Indians in a new way, Atkin took charge of Indian affairs south of the Ohio until his death in 1761.[72]

Neither imperial nor colonial regulations easily reached remote areas. According to Capt. Raymond Demere, commander of Fort Loudoun in east Tennessee, traders and packhorsemen were "worse than the Indians themselves and all Drunkards."[73] After the enactment of the trade act of 1752, illegal traders increasingly challenged provincial authorities in the Cherokee country. In his letter of February 1756 to Governor Glen, Cherokee trader James Beamer accused a man named Williams of Estatoe of "seldom fail[ing] to bring into this Nation considerable Quantities of Rum and Spirits as often almost as he goes from hence to Augusta."

Williams exchanged trade goods for Indians' unprocessed raw skins in "the Woods" and sold these inferior products in Augusta for liquor, which he then sold to the Cherokees at an extraordinary price.[74] What was more problematic to Beamer, Williams boasted defiance of provincial authorities in the presence of Cherokees: "The Governor should not hinder him to bring what Rum he pleased, . . . in any Town in the Nation." His trade partner Cox blatantly asserted that he would leave for Augusta the following day and "bring up a Cargo of Rum only."[75] Captain Demere's reports to newly appointed Gov. William Henry Lyttelton also revealed illicit shipments. Robert Gowdy, for example, furnished pack-horsemen with rum at Fort Ninety Six. Other unscrupulous men also obtained spirituous liquors at Augusta and other places in Georgia and distributed them in the Cherokee country.[76]

During the late 1750s, trader James Elliott instigated most alcohol-related troubles among the Cherokees. In the summer of 1756 Captain Demere reported to Governor Lyttelton that Elliott was smuggling one hundred kegs of rum into Cherokee towns. At that time, many Savannah (Shawnee) Indians were among the Cherokees, and they sought every opportunity to make the tribe abandon the British and side with the French. Fearing that the Cherokees would join these French allies "when they are in Liquor," Demere urged Lyttelton to take countermeasures immediately; but action did not come quickly enough.[77] On August 29, Elliott carried eighty-eight kegs of rum to Fort Prince George near Keowee in upper South Carolina. Without notice, he dispatched twenty-four of the kegs to Cherokee villages. The rest remained in the fort, but the captain was afraid that Cherokees would plunder the warehouse in his absence and steal the rum because, he believed, "they are Devils after Rum."[78]

Two months later, Elliott asked the captain to permit him to transport twenty kegs of rum from Fort Prince George to Fort Loudoun for the officers. When the kegs arrived, Elliott kept two of them in his house, which soon contributed to the death of his packhorseman Thompson. During a drinking binge at Elliott's house, a Cherokee woman tasted a cup of rum and asked Thompson for some more. Instead of giving her more, Thompson took her out of the house and "used her ill." She immediately cried out for help, and her husband and several young Cherokee men came to her aid. Thompson seized a big stick and attempted to drive them off, but the Cherokee woman ran for a gun and handed it to her husband.[79] He promptly pulled the trigger and shot Thompson in the thigh. Hearing that the wounded man had died, Demere concluded that "Mr. Elliott shall have no Liberty from me to bring up any more of his Rum from Fort Prince George," although he still had forty-four kegs in storage. Demere was afraid that Elliott would face the same fate as his packhorseman because "he is hated much by all the Indians."[80]

Elliott did not learn his lesson from this tragic incident. He continued to defy colonial laws and sold alcohol "very dear" to Cherokees.[81] In February 1757, Captain Demere stopped Elliott's illicit shipment at Fort Prince George.[82] Elliott, however, hired several Cherokees and promised to pay them four kegs of rum for carrying a thousand bushels of corn to Fort Loudoun.[83] When these Cherokees safely delivered the corn to the fort, Elliott told them that the army had confiscated his rum at Fort Prince George. Elliott sent the Great Warrior of Chota to ask Captain Demere for the release of the rum, but the captain refused to issue the order. Although Demere reminded Elliott of the death of his packhorseman, the trader had already sent six horses to Savannah

Town to acquire liquor. Demere concluded that Elliott was "cracked-brained," and he expressed concern that the trader had sought advice about the rum trade from a lawyer who "did value more his Fee than the common Wellfare and Tranquility of the Province."[84]

Demere's reports on Elliott's illegal and irresponsible behavior continued. Headman Old Hop complained to Captain Demere that Elliott owed the tribe four kegs of rum since the seizure of his rum at Fort Prince George. Old Hop was so persistent that Demere could not refuse him, and he reluctantly granted Elliott a permit for rum.[85] Soon the Great Warrior of Chota and a group of several headmen petitioned Demere to issue another order for eight kegs of rum. The delegation insisted on "the Rum being justly due to them" because Elliott had promised them eight kegs in payment for their horses. When they urged Demere to release the rum, which they believed was "so reasonable a Request," the captain ordered Elliott to appear at Fort Loudoun. He asked Elliott, in the presence of other officers, whether he wished to have Indians obtain "so many Keggs of Rum." Elliott answered in the affirmative, and Demere felt compelled to release the kegs to permit the trader to pay off his debts to the Cherokees. Now that Elliott's deplorable business practices had become public, Captain Demere ordered that all kegs still in storage at Fort Prince George be destroyed to prevent further mischief by Elliott among the Cherokees.[86]

Illicit and poorly regulated trade threatened to undermine not only colonial authority but also chiefly power over commerce. Still, the role of alcohol in diplomacy continued. The Cherokees' demand for alcohol multiplied precisely when imperial rivalry between the British and the French intensified in the Cherokee country in the late 1750s, and both camps believed alcohol to be instrumental in manipulating

Cherokee sentiments.[87] Native people, however, recognized how to frustrate imperial designs by taking advantage of the Europeans' assumption that Indians loved alcohol. In asking the governor of Georgia for rum, for example, Lower Creek headmen very frankly stated that "we have been used to have Rum from Children and [cannot] do without it and it causes our People to go to the French and [Spaniards] for to get some Rum, which they would not do if we had some from our Friends the English."[88] In these years of upheaval, alcohol became a part of the play-off diplomacy adopted by southeastern Indians.[89]

The French openly used alcohol to cement a diplomatic alliance. On January 2, 1757, a Cherokee headman, the Blind Slave Catcher of Chatuga, informed Captain Demere that Savannah Indians had persuaded the people of Tellico to accompany them to the French camp. The Tellico people, he continued, presented the Savannahs with "a Warr Tomahawk made of Wood," which they subsequently awarded the French. The officer at Fort Toulouse, in a brotherly manner, asked the Tellico people to take their wives and children as well as the Chatuga people to Hiwassee Old Town, where they received "a hundred horse Load of Goods and as many Keggs of Rum," and he reminded them to bring him an English scalp so that they could be "his Children."[90]

Four days later, the pro-French Mankiller of Tellico, along with his party of about thirty young men, appeared at Fort Loudoun. In the presence of about one hundred and fifty Cherokee headmen and British officers, the Mankiller announced that although the French official offered him thirty kegs of rum, he accepted only two of them for his people to enjoy. Apparently, he considered these kegs to be offered in hospitality, not alliance, and on his way home, he burned "a great Deal of Papers with Talks" between his people and the French.[91] Soon after he cleared himself of suspicion, the Mankiller of Tellico asked Captain Demere to send a keg of rum to himself, "not to the Town," and promised to pay for the liquor.[92] To demonstrate that his "Thoughts are good and streight towards all my Brothers, the Cherrockees," Demere violated South Carolina's liquor policy and offered the Mankiller the only keg he had with him.[93] Demere felt compelled to oblige this influential man to prevent an alliance with the French, but for the Mankiller and his young followers, this was a reasonable request because Demere insisted that they side with the British.

In the end, the French used alcohol more overtly in enticing the Tellico people to repudiate the British. When a Creek headman, the Mortar, took two Cherokees to the French fort, officials plied them with rum for ten days and urged them to drive Englishmen out of their country, lest they be "a ruined People, . . . entirely Slaves to the English."[94] The collusion between the French Indians and the people of Tellico soon drove the entire community into conflict. Although some Cherokees, including the Cherokee headman Attakullakulla, adhered to the British cause, others sided with the French.[95] The role of alcohol in diplomacy, however, signaled the persistence of beliefs about alcohol that had emerged in the early years of the trade. Chiefs continued to attempt to control its distribution, and its consumption often took on meanings not entirely understood by Europeans.

Alcohol retained an important ceremonial dimension long after its more deleterious social effects became obvious. When the Mankiller of Tellico requested a keg of rum from Demere, he asked for some paint as well because he needed "a little more to paint himself when he is drinking."[96] Demere provided both rum and paint, probably vermilion.[97] Native people painted themselves on ceremonial occasions to enhance their spiritual power. For the same reason, warriors painted themselves to prepare for battle.[98] By linking paint and alcohol, the Mankiller indicated that his intent was spiritual power and not simply inebriation. Cherokee warriors would not go to war against the French without rum, not because they were lushes, but because rum had become an important war medicine.

As late as the 1790s, the Cherokees consumed alcohol as a war medicine. In 1792, four hundred to five hundred Chickamauga warriors—Cherokees who refused to make peace with the United States following the Revolution and forcefully resisted white encroachments on their land—assembled at Willstown to prepare for an attack on settlements in the Holston River Valley of eastern Tennessee. They "stripped to their flaps, painted black, with their guns and hatchets, and commenced the war dance." These preparations continued for four days, and on the last day, the White Mankiller arrived from Knoxville with whiskey: "Men were immediately despatched to bring it up to the town, and, on its arrival, all hands turned in to drinking." The non-Indian observers of this process interpreted the Cherokee warriors' consumption of alcohol as "neglecting the order for providing for war," but the exact opposite was probably the case. The warriors viewed drinking as appropriate and perhaps even essential to their mission.[99]

The Cherokees apparently conceived of alcohol as possessing spiritual power that those who consumed it could not necessarily control. In a state of intoxication, for example, Attakullakulla visited Captain Demere at Fort Prince George and attempted to hit him in the face with a bottle he brought with him. When he became sober, Attakullakulla apologized for his misconduct, explained that "Rum was the Occasion of it[,] and begged that nothing might be remembered."[100]

Historian Claudio Saunt has suggested that the Creeks also regarded alcohol as "a transformative drug" and associated it with madness and bravery.[101] Spiritual power was dangerous and could bring disaster as well as success. Consequently, as Edmond Atkin observed, Cherokees often excused drunken violence or socially unacceptable behavior by saying "that they are sorry for what hath happened, But that it was not they that did it, 'twas Rum did it."[102]

Cherokee women rarely consumed alcohol unless traders pressed them to do so. The incident involving Thompson, the packhorseman, was typical. Unscrupulous men encouraged Native women to drink so they could assault them sexually. Other women, however, found in drinking frolics an opportunity to recycle alcohol. William Bartram, who traveled the southeastern region extensively in the 1770s, observed how Native women spit the liquor into an empty bottle while feigning to drink with men, "and when the comic farce is over, the wench retails this precious cordial to them at her own price."[103] The only evidence we have of women drinking in the colonial Cherokee country—and even it is indirect—is from Captain Demere, who reported from Fort Prince George. On June 22, 1756, a Cherokee runner informed Demere that the local people planned a dance for him the following day. In the evening, women in the town came to visit Demere and expressed "Thanks for the small Refreshment I had been so good as to send them the Day before." In spite of a current food shortage, each woman, in return for his courtesy, presented the captain a basket full of homemade bread, green peas, and squashes.[104] The "small Refreshment" Demere had sent to the Cherokee women almost certainly was rum.[105] Although it was perhaps gender inappropriate, the gift of rum certainly befitted the ceremonial occasion.

More likely, the consumption of rum played a role similar to black drink in the social bonding of men from various clans and lineages in the Cherokee society. Anthropologist Charles H. Fairbanks has explored the meaning of the exclusive use of black drink by Native men. He argues that in matrilineal societies such as those of southeastern Indians, black drink helped adult males maintain solidarity. By consuming black drink in the square in summer and in the hothouse in winter, Indian men attempted to promote brotherhood among themselves and to satisfactorily perform their economic as well as political duties in society.[106]

Cherokee men increasingly needed to express their solidarity and their maleness in the latter half of the eighteenth century. The dispute over independence between the colonists and British authorities soon replaced the one over European hegemony in North America. The Cherokees divided their loyalties, and military confrontations did not end until 1794. Nearly continuous warfare and multiple invasions devastated their hunting grounds and the lucrative deerskin trade, as well as Cherokee homes and farms. By the end of the eighteenth century, the Cherokees had to find a new livelihood. Although they recognized that they could no longer support themselves by the deerskin trade, the transition to commercial agriculture was not an easy one. Historian William G. McLoughlin defines the years of confusion between 1794 and 1810 as ones of "Cherokee anomie" and argues that some Cherokee men drank to excess and many resorted to horse stealing to appease their rage, frustration, and despair.[107]

At the same time, however, Cherokees increasingly incorporated Anglo-American practices and beliefs. Alcohol, therefore, probably began to have dual meanings, one rooted in ancient culture and one acquired from traders and frontier settlers. By the Revolutionary era, many Cherokee men seemed to crave alcohol. Moravian Brother Martin Schneider, for example, heard on New Year's Day of 1784 that several Americans on the French Broad River had set out for the Cherokee villages with a hogshead of brandy. Col. Joseph Martin prevented the smugglers from selling the liquor, and his prompt action relieved Schneider, who believed American traders and packhorsemen to be "the worst sort of people for morals that breathe the mortal air." He could not bear to see Cherokees exchanging two deerskins per "one quart of miserable Brandy."[108] Such reports contributed to the widespread Anglo-American belief that Indians were drunks, and this stereotype would help shape Cherokee relations with the new U.S. government.

Historian Richard White has argued that by the end of the eighteenth century, the penetration of the market economy and the free use of alcohol by the deerskin traders had made the Choctaws vulnerable and dependent on Euro-Americans.[109] The Cherokee people also engaged in the deerskin trade and became dependent on European manufactured goods and perhaps alcohol, but they were not awash with it. Alcohol posed problems to the Cherokees, and it induced South Carolina's economic sanction against the tribe in the early 1750s. The chiefs, however, had incorporated alcohol into an ancient system of redistribution and attempted to retain their chiefly power while controlling the drinking of their people. Cherokees consumed alcohol as an adjunct to ritual beverages such as black drink in ceremonial contexts that gave it a spiritual meaning. The Cherokees may have regarded liquor as having a distinct spirit that made them behave in extraordinary ways. Although some Cherokees succumbed to alcoholism, most used alcohol on specific occasions including council meetings and warfare. If alcohol became a symbol of Cherokee vulnerability, it also became a symbol of

Cherokee cultural adaptability. In the early nineteenth century, alcohol would become a vehicle for the Cherokee chiefs to accumulate economic wealth and ultimately to assert the political sovereignty of the Cherokee Nation. The Cherokees' struggle with alcohol had just begun.

2

A Struggle for Sovereignty

At the turn of the nineteenth century, Cherokee society began to experience profound changes. A more sophisticated commercial economy emerged, and tribal government began to centralize and assert its sovereignty. Missionaries and U.S. agents attempted to instill a new value system of self-discipline and social reform. All of these changes involved alcohol. Culturally incorporated into the Cherokees' colonial society, alcohol and its consumption in the early nineteenth century began to be enmeshed more thoroughly into the politics of the Cherokee Nation. Alcohol regulation provided the Cherokees a way to assert their nationalism, and the Cherokee Nation and the federal government both manipulated the issue of alcohol to achieve political goals. By prohibiting the sale and consumption of alcohol only among Indians, the U.S. government insisted that it had jurisdiction over the liquor trade. The Cherokees countered that they had the legal authority to regulate the liquor traffic themselves. As a bone of contention between the Cherokee Nation and the United States, the regulation of alcohol in the 1820s reflected larger struggles over sovereignty.

The United States did not immediately introduce alcohol regulations to Native societies. Intercolonial rivalry had hindered the enforcement of antiliquor laws in Indian country, and following the American Revolution, the Articles of Confederation failed to grant the federal government authority to establish regulations. When the U.S. government assumed sole responsibility for Indian affairs under the Constitution, however, it acquired the right to pursue Indian policy without the states' interference. Yet in the first four temporary trade and intercourse acts, U.S. officials did not attempt to prevent the sale of intoxicating liquors among Native people.[1]

Only in the Jefferson administration did the federal government make its first effort to regulate the liquor trade in Indian territories. In his address to Congress in January 1802, Pres. Thomas Jefferson announced that unnamed Indians, aware of the harmful effects of alcohol on their societies, had asked the federal authority to take legal steps.[2] As an ardent advocate of the "civilization" program, Jefferson maintained that most trade functioned as a useful instrument for incorporating the Indians into mainstream American society. By introducing alcohol into Indian communities, however, traders and merchants hampered the efforts of the federal government to maintain peace and order, and they aggravated the destitute and demoralized condition of many Native societies. To keep the peace between the United States and the Indians and to continue its "civilization" program, the federal government believed that it had to take action.

The presence of alcohol in Indian country particularly repulsed federal policy makers of the early republic who promoted Indian "civilization." The "civilization" program aimed to turn Indians into yeoman farmers and to obtain the cession of their "surplus" hunting grounds. To accomplish this, policy makers expected Indians to speak English and to accept American ways of life. The policy also assumed that Native people would assimilate into American society with full citizenship rights and responsibilities. The notoriety of Indian drunkenness, however, troubled the federal policy makers. Under the influence of alcohol, Indians could neither think rationally nor be industrious in learning Anglo-American culture and tradition. Neglecting their work, drunken Indians would never be productive farmers or good Christians. Intemperance threatened the patriarchal family as well: men could not become the heads of what traditionally had been matrilineal and matrilocal households if they were irresponsible, abusive drunkards.[3] Because democracy required the informed judgment of rational citizens, Native drunkards could never learn to participate effectively in orderly government. U.S. policy makers concluded that intemperance challenged the fundamental tenets of "civilization" and therefore jeopardized the whole Indian community. To "civilize" Indians properly, federal officials insisted, they had to regulate the liquor trade and shield the Indians from this source of vice.[4]

At the urgent request of President Jefferson, Congress inserted a special provision for restricting the liquor traffic in the Trade and Intercourse Act of 1802 and authorized the president "to prevent or restrain the vending or distributing of spirituous liquors" among the Indians.[5] In his official instructions, Secretary of War Henry Dearborn reminded Indian superintendents and agents that the law prohibited traders from selling any spirituous liquors to Native people.[6] This provision, however, applied only to non-Indian traders who sold liquor to Indians on tribal lands.[7]

Federal regulation of the liquor traffic, therefore, proved to be enforceable only in Indian country, not in frontier American settlements, which came under state jurisdiction. Native people could go across the border, enter neighboring towns, and return to their own nation with the liquor they legally had purchased. Aware of the loopholes in the Intercourse Act, President Jefferson, in a letter of December 31, 1808, asked the governors of the states and territories to prohibit their citizens from selling liquor to Indians.[8] Largely ignored, this request did not effectively help restrain the flow.[9]

The loopholes and ambiguities in the Intercourse Act encouraged American traders to continue selling liquor to Indians. With Native partners who acted as covers for them, American traders legally sold whiskey in the Indian nations. This was exactly how the Cherokees obtained alcohol in their Nation after 1802. Cherokee headmen formed partnerships with Americans who ran alcohol-related businesses for them and began to engage directly in the liquor trade. By allowing Americans to manage taverns owned by Indians, these chiefs encouraged the liquor traffic within the boundaries of the Nation, and many of them profited substantially from the practice.[10] Most of these men sat on the Cherokee Council, and they knew that their actions were absolutely legal. The Trade and Intercourse Act did not regulate the actions of Indians who were conducting business with other Indians within their own nations. The Cherokee Council enacted legislation that applied to Cherokees within the boundaries of the Cherokee Nation, and it had not outlawed such sales. The council regulated alcohol sales simply by authorizing contracts and businesses.

The practice of contracts between Indians and Americans began on May 11, 1803, when Cherokee Chief Tolluntuskee made an agreement with Thomas N. Clark to establish two taverns on the Cumberland Road. This five-year contract permitted Clark to "keep good & reputable persons in said Houses" and to "furnish liquors & good provisions" for travelers. Tolluntuskee agreed to live in one of the houses for "keeping good order perticularly [*sic*] amongst the Cherokees" and more precisely to comply with regulations prohibiting non-Cherokees from operating taverns in the Cherokee Nation.[11] The chiefs approved these terms in council on July 22.[12]

Three months later, another prominent Cherokee, Doublehead, entered into a five-year contract with an American named William Tharp. Under this agreement, Doublehead and Tharp, as partners, planned to operate a ferry at the junction of the Tennessee and Clinch rivers and establish taverns along major thoroughfares. Although the contract stipulated that Doublehead and Tharp divide the income equally, Tharp obtained the right, in the name of Doublehead, to start the business and to run two "stands" serving alcohol at "the Flat Rock" and at the forks of the Cumberland Road. The agreement specifically noted: "The said Double Head[']s name in this transaction is only intended to receive the rights of the Nation and prevent any infringement of the law."[13]

Although they expressed their reluctance to authorize another stand, the Cherokee chiefs soon agreed to open three new "houses of entertainment" on the Cumberland Road. These leaders, moreover, permitted the United States to build a public road from Tennessee to Georgia through their Nation, and Chief James Vann made plans to operate a stand on the new road.[14] Turnpikes and waterways soon brought more Americans, more taverns, and more alcohol into the Nation, and the council continued to regulate—but not prohibit—the liquor trade.

At times, the Cherokee Council seemed to take measures to intentionally circumvent the Trade and Intercourse Act. On November 20, 1816, for example, Marston Mead of Fort Deposit, Alabama, complained to Cherokee Agent Return J. Meigs that Lenoard Bowerman, living within the Cherokee

Nation "on the [s]outh bank of the Tennessee River," had sold whiskey to the Indians for two years. According to Mead, Gen. Andrew Jackson, during a short stop at Fort Deposit, learned of Bowerman's illegal conduct. He warned Bowerman never to sell "another gallon of whiskey" and to leave the Nation "within thirty days"; otherwise, he must pay the penalty. Bowerman, however, "violated those orders in less than thirty minutes after the General had crossed the River," and, as Mead reported, he continued his business by selling "about one thousand gallons" of whiskey. As a responsible U.S. citizen, Mead did not think it right to let Bowerman stay within the Nation any longer. He asked Meigs to punish this illicit dealer according to the federal law, but it was too late. The Cherokee Council had already granted a permit for Bowerman to stay in the Nation.[15]

U.S. officials recognized that they had failed to stop the liquor flow into Indian country. Cherokee entrepreneurs, together with their American partners, sold alcohol to Indian and non-Indian travelers on the federal road and to Indians who simply lived in the neighborhood. Some Americans in communities adjacent to the Cherokee Nation legally retailed whiskey to Cherokees, who took it home with them, while others successfully smuggled liquor into the Nation in defiance of federal law. Easily accessible, alcohol became more thoroughly incorporated into the everyday lives of the Cherokees. Whereas the Cherokees had initially allowed the limited consumption of alcohol in relation to war, at the opening of the tribal council, or at a ball game, by the early nineteenth century such spiritual and ceremonial meanings of alcohol had faded away, and men, women, and children drank socially rather than ritually at public gatherings.[16] Observing a ball game in Chickamauga on his journey of 1809–1810 to the Cherokee country, for example, a Mohawk, Maj. John

Norton, noted that "those who desire[d] to make a little money" carried whiskey to the ball ground; "a small number however only appeared to be affected by liquor, and these only in a moderate degree." In the Green Corn Ceremony he observed, moreover, only a few Cherokees drank to excess although "many appeared in a merry mood."[17]

Most Americans found such drinking scenes problematic and left highly critical accounts. Indians were the only people in America whom the U.S. government tried to keep from drinking, and their consumption of alcohol seemed particularly sordid and objectionable, even in contexts in which drinking might have been acceptable for other Americans. Relying on his two years of residence in the Cherokee Nation, J. P. Evans wrote in the mid-1830s that Cherokee ballplayers spent "the greater part of the time in drinking," quarreling, and fighting with one another. Failing to understand the Cherokees' incorporation of alcohol in a "common dance," Evans noted that "a scarcity of whiskey," not "the want of company," often brought the ceremony to a close. The Green Corn Dance, Evans continued, sparked drunkenness and its accompanying lawlessness, and many young people engaged in a drinking frolic while older Cherokees performed their "solemn duty."[18] Such accounts of drunkenness soon typified American reports of the Cherokees, embarrassing Cherokee leaders who tried to fulfill policy makers' expectations and cultivate an image of the Cherokees as a sober, industrious, "civilized" people.

The greatest threat to that image came not from the recreational use of alcohol by young Cherokees but from the occasional incidents of violence in which drunkenness figured prominently. Most dangerous of all were conflicts between Cherokees and their non-Indian neighbors. Bloodshed on the border with Georgia in 1802, for example, provoked on both sides "a deep sensation" of fear. A drunken Cherokee seriously injured a Georgian's wife. The husband retaliated by shooting the Cherokee. Before he died, the drunkard, in a fit of anger, "threw a child into the fire" and struck a young woman with "a Mattock," which split "her face from the forehead to the chin." Agent Meigs and Chief James Vann both feared "further mischief" between Cherokees and Americans. Vann promised that the Nation would try its best to "preserve Tranquillity," and Meigs replied that neither the Cherokees nor the Georgians should consider this incident "an Act of hostility."[19] Nevertheless, alcohol in the early nineteenth century gradually cast a shadow on the Cherokees' peaceful and stable society.

Intemperance resulted in seven more murders between 1802 and 1817 within the limits of the Cherokee Nation.[20] In 1807, four years after the establishment of the taverns on the Cumberland Road, American travelers on the road in Tennessee urged a Cherokee to drink whiskey with them. In a drunken frenzy, the Cherokee killed an African American slave belonging to one of the travelers. State authorities arrested the Cherokee and put him in jail at Carthage, Tennessee. The Cherokee Nation insisted that the state court could not adjudicate the case between its citizen and a citizen of the United States, but the slave owner brought suit, and the superior court of Tennessee put the Cherokee on trial. The state, however, did not have a statute to deal with killing slaves, and the court freed the Cherokee.[21]

Intoxicated Indians were not always so fortunate. In March 1807, for example, several Creeks who lived among the Cherokees purchased whiskey on the banks of the Tennessee River. After consuming a substantial amount, these Creeks started a quarrel with an American named Stinson during which two of them "fell upon Stinson[,] threw him down[,]

& Stubbed [*sic*] him in the throat with a knife." While Stinson breathed his last, the Cherokees arrested the two Creeks and "shot them both." Although he blamed whiskey smugglers, Meigs regretted "the willingness of Indians to purchase" whiskey and observed that "it is impossible to prevent" the vicious circle of murder and violence caused by alcohol.[22]

Some Cherokees, although they did not commit murder, resorted to violence to obtain liquor from Americans. In December 1807, hog drover James Lusk asked a Cherokee woman for a night's lodging. The following morning, a Cherokee man pointed a gun at Lusk and demanded whiskey. When Lusk answered that he had no whiskey, the man shot and killed the largest of Lusk's 230 hogs. Lusk attempted to protest, but the Cherokee threatened to kill him, saying that Agent Meigs ordered him to get meat.[23]

Such behavior on the part of the Cherokees contributed to the stereotype of the "drunken Indian." Americans who interacted with Cherokees on the basis of this image sometimes exacerbated the alcohol-related violence in the Nation. In the winter of 1807–1808, several men who had an exaggerated misconception of the Indians' love for drink asked a Cherokee named Seed to exchange his gun for whiskey. When he refused their offer, the men violently snatched the twenty-dollar gun from Seed's hands and fled without leaving him a single drop of whiskey.[24]

While intemperance increasingly damaged the Nation's reputation and relations with non-Cherokees, Cherokee leaders recognized that the tribal government had an important stake in regulating the liquor trade, and they seized the opportunity to act. On August 12, 1816, two Cherokees were drinking near Muscle Shoals, Alabama, with a black man named Fox who had resided within the Nation for several years and who "had whiskey to sell." When the Cherokees asked him for more, Fox refused and carried the keg into a cornfield to hide it. The two drunkards, however, soon discovered the keg, driving its owner into a rage. At the request of Fox, ten or twelve Americans, armed with guns, followed the two Cherokees to their home. Upon finding these two troublemakers with other Cherokees, the vigilantes set fire to everything they could, killed two Natives, and wounded two others.

Arguing that Fox was "one of our people," the Cherokee chiefs informed Meigs that they intended to try him by "our own laws." Goard, a Cherokee spokesman, also claimed that the Americans should not have killed the two Cherokee citizens because the incident had nothing to do with them. On August 18, Meigs authorized the Cherokee police under Col. Richard Brown and Col. John Lowrey to arrest Fox and question him about the names of the American suspects. Fox apparently evaded them, however, and Meigs dropped the matter.[25]

At this point, the Cherokees began to assert control over the liquor traffic and suppress "the noxious vapours of intemperance" with their own laws.[26] On October 28, 1819, the Nation passed a law for regulating trade within its boundaries. The law authorized the Nation to levy taxes from citizens and noncitizens who intended to establish businesses. Cherokee merchants had to pay a tax of twenty-five dollars per year. The law required noncitizens, after "obtaining lisense from the Agent of the United States for the Cherokee Nation," to pay an annual tax of eighty dollars to the Treasury of the Nation. Failure on the part of noncitizens to pay the tax resulted in a fine of two hundred dollars. This decree of 1819, moreover, included a provision to regulate liquor traffic within the borders of the Nation. It provided that no person or persons, not citizens of the Nation, shall bring into the Nation and sell, any spirituous liquors, and all such person or persons so offending, shall forfeit the whole of the spirituous liquors that may be found in his or their possession, and the same shall be disposed of for the benefit of the Nation; and if any person or persons, citizens of the Nation, shall receive and bring into the Nation, spirituous liquors for disposal, and the same or any part thereof, be found to be the property of person or persons not citizens of the Nation, and satisfactory proof be made of the fact, he or they shall forfeit and pay the sum of one hundred dollars, and the whiskey be subject to confiscation as aforesaid, . . .[27]

The law was intended to prohibit noncitizens from selling alcohol to Cherokees and to end the practice of Cherokees acting as covers for noncitizens. Still, the law did not interfere with Cherokee citizens selling their own liquor. Within the boundaries of the Nation, Cherokee leaders did not entirely prohibit the sale of alcohol. By imposing a heavier tax on non-Cherokees, the chiefs tried to protect Native merchants and traders and to restrict competition between Americans and Cherokees. Since members of the Cherokee National Council were among the few people who could afford to run businesses in the Nation, they eliminated, through trade regulations, non-Cherokee competition from the tribal alcohol market and promoted their own economic interests.[28]

Although he once wrote that "I sincerely wish to restrain as much as possible the sale of spirituous liquors" among his "good neighbors & friends" in the Nation, Agent Meigs did not want the Cherokees to take control of their own internal affairs by usurping federal regulation of commerce.[29] Meigs's frustration provoked him into making insulting remarks about Cherokee leaders. In correspondence with Secretary of War John C. Calhoun in 1822, Meigs described the Cherokee government as "an aristocracy . . . control[l]ed by perhaps twenty Speculating individuals. Some of these individuals are making fortunes" by dealing in "whiskey, & other ardent spirits." Continuing his critique of the Cherokee chiefs, Meigs railed, "The tendency of the conduct of these individuals is to perpetuate barbarism by encouraging indolence."[30] Meigs was particularly upset because legislation such as the 1819 trade regulation and tax act demonstrated that the Cherokees had no plans to become part of American society. Instead, the Cherokees' actions indicated that they intended "to raise up a Government within a Government." This evidence of Cherokee nationalism, Meigs declared, "cannot be possibly permitted."[31]

However severely Meigs criticized them, the Cherokees had no doubt about their right to manage their own affairs. Expressing the love of "our Country & our Laws," as early as 1803 the Cherokee chiefs asserted that the trade was "subject only to the Laws made by us in Council."[32] To the Cherokees, the law of 1819 was simply a written expression of an ancient tribal prerogative, and the defense of Cherokee rights, along with commercial success, became an important marker of Cherokee manhood. Alcohol provided the means by which they could accomplish both.

Faced with opposition from American merchants, the Cherokees did not enforce the taxation provisions of the law of 1819 until 1823, when they received a supportive opinion from Judge Hugh Lawson White of Tennessee.[33] White wrote that he believed the chiefs of "the Nation have the right to impose this tax" on licensed traders. Under the treaties, "the United States have the power, to regulate *trade* and *intercourse* with the Cherokee Indians," but White did not think that the federal government could "take from the Nation, the right of judging; whether" its citizens "should trade with him or not; nor the right of fixing the terms and conditions, upon which such trade should be concluded."[34]

Supported by Judge White's legal opinion, the Cherokee Nation finally enforced the law and imposed taxation on licensed traders. Some of these traders, however, refused to pay taxes to the Nation. When the Cherokees confiscated their goods "to satisfy the amount of their Taxes," these merchants promptly claimed compensation for the lost merchandise from the Nation and asked the Cherokee Agency and the War Department for assistance in recovering the value of their goods.[35]

The Cherokee National Council disputed their claims. The council also maintained that it had the right to tax American traders and that taxation did not violate treaties between the Cherokee Nation and the United States. Having "a Government of [our] own," the councilors contended, the Nation had the right "to raise a revenue for its support." The Cherokee leaders insisted that they never "conceded their own right of making municipal regulations for themselves."[36]

U.S. Attorney General William Wirt ruled, however, that "the Indians have no right to impose this tax on traders licensed under the authority of the U.S." To him, Judge White's opinion, which upheld the rights of both the federal government and the Cherokee Nation, was merely "a political solecism." Although he recommended that the federal government consider the changing nature of the Cherokee Nation, Wirt rejected the Cherokee claim that their Nation was independent and sovereign because "by the treaties of [17]'85 & '91 the Cherokees placed themselves under the protection of the United States, and of no other sovereign whatsoever."[37]

Moreover, they granted to the United States "the sole and exclusive right of regulating *their* trade." Referring to John Marshall's decision in *McCulloch v. Maryland* (1819), Wirt argued that only Congress had "the right to create those regulations of trade" and that "a power to destroy them is a wholly incompatible power, and [the Cherokees'] power to tax . . . is, virtually, a power to destroy" the authority of Congress.[38]

Once he denied the Cherokee Nation's right to levy taxes, Wirt proceeded to a discussion of the Indian tribes' prerogative "to prohibit, altogether, a trade which Congress has declared to be open." Again he stated that "*Congress alone* has the right to say when this trade shall be open and when it shall be shut." "So long as their treaties remain in force," he continued, "the Indians have no power to interfere with their regulations, either by addition or subtraction." In his opinion, the Cherokees ought to be ordered immediately to give up their arbitrary action against the authority of the United States.[39]

The Cherokees contended, however, that until Congress decided against the Nation, they would continue to levy taxes, neither yielding to federal authority nor refunding collected money to the claimants.[40] Nevertheless, on February 22, 1825, Thomas L. McKenney of the Office of Indian Affairs informed the Cherokee delegation that the Department of War had decided to deduct the sum of $1,539.25 from their annuity payment to refund the claimants.[41] Referring to the decision of William Wirt, McKenney declared it "final."[42] Although the Nation maintained that its stance on internal taxation was "still . . . in ful [*sic*] force," the federal officials denied the Cherokees the right to tax U.S. citizens and continued to refund tax payments by taking the funds out of the Cherokees' annuity.[43] The U.S. government determined to stifle this expression of Cherokee nationalism and to undermine claims to tribal sovereignty.

Meanwhile, the federal government continued its efforts to regulate the liquor trade among the Indians. An amendment to the Intercourse Act of 1802, passed on May 6, 1822, gave military officers, as well as Indian agents and superintendents, the right to inspect the stores and packages of American traders suspected of carrying intoxicating liquors into Indian country. When federal officials found alcohol, they confiscated all the goods, rewarded the informant with half, and kept the other half for the benefit of the U.S. government. Furthermore, they retained the bond the trader had posted and canceled his license.[44]

In spite of intensified federal interference in its internal affairs in the early 1820s, the Cherokee Nation passed a series of laws to suppress drunkenness among its citizens. Cherokee leaders felt compelled to prevent alcohol-related disruption in the Nation. The first step the Cherokees took was the elimination of spirituous liquors from public events. Believing that "no nation of people can prosper and flourish" in a state of intoxication, the National Committee passed a law on November 8, 1822, prohibiting spirituous liquors "within three miles of the General Council House, or to any of the court houses within the several Districts during the general Council, or the sitting of the courts." The law authorized confiscation and destruction of any whiskey discovered.[45] The Cherokee National Council also recognized that alcohol at ball games and all-night dances had disruptive effects on the social stability of the Nation. Therefore, on January 1, 1825, the law extended prohibition to include these occasions. Lighthorsemen, marshals, sheriffs, deputies, and constables were responsible for executing this law. If they neglected their duties, they had to pay a fine imposed on them by the court.[46]

A supplement to the 1819 Cherokee tax law, enacted on

November 11, 1824, further reinforced the regulation of the liquor traffic within the Nation. If noncitizens illegally distributed alcohol in the Nation, they not only had to forfeit the liquor but also had to pay a fine of one hundred dollars with half going to the informer and the other half to the Cherokee National Treasury. Citizens of the Nation were assessed the same fine for purchasing spirituous liquors from noncitizens within the limits of the Nation.[47] An American trader, Samuel Henry, violated this law by selling brandy within the Nation, but the National Council decided not to fine Henry when he swore never to break the Nation's laws again.[48]

The Cherokees, however, were not always so lenient. In the winter of 1825, brothers James and Samuel Reid, unlicensed U.S. traders, sold liquor to some Cherokees on the banks of the Conasauga River in the Cherokee Nation. On December 21, Cherokee officer John Walker Jr. and several other Cherokees seized from the Reids "six hundred & fifty three Gallons of whiskey and seventy three gallons of peach Brandy." Two days later, another officer, John Shepherd, demanded that the Reids pay a fine of one hundred dollars. The Reids declined to pay and eventually forfeited "Twenty Barrels of flour" from their boat. The Nation also tried its citizens who, in violation of tribal law, purchased spirituous liquors from the Reids.[49]

Indian Agent Hugh Montgomery admitted that James and Samuel Reid "did sell some whiskey" to Cherokee citizens within the boundaries of the Nation, but he complained that the Cherokees had prevented federal authorities from investigating whether or not the Reids had violated the Trade and Intercourse Acts. The Reids' case once again brought up the issue of the Cherokees' legal right to regulate the trade within the Cherokee Nation. Regarding the "questions Touching the right of passing laws affecting trade and intercourse between the Citizens of the U. States and the Cherokees," Montgomery referred to the eighth and ninth sections of the first article of the U.S. Constitution, the ninth article of the 1785 Treaty of Hopewell, and the sixth article of the 1791 Treaty of Holston. He asserted that these stipulations were "the Supreme Laws of the Land" concerning regulations of the trade. "They are," moreover, "[the Cherokees'] Constitution." According to Montgomery, the Cherokee tax laws and other trade regulations were void unless they were compatible with these provisions. Arguing that they were not, Montgomery concluded that the only thing the Nation could do was to report violations of the Trade and Intercourse Acts to the agent.[50]

On December 11, 1826, in reply to Montgomery, Assistant Principal Chief Charles Hicks and the president of the National Committee, John Ross, presented their own interpretation of the eighth section of the first article of the U.S. Constitution, which provided that "Congress shall have power to regulate Commerce with Foreign nations, and among the Several States, and with the Indian Tribes." Hicks and Ross observed that under this section, "we are placed precisely on the Same footing with Foreign nations & the Several States." Then they asked, "have not the Several States ever exercised the right of Taxing merchants Pedlors [*sic*] & c. . . . , for the purpose of creating a revenue?" Hicks and Ross never doubted that the Nation had "the Same right . . . as any other nation" to make "municipal regulations for their internal Government" to raise revenue. They restated that they would continue to exercise their legal right to tax licensed American traders "until [the] Congress or Supreme Court of the U. States shall have made a final decision on this question . . . denying . . . us the right" to levy taxes and regulate trade with the United States.[51]

On the matter of James and Samuel Reid, Hicks and Ross considered this to be a subject "of a different character." By selling whiskey to Cherokee citizens within the boundaries of the Nation, the Reids had violated the laws of the federal government as well as those of the Cherokee Nation. Hicks and Ross believed, however, that the Reids had "placed themselves completely under the Contract of the laws of the Cherokee Nation" when they entered the Nation "without a passport or a license to trade." As the eighth and ninth articles of the 1791 Treaty of Holston precisely stipulated, a noncitizens of the Cherokee Nation who settled within its boundaries "Shall forfeit the protection of the U. States, & the Cherokees may punish him or not as they please."[52]

The issue remained undecided until December 1828 because Secretary of War James Barbour failed to act on it during his term of office. In response to the urgent request of J. C. Mitchell of Tennessee, Thomas L. McKenney of the Indian Office, under the supervision of Barbour's successor Peter B. Porter, ordered Agent Montgomery to pay the Reids $779.10, the value of the losses they claimed. Once again, the sum was deducted from the Cherokee annuity.[53]

By the end of the 1820s, alcohol had become a serious issue of contention between the Cherokee Nation and the United States. Both governments felt compelled to regulate the liquor traffic, but any Cherokee effort to do so conveyed the impression that this Indian nation had the sovereign right to legislate over U.S. as well as Cherokee citizens within its bounds. U.S. officials feared that recognition of such regulations would legitimize the Cherokee constitutional government established in 1827 in the midst of their controversy. Washington officials believed that nothing should encourage assertions of Cherokee nationhood; doing so contravened a federal Indian policy designed to promote assimilation, not nationalism. Thus, the federal government opposed Cherokee initiatives in alcohol regulations. Cherokee leaders doubted neither their right nor their ability to handle the internal affairs of the tribe, however, and persisted in their policies. A clash of interests between the two powers caused prolonged disputes throughout the 1820s over who had the right to regulate trade within the boundaries of the Cherokee Nation, and the election of Andrew Jackson in 1828 further exacerbated this battle over sovereignty.

On May 26, 1830, under the Jackson administration, Congress, by a narrow margin, passed the Indian Removal Bill, which authorized negotiation for removal of eastern Indians west of the Mississippi. On June 1, the state of Georgia enforced a code of law over the part of the Cherokee Nation within its boundaries, denied the Cherokees' title to their tribal land, and forbade the national government to function.[54] Thereafter, in the eyes of the Georgians, the Cherokee Nation ceased to exist, and so did every single prohibition the Cherokee National Council had passed against the liquor traffic. Furthermore, on March 1, 1831, the Georgians' harassment extended to U.S. citizens residing within the Cherokee Nation. State law stipulated that American citizens could not stay in the Cherokee part of Georgia unless they took an oath of allegiance to the state. As soon as the Georgia Guard arrested postmaster and American Board missionary Samuel A. Worcester for violation of state law, a licensed American trader, William J. Tarvin, swore allegiance to Georgia and replaced Worcester as postmaster. Notably, Tarvin took office even though he had, for some time, sold whiskey to the Cherokees in defiance of the laws of the United States and those of the Cherokee Nation.[55] In 1832 Alabama also extended state authority over the Cherokee Nation and denied the validity of Cherokee and federal laws.[56] State laws, which offered no protection to Indians against whiskey traders, prevailed. The inability to regulate alcohol became one of the most personally damaging effects of the Cherokee Nation's loss of sovereignty during the removal crisis.

The Cherokees' regulation of alcohol was an integral part of what historian William G. McLoughlin calls the "Cherokee renascence": "The essence of Cherokee renascence was to establish a distinct national identity, firmly grounded in economic self-sufficiency and political self-determination."[57] By revitalization through political, economic, cultural, and social change, the Cherokees in the early nineteenth century sought to preserve the integrity of their people and their Native land. Cherokee political leaders used the issue of alcohol to assert their national sovereignty and establish their reputation as having "made further advances in civilization than the neighboring tribes."[58] Certainly alcohol caused problems in Cherokee society, but it also gave Cherokees an opportunity to demonstrate that they could use political sovereignty to solve their problems. The Cherokees soon augmented their case for political control of alcohol by laying claim to the moral high ground.

3

The Moral High Ground

When tribal alcohol regulations challenged the U.S. government and generated interference in Cherokee internal affairs, the Cherokees strengthened their legal claims by asserting moral authority over drinking through their temperance activities. Evangelical missionaries, particularly those of the American Board of Commissioners for Foreign Missions, assisted them. Although the pietistic Moravians had been in the Nation since the beginning of the nineteenth century, and evangelicals sporadically had attempted to convert the Cherokees, the missions established after the War of 1812 by the American Board (a Presbyterian/Congregationalist organization), Methodists, and Baptists introduced social reform as well as religious conversion. Cherokee laws regulating alcohol impressed them with Native morality. Failing to comprehend the fundamentally political nature of regulation, missionaries nevertheless came to embrace Cherokee nationalism in large part because of their perception of the Cherokee government's commitment to "civilization," including temperance.

The emergence of the temperance movement in the Cherokee Nation coincided with the election of Andrew Jackson, who invigorated federal commitment to rid the East of Indians. In 1829, a reader who took the pen name of "Philanthropist" wrote the editor of the bilingual newspaper of the tribe, the *Cherokee Phoenix*, to promote temperance. By presenting a persuasive dialogue between "Mr. Take-care" and "Mr. No-harm," "Philanthropist" made an appeal for the Cherokees to establish a temperance society. The names of these two characters symbolized their stances on temperance. While "Mr. Take-care" emphasized the importance of total abstinence, "Mr. No-harm" argued that no one would become a slave to alcohol. In concluding the dialogue, "Philanthropist" made "Mr. Take-care" assert that a "Temperance Society ought to be immediately formed in this Nation, in imitation of many such benevolent institutions in different parts of the United States."[1] In his editorial, Elias Boudinot responded positively to his correspondent's recommendation and observed that it was high time for the Nation to form a temperance society.[2]

"Philanthropist" reflected a growing sentiment in the United States. American citizens began to subscribe to the cause of temperance and to organize temperance societies during this period. Temperance historian Ian R. Tyrrell's *Sobering Up: From Temperance to Prohibition in Antebellum America, 1800–1860* traces the evolution of reform thought in the crusade against alcohol in the United States. Tyrrell observes that during the first six decades of the nineteenth century, reform thought developed from temperance (the 1810s), to total abstinence (the late 1820s and 1830s), into prohibition (the late 1840s and 1850s). Temperance reformers in antebellum America aimed at not only suppressing the liquor traffic but also solving serious social problems such as crime, violence, poverty, and immorality in the Jacksonian era. With many people identifying drunkenness as the root of all these social evils, temperance reformers advocated sobriety as the means to ensure social stability.[3]

In early America, however, drinking was widely accepted in society. On both public and private occasions, many drank, particularly those in the working class who considered alcohol a stimulant to labor.[4] The Massachusetts Society for the Suppression of Intemperance (MSSI) was the first to publicly associate excessive drinking with the laboring class. Established in 1813 as the first temperance society in the United States, the MSSI attempted, in conjunction with the state license laws, to suppress excessive drinking among the lower classes and to make them moderate drinkers. The tenet of the MSSI was, as Tyrrell puts it, "social control by one group over another."[5]

When the temperance reformers' first attempt ended in failure, the American Temperance Society (ATS) organized in 1826 with different targets and strategies from those of the MSSI. Believing that self-reform, rather than social control, would reduce intemperance and alcohol-related problems, temperance reformers of the ATS targeted "respectable" people, instead of laborers. Further diverging from the Massachusetts crusade, the ATS advocated total abstinence from alcohol. Those people who refrained from alcohol were supposed to demonstrate "the virtues of abstinence" in society. Christians, so the theory ran, should take the initiative in sobering up.[6]

From the first stage of the U.S. temperance movement, members of the American Board of Commissioners for Foreign Missions, an interdenominational group heavily engaged in Indian missions, participated in the crusade against alcohol. Three American Board missionaries were involved in the formation of the MSSI; all leaders of the ATS except one were American Board missionaries.[7]

The missionaries of the American Board had also deeply committed themselves to "civilizing" the Cherokee Indians.

In 1817 they established their first station at Brainerd and, over the next several years, steadily expanded their presence in the Nation. Described as "agricultural agents as well as messengers of Christ's Gospel," the missionaries taught Cherokee men to farm and women to spin and weave while they spread Christianity.[8] In mission schools, Cherokee children learned reading, writing, and arithmetic as well as American culture and customs. The missionaries were pleased to see the Cherokees' progress toward "civilization," but sensitized to the evils of alcohol and influenced by the stereotype of "drunken Indians," they came to believe that the Nation suffered from serious alcohol-related social ills.

American Board missionaries deplored the Cherokees' drinking habits and the consequences of alcohol consumption. Drinking promoted idleness, Sabbath-breaking, poverty, and crime, they argued, and it disrupted moral order. Alcohol undermined the integrity of Cherokee society, steadily depriving the people of control over their own lives. American Board missionaries sincerely believed that their religious influence would save the souls of drunken Cherokees. Christianity assured sobriety, and sobriety was a positive step toward being a good Christian. The missionaries often described how quickly the Cherokees reformed themselves and sought orderly lives. Within a couple of years of their arrival, the missionaries claimed to observe less intoxication around their stations.[9]

Missionary journal entries often cited the improvement of morals through temperance. On February 8, 1823, for example, one missionary wrote that a Cherokee called Jack Wicket (missionaries first thought that the name of this Indian man was "Wicked Jack") came to his station to learn the teachings of Christ. Deserted by his family and relatives, Wicket had, until recently, spent his life wandering and drinking.

Once he met Brother Samuel J. Mills, who admonished him for drinking, Wicket decided to abstain from alcohol and pursue a sober Christian life.[10]

Another missionary challenged the stereotype of "drunken Indians," which was widely believed in the United States. He pointed out that the lives of well-informed, civilized Cherokees proved "this hypothesis at least doubtful." Linking "civilization" and temperance, he lamented that U.S. citizens, with "floods of whiskey," still tempted those Cherokees who "remain in their ignorant state."[11] As agents of "civilization" and dedicated temperance reformers, American Board missionaries promoted total abstinence among the Cherokee Indians and assisted in the formation of temperance societies in the Nation.

The temperance cause became widespread throughout the Cherokee Nation, and aided by the correspondence from "Philanthropist" in 1829, a voluntary temperance movement emerged. A month after the exchange between "Mr. Take-care" and "Mr. No-harm," the Reverend Samuel A. Worcester of the American Board reported to the *Cherokee Phoenix* that a group of Cherokee citizens had adopted four resolutions to encourage total abstinence from alcohol, except as a medicine, and that copies of these resolutions, with space for signatures, would soon be available both in Cherokee and in English.[12] At their mission stations, moreover, the American Board missionaries helped the Cherokees form temperance societies. Believing that "the power of religion," rather than the enforcement of Cherokee laws, promoted temperance, these missionaries incorporated abstinence into their Christian message.[13] William Holland at Candy's Creek, Tennessee, triumphantly reported that almost all the church members—eleven Cherokee men and thirteen women—subscribed to the constitutions of the men's and women's temperance societies. He was gratified to see that more than half of the adults within four miles of his station had embraced the temperance cause.[14]

In the fall of 1829,[15] the Cherokee Temperance Society formally organized. In the presence of the Methodist Reverend James J. Trott[16] and Reverend Worcester of the American Board, a written constitution, which required total abstinence of members except in cases of illness, was presented, interpreted, and then adopted. The forty gentlemen present elected as president George Lowrey,[17] assistant principal chief, and as vice president Richard Taylor,[18] former agency interpreter. The society encouraged the members to organize auxiliary societies in their districts and entitled two representatives of each district society to attend its annual national meeting.[19]

Alcohol was not solely a concern of the eastern Cherokees. Cherokees had emigrated to Arkansas between 1808 and 1810 and between 1817 and 1819, and in 1828 they moved farther west into what is today northeastern Oklahoma. Although they left behind the constant pressure from government officials and local whites to remove, as well as some of the internal dissension related to removal, the western Cherokees struggled with alcohol-related problems. In fact, they seemed to suffer more from drunkenness than did their counterparts in the East. American Board missionary Dr. Marcus Palmer wrote in 1830:

> Indeed, intemperance with all its horrid train of evils, seems now to threaten a speedy destruction of the Nation. A few weeks ago I found at Mr. Price[']s, one Sabbath morning, as I came there to preach, several drunken persons very loud and noisy, but they moved off out of sight, when divine service began. After the

close of the exercises Mr. Price informed me, that these drunken fellows, with several others had been round his house all night, that near by, there had been on Saturday, a large collection of idle people, to attend a shooting match, and that some of them continued drinking and carousing all night, to his great annoyance.

Deploring his brethren's dissipated lives, Price asked Dr. Palmer for help. As soon as Dr. Palmer suggested that the western Cherokees form a temperance society similar to those organized in the East, Price and his friends showed a keen interest in his plan. Dr. Palmer promptly fixed a public meeting for July 10.

In the first meeting of the Arkansas Cherokee Temperance Society, thirteen gentlemen pledged total abstinence, except as a medicine, and signed the constitution of the society.[20] Membership required the emotional commitment of each member. One notorious drunk, with tears rolling down his cheeks, solemnly swore, "I hope to drink no more, and to expose my life and limbs only in doing good." Another Cherokee, David Brown,[21] could not sign his name in Cherokee because his hands trembled so much. He had to ask another person to enter his name on the list, beside which he managed to make his mark.[22] Dr. Palmer noted, "This number [thirteen] may be thought small but all the friends of the society are sanguine of the ultimate success."[23] In the course of six months, the society added nineteen Cherokee men to its membership. Functioning as the bulwark of morality, the society unanimously amended its constitution in February 1831 to prohibit members from attending places that offered entertainment such as gambling, horse racing, and ball playing where alcohol was served.[24]

Unlike their counterparts in the East, the Cherokee men

in the West encouraged women to join them in the cause of temperance. On August 8, 1830, a group of women established the Cherokee Female Society for Doing Good. Article IV of its constitution required the total abstinence of members. Embracing forty women by the end of 1831, the society cooperated with the Arkansas Cherokee Temperance Society and spread the message of the fatal effects of alcohol among the Cherokees.[25]

Except at Candy's Creek where there seems to have been a women's temperance society, at least briefly, formal temperance activities in the East involved only men. Men had a stronger tradition of drinking than women, who apparently had found few ways to incorporate alcohol into their rituals or activities. Furthermore, the men who formed the Cherokee Temperance Society were the very ones who had recently excluded women from public political life. The Cherokee constitution adopted in 1827, the culmination of a trend toward limiting political participation that began in the late eighteenth century, did not permit women to cast votes or hold office.[26] Temperance gave men an opportunity to demonstrate their ability to assert self-control at the same time that they were centralizing political institutions and implementing a system of delegated political power that they dominated.

The *Cherokee Phoenix* provided a forum for Cherokees to acknowledge their own moral failings and extol the virtue of self-control. In 1828, the *Phoenix* reported five instances of Native murders caused by the use of spirituous liquors. In one of these incidents, a drunken Cherokee "thrust a butcher-knife into the temple of another."[27] Although the event was shameful, editor Elias Boudinot carried such news in the hope that publicizing "the evil effects of ardent spirits will prove a warning to our Citizens."[28] By using a clear and plain message, the *Phoenix* reminded Cherokees of the desirability of self-control and the threat alcohol posed to this objective. The letter from a Christian Cherokee to his brother described an intemperate life:

> [G]et drunk and you will do any thing. If you want to kill a man, get drunk. If you want to fight, get drunk. If you want to be poor, or if you want to be covered with rags, get drunk. If you want to fall out with your best friend, get drunk. If you want to make all your friends and neighbors enemies, get drunk. If you want to shorten your life, get drunk. . . . Lastly, if you want to be sure to have your soul go to hell, get drunk again and again, and continue to become drunk, and it will go there.[29]

To succeed in the Cherokee republic and be a good citizen, none should remain drunk. In many ways, the Cherokee republic inaugurated by the constitution of 1827 and the temperance society cultivated by Cherokee leaders, U.S. agents, and missionaries reflected the state of the United States. In the advocacy of temperance, however, Cherokees often pointed to the failings of U.S. citizens to demonstrate the evils of alcohol. The editor of the *Phoenix*, in particular, combed the non-Indian press for sordid revelations. One example is the confession of a whiskey dealer: "I have no more doubt that I have killed a hundred men than if I had taken a gun and shot them."[30] Such tales underscored editor Boudinot's message that a drunkard lost his reason, destroyed his property, family, and health, suffered from diseases, and then died a miserable death, or he fought, made trouble, committed a crime, and went to the penitentiary. Repeatedly published in the *Cherokee Phoenix*, examples of American drunkards showed the Cherokees how spirituous liquors subverted the happy lives and undermined the morals and health of white people. One American prisoner, a victim of intemperance, confessed that "the separation from the bottle seemed like the separation of the 'joints and marrow.'" To satisfy his appetite for drink, he had tried in vain to earn a living as a teacher, an editor, and a printer. He had changed his workplace more than fifty times. He had often spent a month's earnings in one week at the tavern or the liquor shop. He continued:

> But an empty purse was the least of all the evils occasioned by this besetting and besotting sin. The same stimulates [*sic*] which heated the blood, and inflamed the animal spirits, overpowered reason; while the feet tottered, the arms trembled, and the tongue faltered, the soul was in the wildest frenzy. Three times I have been led to excesses which fell within the cognizance of municipal law; and imprisonment followed; . . . [31]

From such stories, the Cherokee people learned about the disruptive consequences of drinking as well as the moral degradation of supposedly "civilized" American citizens.

By using anecdotes about American families rather than "abstract moral precept," the *Cherokee Phoenix* conveyed to its readers the message that alcohol also destroyed family life.[32] The typical story focused on a well-educated man who enjoyed his job, achieved prosperity, and won the respect of his friends and neighbors. Marrying a pious woman, he lived a happy life with his wife and children. Once this husband and father began drinking, however, family life disintegrated. Drunkenness, often followed by poverty and domestic violence, brought tears to his wife and children who had to take shelter under a neighbor's roof. Although his wife tried to make him sober again, she, in the end, either left him or "kiss[ed] for the last time the cold lips of her dead husband, and la[id] his body for ever in the dust."[33]

In remarkable contrast to apparently rampant intemperance among Americans, the *Cherokee Phoenix* described tribal efforts to control alcohol and the success of its temperance movement. Although the *Phoenix* also reported on the temperance movement in American communities, it focused on failures and placed little emphasis on victories.[34] By contrast, the Cherokees had laws that regulated the sale and consumption of alcohol. The sobriety of the Cherokees in comparison to the citizens of the United States was a point of honor that the *Phoenix* made repeatedly. The *Phoenix* reprinted a letter originally published in the *Connecticut Observer*. Just as "A traveller" described his experience in the Cherokee Nation, the Cherokees' success in alcohol regulations and temperance reform, particularly by comparison to their white American neighbors, did not escape the attention of Americans:

> I saw but one drunken Indian, [i]n the limits of the nation, but *did* see within the same limits more than one drunken white man. There is a large Temperance Society among the Cherokees. I also learned that they have a law that no ardent spirits shall be brought within a given distance, of an election or a court of justice. A person informed me, that he was a little time before at a court, and the judge learned that some whiskey had been brought into the neighborhood. He directed the Sheriff to search for it, and dispose of it according to law.—He did so. After finding it he poured it all upon the ground, as the law directs.[35]

The Cherokees were making headway in transforming the popular image of Indians.

The Cherokees' ability to control alcohol consumption strengthened their claims to sovereignty, particularly in light of the failure of the United States to control the drunkenness of its own citizens. On April 21, 1830, the *Cherokee Phoenix* carried excerpts from a report prepared by the Committee on Indian Affairs in the House of Representatives, along with Boudinot's counterargument. Boudinot protested the committee's statement that "the condition of the common Indian is perceptibly declining," and he proudly asserted that "*the common Indian among the Cherokees is not declining, but rising.*" Boudinot compared the Cherokee Nation's rigid application of laws with the intemperance that undermined American communities:

> [A]mong the whites of the surrounding counties intemperance and brutal intoxication . . . may be witnessed in every neighborhood. Go to their elections and courts and number those who are under the influence of inebriating drink, and then come into the nation, and visit the Indian elections, courts and the General Council and make a disinterested comparison, and we pledge ourselves that there is less intemperance exhibited here on these occasions than among the whites. It is an incontrovertible fact, for the truth of which we appeal to all honest eye-witnesses, that on those public occasions, particularly at the General Council, which continues four weeks, a drunken Indian is seldom to be seen. We are sorry that intemperance does exist, but is it not universal? There has been of late considerable reformation among the Cherokees, in common with other parts of the country.[36]

Boudinot's editorial portrayed the Cherokees not as the

equal of the white American neighbors but as their moral superiors.

Despite the considerable evidence that the Cherokees presented, U.S. policy makers in the 1820s increasingly concluded that the vices of "civilization," including alcohol, had overtaken its virtues in Indian country. To save Native people, U.S. policy makers argued, the federal government had to isolate the Indians west of the Mississippi and make the encroachment and depredation of American intruders "unhappy memories of the past."[37] Removal also would presumably rescue Indians from their unscrupulous American neighbors and shield them from the corrupting influence of the Euro-Americans' liquor.

On March 31, 1832, the *Cherokee Phoenix* carried a letter written by a supposedly sympathetic gentleman in Tennessee. The letter originally appeared in the *Journal of Communication*:

> While the white man can go and come without fear of robbery, oppression or murder, the poor Indian must watch night and day, to preserve even one little poney [*sic*] to plough his field, or one poor cow to nourish his children, . . . White women can pass and repass with safety among the Indians, yet the Indians must watch with the most anxious solicitude, or their wives and daughters will be betrayed, debauched, & worse than murdered by *American citizens*. Mhey [*sic*] must watch also every motion of their own hearts, or they are made drunkards before they know it by *American citizens*, who are constantly forcing intoxicating poison into their hands. Wherever they go, which way soever they turn, they find American citizens with some dark and deep laid plan to rob them of their property, their friends, their virtue, their good name, their all.

The letter writer's account of the suffering of the Cherokees seemed quite reliable, although the editor of the *Journal of Communication* noted that "his remarks are by no means intended to apply to the whole population who surround the Cherokees, or indeed to any considerable part of them." The Tennessean, however, reached the following conclusion:

> They cannot live with such wretches. They must go to the more virtuous Comanches of the West! If American citizens were not insensible to shame, they would blush at the recital of their deeds; but they now glory in their shame. . . . Yes, *American citizens* are so much worse than the Indians, that the latter cannot live near them without being robbed, corrupted and debased: therefore they must remove. Let all the world know this.[38]

His statement reflected an important argument in favor of Indian removal. Justifying the Removal Act as humanitarian, policy makers maintained that in the West, the Indians could pursue a peaceful and "civilized" life at their own pace, without the interference of the states, including state laws that permitted the sale of alcohol to Indians, or the vices of U.S. citizens.[39] However benevolent the stated rationale, removal was the last thing most Cherokees wanted, and they believed that one way to avoid removal was to prove that temperate and responsible Cherokee citizens could coexist with Americans, even those who were considerably less sober and respectable than they were. The Cherokees desperately wanted to remain where they were because they loved their ancestral land, owned many improvements to that land, and linked their national identity with their geographic location.[40]

In passing the Indian Removal Bill on May 26, 1830, policy makers assured the Indians that they could live a peaceful and quiet life west of the Mississippi, but to Jeremiah Evarts, secretary of the American Board, the West could never be "a sanctuary for Indians, to which their corrupters and tempters could never gain access."[41] Evarts was the most powerful lobbyist against Indian removal. Publishing the "William Penn" essays on behalf of the Indians in 1829, Evarts defended the Indian cause, appealed to the conscience of U.S. citizens, and urged them to oppose this immoral bill. Even after Pres. Andrew Jackson signed the Removal Bill, Evarts did not give up hope and attempted to prevent the enforcement of the removal policy.

In a memorial of the American Board to Congress dated January 26, 1831, Evarts contended that even "a general removal of a community can never be achieved without exposure to a serious deterioration, in regard to morals, manners, and enjoyments; and it needs very high attainments of mind & hearts to preserve a community, in such circumstances, from a most ruinous catastrophe." For those "who have just begun to form such habits as are indispensable to the whole process of civilization," therefore, removal would be particularly disastrous, and it would only further the Indians' disintegration. More problematic, Evarts continued, was the presence of alcohol. As earlier removals had demonstrated, liquor was "always within the reach of the emigrants," and alcohol, brought with American intruders, remained "the bane of the Indian tribes" in the West.[42] Evarts squarely placed the blame for Indian drunkenness on Americans, not on Natives.

Evarts's strong defense of Cherokee rights failed to protect the Cherokees from the harassment of the neighboring states. His prediction of the corrupting influence of American citizens proved true. In particular, Georgia's actions in the early 1830s that suspended Cherokee law and extended state law over much of the Cherokee Nation became the "fountain cause of the growing intemperance of the Cherokees and the loss of lives."[43] Unrestrained by Georgia law, liquor dealers flooded the Nation. The missionaries observed that "a dark cloud" lay low over the Cherokee people.[44] The influence of the corrupt world reached every corner of the Cherokee Nation and destroyed the religious family life that they had carefully cultivated among the Cherokees. "With great professions of friendship for the Indians," liquor dealers approached Cherokee men and women and gave them whiskey "as medicine." Easily obtaining liquor in the intruders' shops, even church members yielded to the temptation of alcohol. Among teenagers, too, drinking and gambling spread. Intruders brought whiskey onto playgrounds and invited Cherokee children to drink. To acquire whiskey, drunken parents took bread from their children's mouths. Easily victimized by demon rum, the missionaries bemoaned, the Cherokees became a tragically tormented people.[45] When Alabama extended state authority over the Cherokee Nation in 1832, the Reverend William Chamberlain at Willstown reported that a man opened a dram shop within a mile of his mission station and began selling liquor to the Cherokees. To his regret, even those Cherokees who had long refrained from alcohol became regular customers.[46] The missionaries held white Georgians and Alabamans, not Cherokees, accountable for the distressing situation.

Although the missionaries may have sensationalized Cherokee victimization in order to further their own evangelical goals, secular sources also decried the flood of alcohol that threatened to swamp the Cherokee Nation. Cherokee Agent Hugh Montgomery lamented in 1833 that the Nation not only had many successful liquor smugglers but also had "stills, and retail shops all around our borders." Those who wished to purchase liquor could do so "without regard to colour or sex." Only the neighboring states could prevent the introduction of spirituous liquors into the Nation, but neither Georgia nor Alabama enacted laws to regulate alcohol.[47] This situation led Principal Chief John Ross to accuse the federal government of failing to fulfill its duty.[48] Elbert Herring, commissioner of Indian affairs, agreed that the government had the "duty to give to the law all possible efficiency," but he freely admitted that alcohol regulations would be much easier "[a]fter their removal west" to land not claimed by any state.[49]

While the Nation tried to suppress drunkenness, the federal and neighboring state governments pressured the Cherokees to negotiate removal. Although Chief Justice of the United States John Marshall recognized Cherokee sovereignty in *Worcester v. Georgia* (1832), denied Georgia's authority to enforce its laws within the boundaries of the Cherokee Nation, and ordered Georgia to release missionaries imprisoned for their refusal to take an oath of allegiance to that state, the state refused to do so, and the federal government encouraged it to ignore the ruling. Georgia continued to threaten the existence of the Cherokee Nation by distributing Cherokee land within the state boundaries to its citizens who registered for land lotteries. Once the drawings of the Georgia lottery began on October 22, 1832, many "fortune drawers" entered the Nation and harassed the Cherokees in every possible way. Powerless in the midst of land-hungry Americans, many Cherokee men, in particular, drank excessively.[50]

Georgia law had suspended the operation of the Cherokee government and made it impossible for the National Council to meet openly. In this breach, temperance became a subterfuge by which the Cherokees continued their banned republican government. On October 20, 1833, the Cherokee Temperance Society, founded originally in 1829, reorganized as the Cherokee National Temperance Society. Headed by Principal Chief John Ross, the society became centralized. Eight vice presidents, one from each of the electoral districts in the Nation, assumed responsibility for establishing societies in their respective districts. The society's constitution also provided that it "shall meet annually on the 3d Monday in Oct., at the place where the General Council shall convene." By 1833 the council no longer met at the capital New Echota, which was in the territory claimed by Georgia, but met instead at Red Clay, which was within the boundaries of Tennessee; its decisions were not enforceable in Georgia. Council members could not stand for election nor could they meet to discuss political issues. They could, however, take the pledge. After unanimous adoption of the new society's constitution, almost all the members of the former General Council of the Cherokee Nation subscribed to the pledge of total abstinence and became members of the society.[51] The moral high ground became a political refuge. The National Temperance Society kept no records—or, at least, no records beyond the inaugural one survive—so we do not know exactly how it functioned. Still, the society kept lines of communication open throughout the Nation, including that part that lay within Georgia, and provided opportunities for political leaders to meet and discuss issues of national concern. Unlike with the outlawed Cherokee government, Georgians could not assert that such a benevolent group violated the sovereignty of their state.

Elias Boudinot, his cousin John Ridge, and his uncle Major Ridge became increasingly disillusioned by the disorder in the Cherokee Nation and ultimately formed a pro-treaty party. Although most of the members of the Treaty party advocated removal due to their economic and political ambitions, Boudinot believed that removal would save the Nation and his fellow Cherokees from national disintegration and moral degradation.[52] The systematic actions on the part of the federal government to dispossess the Cherokees of their land culminated in the *"Christmas trick"* of 1835. U.S. treaty commissioner John F. Schermerhorn appointed twenty pro-removal Cherokees to negotiate on Christmas Day, but they were too intoxicated to discuss provisions with the commissioner. Four days later, the members of the Treaty party finally signed the Treaty of New Echota. Ceding the tribal land for $5 million, this small group of people determined the fate of the entire Nation.[53]

Although Chief Ross had soon to give up the idea of abrogating the treaty, he attempted to amend it by asking Congress to increase the amount of money the Cherokees were to receive under its provisions. Boudinot accused Ross: "Mr. Ross is using his influence to defeat the only measure that can give relief to his suffering people."[54] "You seem to be absorbed altogether in the pecuniary aspects of this nation's affairs," he continued, and when many more American intruders overran the Nation and dispossessed the people of their land and property, "you say little or nothing about the moral condition of this people, as affected by present circumstances." Boudinot condemned Ross for his nonchalance of "the depression of the mind, and the degradation and pollution of the soul" among his fellow citizens. They were "dying a moral death" in the midst of American intruders, Boudinot insisted, and intemperance, murders, and prostitution produced "a general immorality and debasement" of the Cherokees.[55]

Some Cherokees left for the West under the supervision of the United States before the time specified by the Treaty of New Echota, but the majority of the tribe remained in the East. They hoped that they could stay where they were, but the constant presence of alcohol made their situation miserable. In 1837, for example, an American named Robert Kirkham Jr. sold whiskey to the Cherokees who stayed within the garrison at New Echota for consultation with the U.S. treaty commissioners. Faced with "great irregularity, inconvenience, and disorder," Gen. John Ellis Wool told Kirkham to stop his illegal activity, but he refused to obey the order. When Lt. George W. Paschall, under the direction of General Wool, confiscated the whiskey and disposed of it, Kirkham sued the lieutenant for damages in the Supreme Court of Georgia, and Paschall had to pay the sum of $291.62 to Kirkham.[56]

Contending that the Cherokees would soon become "an easy prey to speculators" and that "the retailer of ardent spirits, . . . will complete the work of degradation and ruin which the speculator has commenced," the state of Alabama in 1836 refused to provide reservations for the Cherokees within its boundaries.[57] When General Wool, in response to Cherokees' complaints, attempted to halt the sale of spirituous liquors to the Cherokees, Alabama, on July 3, 1837, accused Wool of having "usurped the powers of the civil tribunals, disturbed the peace of the community, and trampled upon the rights of the citizens."[58] Many in the adjoining states failed to show an ounce of mercy to the Cherokees and abhorred those citizens who sympathized with the Indians.

In the early summer of 1838, the U.S. Army confined the Cherokees in stockades to await removal to the West. Capt. L. B. Webster, who led eight hundred Cherokees in western North Carolina into the central depot at Calhoun, Tennessee, wrote to his wife on June 28 that the Cherokees in the stockades "are the most quiet people you ever saw."[59] They were a depressed and discouraged people who had been driven from their homeland.

Forced removal of the Cherokees began immediately after completion of the roundup and confinement. Considering the mortality of the first three contingents, however, Gen. Winfield Scott allowed the Cherokees to postpone the major deportation until autumn, and Pres. Martin Van Buren agreed. "The most quiet people" in the stockades remained victims of the Americans—this time, the victims of those soldiers who were supposed to keep order. Deploring the Cherokees' "moral desolation," including their "almost universal Saturday night frolicks, carried through the Holy Sabbath," the American Board missionary Daniel S. Butrick wrote:

> The other day a gentleman informed me that he saw six soldiers about two Cherokee women. The women stood by a tree, and the soldiers with a bottle of liquor were endeavouring to entice them to drink, though the women, as yet were resisting them. He made this known to the commanding officer but we presume no notice was taken of it, as it was reported that those soldiers had these women with them the whole night afterwards. A young married woman, a member of the Methodist society, was at the camps with her friends, though her husband was not there at the time. The soldiers, it is said, caught her, dragged her about, and at length, either through fear, or otherwise, induced her to drink; and then seduced her away, so that she is now an outcast even among her own relatives.[60]

A substantial number of Cherokee women probably became the victims of alcohol-induced abuse.

On July 26, 1838, General Scott entrusted the Cherokees with full powers to manage their own emigration.[61] Chief Ross promptly appointed thirteen conductors to lead the detachments to the new country.[62] On October 4, Butrick left Brainerd with his wife to join the Cherokees in the stockades to set out for the Indian territory.[63] From the following day, "the almost constant yell of drunkards passing & repassing to & from a whiskey shop set up by a white man to ensnare the poor Indians" disturbed their nights.[64] Throughout their westward journey, Butrick and his wife "exposed [themselves] to hear the Name of our Blessed God and Saviour thus blasphemed."[65] Americans continued to serve liquor to the Cherokees on their way west, and all-night drinking bouts disturbed many emigrants.[66] A woman visited Butrick's tent one night: "She had been kept awake all night long by drunkards, and was almost worn out."[67] Although Cherokees succumbed to the temptation or pressure to drink, responsibility for the situation rested largely with Americans who preyed on the emigrants. When Butrick preached to lawless Americans about the sin of profane swearing, "[a]ll seemed still for the moment, but soon after the exercise closed, the white men commenced their awful career for the night." Their riotous behavior frightened the Cherokees and caused the Indian men to remain "very sober during the night."[68]

On the day he left Brainerd, Butrick wrote: "O what scenes of distress we have experienced here for two years past."[69] Drunkenness was a major cause of the distress, but Butrick and other missionaries did not hold the Cherokees accountable. Over the preceding decade, the Cherokees had demonstrated their commitment to temperance not merely through their laws but also in the organization of temperance societies. Their national newspaper promoted the virtue of sobriety and pointed to the moral failings of the Cherokees' supposedly "civilized" American neighbors. The suspension of Cherokee law by the states of Alabama and Georgia led to the unbridled marketing of alcohol by white Americans within the Cherokee Nation, and many Cherokees, disheartened by political events and frightened about the future, turned to alcohol for solace. As much as Cherokee leaders and their sympathizers decried this weakness, they placed blame firmly on white purveyors of liquor and depicted the Cherokees as victims. While the Cherokees lost the battle against removal, they clearly won, in the eyes of many Americans, the contest over the moral high ground.

4

Alcohol and Dislocation

Alcohol took a serious toll on the Cherokees in the years surrounding removal. Unregulated and widely available, liquor offered comfort to disillusioned Cherokees, particularly men. The justice of their cause and the moral fiber of their people seemed to carry little sway in the United States. The Nation they had established in the Southeast and the cultural transformation that many had achieved offered the Cherokees no protection from the greed and racism of white southerners. Alcohol eased the pain and indignity of their forced migration to the West and the political chaos that marked the reestablishment of their Nation. One of the great challenges presented by removal was reclaiming the legacy of sovereignty and morality, both rooted in the control of alcohol, that the Cherokees had created in the Southeast.

In contrast to their previous sobriety, Cherokee alcohol abuse after 1835 exacerbated the trauma of removal, and Cherokee women and children, in particular, suffered enormously. Recollecting the scenes of Cherokee family disintegration still vivid in her mind, for example, the wife of a Georgia intruder, Zillah Haynie Brandon, wrote that "the wives of those drunken savages knew the least about a resting place." She continued, "[H]usbands would drink to drunkenness, and were very cruel when under the influence of the fire water." Although the Cherokee men of Brandon's acquaintance might refrain from drinking for a couple of weeks, "the poisoned cup was again placed to their lips." Brandon admitted that Cherokee men posed no threat when they were sober, but she never knew when her safety would be jeopardized by an American intruder selling whiskey to the Cherokees in her vicinity.[1]

Once, in her husband's absence, a group of Cherokee men started drinking in her neighborhood. One man uttered "shrill panther-like screams," and his wife had to flee with her children. Brandon briefly sheltered them inside her house. Fearing that the Brandon household was too obvious a haven, the Cherokee mother and children soon left. Danger was, indeed, close at hand. With gun at the ready, the furious husband headed for the Brandon dwelling. Brandon immediately took her children to another neighbor's house and escaped injury, but they did not feel secure until the neighborhood liquor store closed its door.[2] Drunkenness provoked lawlessness, destroyed family life, threatened the entire community, and dismayed the Cherokees even more in the years to come.

Under the terms of the New Echota Treaty, the federal government conducted three Cherokee detachments in 1837 and early 1838 to the new Cherokee Nation in what is today eastern Oklahoma. Accompanying the first party in March 1837, physician C. Lillybridge recorded the events of the monthlong journey in his journal. As his account reveals, the party experienced considerable intoxication and lawlessness the entire way. From the first day of the journey, several Cherokees drank whiskey and became "a very rude and noisy set."[3] When they reached Gunter's Landing in Alabama on March 6, officials decided to anchor the boats at Gunter's Island in the hope of preventing the Cherokees from getting drunk in the town. Some Cherokees, however, dared to swim across the Tennessee River to acquire alcohol. Afraid of drowning, the Cherokee Alexander Brown seized a canoe and attempted to climb inside, but because of the strong current, he lost his balance and fell into the water. When he finally managed to regain his footing, the river had swept Brown two hundred yards from the bank.[4] Five days later, another Cherokee, Killanica, who had received a blow to his left eye on a spree, came to see Lillybridge. He treated Killanica's inflamed eye and noted that the patient had a splitting headache as well.[5] When the Cherokees "had free access to the Whiskey shops" at Montgomery Point on March 18, many drank, and some even brought whiskey into the boats, which produced a drinking bout and "a number of quarrels" on board.[6]

Although they did not suffer as much as their earlier counterparts did, the second detachment of Cherokees heading west to Indian Territory in the winter of 1837 also experienced intemperance on their overland journey.[7] On November 20, for example, conductor B. B. Cannon had to "get out of bed about midnight" to deal with a group of drunken Cherokees.[8]

Nor could the third party prevent "rioting, fighting, or disorder" caused by the use of intoxicating liquors.[9] During his detachment's emigration in the spring of 1838, Lt. Edward Deas had to remain fully alert to the ways in which he could block Native access to alcohol. To prevent Indian drunkenness, Lieutenant Deas anchored the boats as far from the towns as possible.[10] On the last day of his tour of duty, the lieutenant confessed that spirituous liquors were the "only source of annoyance" on the one-month journey and further noted that he had no difficulty in controlling the Cherokees when they were sober but that once they were placed under the influence of alcohol, they became "unmanageable."[11]

The treaty required the Cherokees to leave for the western land by May 23, 1838, but most of them continued to live in the East. In spite of Gen. Winfield Scott's warning on May 10 that his soldiers were about to begin rounding up Cherokees for deportation, the mass of Cherokees could not imagine what would soon happen to them.[12]

In the summer of 1838, the first three detachments of Cherokees under forced removal successively departed for the West. Alcohol once again generated disorder en route. While the second party waited in Tuscumbia, Alabama, to sail for Waterloo, for example, the guard's unauthorized absence permitted the introduction of whiskey, and more than one hundred Cherokees escaped from the camp.[13] The vice of alcohol followed the Cherokees along the Trail of Tears to their new homes, which were also abundant in alcohol. The march westward did not secure a peaceful life for the Cherokees.

The experiences of the "Old Settlers," who had removed decades earlier, did not bode well for these new emigrants. Until 1828, the Old Settlers had lived in Arkansas where they constantly were exposed to the evils of intemperance. They also confronted the issues of sovereignty and removal just as had their brethren in the East. When U.S. officials tightened alcohol regulations in Indian country, western Cherokees recognized it as an attempt to undermine the autonomy of their tribe. The greatest challenge, however, came in 1828 when the United States forced them to move farther west. Removal precipitated an increase in alcohol abuse. The Reverend Cephas Washburn had to admit the distressing fact in 1830: "There has been more drunkenness in the nation during the last *six months*, than for the whole ... *six years* preceding."[14]

Having worked among the western Cherokees since 1821,

Washburn came to think of "their connection with the white population on their borders as the circumstance[s] most unfavorable to their improvement." He had followed this small group of people when the Treaty of 1828 removed them farther west where, he hoped, "they are no more to be surrounded by a white population." Washburn, however, soon realized that the migration did not help the Old Settlers: "The evil is not diminished in the least. Indeed it is greatly increased."[15] The trauma of removal almost certainly challenged the Cherokees' will to resist and made them more susceptible to the temptation of alcohol.

Alcohol abuse threatened all aspects of tribal life in the West. Intemperance produced Native whiskey dealers, idleness, and assault and murder. Stating that "I would not, I need not, I do not exaggerate" the present conditions of the western Cherokees, Washburn continued his report of 1830 by recounting the spread of "the liquid fire" and its accompanying miseries. Knowing that the federal government would soon make monetary compensation to the Cherokees for their lands in Arkansas, merchants and traders carried large amounts of whiskey into the Nation. Both Cherokees and Americans with Cherokee families bought whiskey and, as go-betweens, sold the product to others. Washburn estimated that between fifty and one hundred men married to Cherokee women had liquor to sell around the Nation. As a result, many Cherokees gave themselves up to debauchery. Drunken Cherokees neglected their work and left their farmlands uncultivated. Gambling, fighting, and murder became prevalent. Within the period of eight months, about fifty Cherokees lost their lives in alcohol-related incidents. Washburn lamented that the Indian agents, without effective federal intercourse acts or a tribal law to regulate the flow of alcohol within the western Cherokee country, could not suppress intemperance. He warned Thomas L. McKenney of the Office of Indian Affairs that this situation would encourage the eastern Cherokees to resist removal to the West.[16]

The U.S. government failed to enforce the Trade and Intercourse Acts of 1802 and 1822, which prohibited the introduction of whiskey into Indian country, and liquor flowed freely into Cherokee communities, particularly in the vicinity of the Cherokee-Arkansas line.[17] In 1831, for example, George Vashon, the agent for the western Cherokees, learned that the Fort Smith trading firm of Colville & Coffee had employed James M. Randolph as a clerk and instructed him to sell whiskey to Indians on the Cherokee-Arkansas border. Vashon warned the company that he would not renew its license as long as it continued this illicit activity.[18] Nevertheless, Vashon only briefly hesitated when William DuVal and Peter A. Carnes, both American citizens, applied on April 3 for a license to trade in the Cherokee Nation. DuVal and Carnes admitted "verbally" that they were "in the constant habit of selling large quantities of whiskey to the Indians," and they asserted that "every citizen of the U.S. [was] legally authorized to do so." Although he asked Secretary of War John H. Eaton for further instructions, Vashon, in the meantime, permitted the two to open a retail shop in the Cherokee Nation on condition that they did not violate provisions in the Trade and Intercourse Acts, presumably including those prohibiting the liquor traffic.[19]

Such irregularities on the part of Agent Vashon created consternation among the western Cherokees, but his insistence on enforcing prohibition within their communities concerned these Cherokees even more. On July 9, 1832, Congress passed an absolute alcohol ban that stated: "No ardent spirits shall be hereafter introduced, under any pretence, into the Indian country."[20] Although Agent Vashon notified the western Cherokees' General Council of the law on September 26, the council refused to consent to federal control of Cherokee liquor traders and distillers within the Nation. The chiefs considered internal liquor questions and trade regulations to be within their exclusive purview. Western Cherokee councilmen clearly saw the 1832 prohibitory act as a federal infringement of "our Rights & Privileges."[21] Vashon ignored the council's pronouncement, however, and in November 1832, he confiscated forty barrels of whiskey in the Nation from the Cherokees James Cary, Walter Webber, and Peter Harper.[22] Vashon also tried in vain to seize liquor from the Cherokee merchant John Drew, who refused to surrender himself to federal authorities until Maj. Francis W. Armstrong, the agent for the Choctaws, finally "overpowered" him and confiscated the four barrels from him.[23] Charles Rogers, a Cherokee distiller, suffered similar treatment when U.S. troops destroyed his distillery and gristmill in June 1833.[24]

On March 6, 1833, John Drew petitioned Secretary of War Lewis Cass for monetary compensation. Also acting as a representative of Cary and Harper, Drew contended that they had introduced the whiskey prior to the 1832 prohibitory enactment and, therefore, the agents had seized "his and their lawfull property."[25]

Vashon welcomed the opportunity to demonstrate to Washington his scrupulous performance of duty as an Indian agent. Vashon insisted that Harper, as a U.S. citizen, had introduced whiskey into the Nation "in direct violation of and after the promulgation of the [1832] prohibitory act" although Harper lived in the Nation with his Cherokee family, and the Cherokees regarded him as an adopted citizen.[26] Vashon could not make a similar claim about Cary and Webber, prominent members of the tribe, and he assured them of a fair price for the damage caused by the seizures. In correspondence of April 1833 to Commissioner of Indian Affairs Elbert Herring, Vashon confessed that he was aware Cary and Webber had introduced whiskey into the Nation several months before the passage of the prohibitory act and the "said whiskey was not legally liable to seizure." Vashon had seized the property, not because he believed that these Cherokees violated the federal law, but because he appreciated the federal efforts to restrain liquor traffic in Indian country, and he felt compelled to "endeavor to effect the benevolent views of the government upon the subject."[27] In an attempt to secure prompt remuneration for these illegal seizures, Vashon disingenuously wrote the commissioner that "a highly respectable portion of the Cherokee Nation was decidedly in favor of the law" and that he would seek "their cordial cooperation to prevent the introduction of ardent spirits" in the Nation.[28] Lack of funds in the War Department and protest of the estimates of loss, however, ultimately prevented Vashon from getting reimbursement for these Cherokees.[29]

Capt. John Stuart, the commanding officer at Fort Smith, reported to Secretary of War Lewis Cass in 1833 that the Cherokees were "determined to Seize upon — every possible Occasion, to annoy the officers of Government, engaged in enforcing" the liquor law, but the 1832 incident did not develop into a political dispute between the United States and the Cherokee Nation, nor did it encourage Cherokee initiative in alcohol regulations in the West.[30] Still, successive raids and seizures of private property by the U.S. officers and troops reinforced the idea among the western Cherokees that the 1832 prohibitory act was "oppressive, arbit[r]ary, and unlawful." Captain Stuart informed Secretary Cass that prominent members of the Cherokee tribe "are almost unanimously opposed to the late Acts of Congress in relation to the introduction of Ardent Spirits into their nation." The Cherokees drank much less than other Indian tribes, he believed, and "their civilized condition" helped them "not when drunk [to] show one half the savage Ferosity of other Indians."[31] Stuart's observations on this particular Indian tribe, however, were never persuasive enough to affect U.S. Indian policy regarding the internal liquor traffic, and the confiscation of private property continued.

By this time the Arkansas Cherokee Temperance Society and the Cherokee Female Society for Doing Good had ceased to function, largely because their reforming efforts did not long sustain public interest. Another reason for their decline was the pledge they formulated. The pledge required the members to abstain from distilled liquors, but not from fermented drinks such as cider and wine. A substantial number of subscribers, therefore, became intoxicated "without having broken their pledge." The first secretary of the Arkansas Cherokee Temperance Society was among those so disgraced.[32] Despite an awareness of the intoxicating effects of weaker beverages, the thrust of prohibition was still toward the introduction and sale of liquor.

A year after the 1832 liquor law, Commissioner Herring, in a circular, reminded Indian superintendents and agents throughout the country that "Indians[,] equally with white persons, are liable to" indictment when they introduced alcohol into Indian country.[33] The Trade and Intercourse Act, passed on June 30, 1834, addressed directly this subjection of Indian individuals in Indian country to the federal alcohol regulations. The law required Indian superintendents, agents, and subagents as well as military officers to search the stores, packages, boats, and warehouses of the American and Indian liquor traders suspected of introduction and, if they found alcohol, to seize all of the trader's goods and property. Civilian officers were also responsible for imposing a fine of one thousand dollars on distillers and ordering the military forces to destroy stills in Indian country.[34]

Notably, the 1834 Intercourse Act granted "any Indian," together with U.S. officials, a right to destroy spirituous liquors and wine when found in Indian country, but the law, to the western Cherokee chiefs, was still "oppressive, and restricts their liberties as free citizens." They complained that the law was unevenly enforced in Indian country and that while one whiskey peddler was under arrest, "twenty others, on other roads & routes, will escape observation or detection."[35]

Inconsistency among federal officers in Indian country prevented proper enforcement of the trade regulations. In July 1837, for example, a U.S. citizen, Maj. Elbert Harris, obtained from the Western Cherokee General Council a permit for him and his partner Wood to establish a store in the Nation, on the Arkansas River, opposite Fort Smith. Wood and Harris then applied to Indian Agent Montfort Stokes for a license to trade in the Cherokee Nation.[36] The 1834 Intercourse Act required Agent Stokes to designate a "certain suitable and convenient" spot for traders, but, in issuing a license, he announced that "it is altogether impossible for me to select suitable places for trade" and abdicated his responsibility: "I have uniformly left it to the traders themselves to *choose* their own stations and have granted them licenses accordingly."[37]

William Armstrong, the acting superintendent of Indian affairs of the western territory, took issue with Stokes's lack of decision: "The location of Messrs[.] Wood & Harris according to my view is the worst that could be made for the benefit of the Indians." Far from minimizing contact between Cherokees and the tavern keepers in Arkansas, Armstrong observed, Agent Stokes had allowed Wood and Harris to build a trading house "among the largest Whiskey dealers on the line." Indians would soon cross the river and obtain liquor in the state of Arkansas. Armstrong, moreover, feared that Wood and Harris would eventually engage in this illicit yet lucrative business themselves.[38] In December 1837, Armstrong revoked their trading license.[39] In March 1838, he ordered Captain Stuart to confiscate the goods in Wood and Harris's store, and a month later, Lt. Henry McKavitt and his twenty men seized the store but found no liquor within.[40] Although he did not dispute the acting superintendent's action against Harris and Wood, Agent Stokes, without much screening, continued to issue licenses to trade in the Nation "almost at will."[41] In 1839, when the eastern Cherokees joined the Old Settlers in the West, whiskey peddlers welcomed them.

Having accompanied the Cherokees on the Trail of Tears and shared their sufferings, American Board missionary Daniel S. Butrick encountered another deplorable scene soon after he completed his trek to the West. He discovered that a storekeeper named D. Sanders retailed liquor to the Cherokees in his grocery. Butrick rebuked Sanders: "If I wished to kill off the Indians I could take no more direct method than to fill the country with whiskey." Sanders did not flinch and retorted that "all must have some way to get a living." Butrick replied that "the thief & robber would say the same." Although Sanders "did not wish any one to come to his house to trouble him," Butrick decided to "trouble him as long as" he kept whiskey for sale in the store.[42]

The yet-to-be-unified Cherokee Nation invested much of its early nation-making effort in the trans-Mississippi West in the restoration of peace and order and the reestablishment of political unity. The Ross party was at virtual civil war with the Treaty party, and the Old Settlers regarded Chief Ross as a usurper. Furthermore, the Old Settlers were much less likely to regulate individual behavior, especially economic behavior, and less interested in moral reform than the Ross people. Still, to Cherokee leaders who had migrated recently from the East, the termination of the surreptitious liquor traffic and prevention of abusive drinking among their citizens remained pressing issues.

On September 28, 1839, in its new capital, Tahlequah, the National Council, under the control of the Ross party, passed a law prohibiting alcohol in public places. Cherokee officials, as well as persons appointed by the sheriffs, were responsible for destroying spirituous liquors introduced within five miles of the National Council and one mile of the courts while in session. They were also to keep the area within one mile of any public gathering or meeting alcohol-free.[43] On October 25, 1841, Acting Chief Andrew Vann approved an act that provided, "from and after the first day of January, 1842, the introduction and vending of ardent spirits in this Nation shall be unlawful; and any and all persons are prohibited from selling or retailing spirituous liquors within the limits of the Nation, under the penalty of having the same wasted or destroyed by any lawful officer, or person authorized by the Sheriff for that purpose." When found guilty, the offenders, Cherokee or non-Cherokee, had to pay a fine of between ten dollars and five hundred dollars.[44] The alcohol regulations of the postremoval era, unlike the laws exercised in the past, did not exempt Cherokee citizens. The Cherokee people did not unanimously approve these laws, but total prohibition became the general rule within the boundaries of the Nation.

Although the Nation did not have a unified tribal government, the Cherokee officers diligently enforced the liquor laws. Maj. Ethan Allen Hitchcock observed during his official trip to Indian territory between November 1841 and March 1842: "I have not yet seen a drunken man since I came into the [Cherokee] nation. . . . I have never seen any assembly of people more orderly than this at Tahlequah."[45] He witnessed Cherokee sheriffs destroy whiskey on the council ground "by bursting the head of the barrel." They "also broke a gallon jug and a quart bottle wasting the liquor contents of each." Although the whiskey vendor sought a quarrel with one of the sheriffs that night, the Cherokee officer "found no difficulty in protecting his dignity."[46] At the house of Young Wolfe, a Cherokee preacher, Hitchcock heard the preacher's daughter explaining her reaction to a tribal law sanctioning intermarriage between non-Cherokee men and Cherokee women: "The Cherokee men had better behave better and stop drinking whiskey and then the 'Cherokee girls would marry them.'"[47] More frequently, however, U.S. citizens who resided in the Nation suffered by comparison to Cherokees. Gen. Matthew Arbuckle maintained that the Americans were "men of bad character" and that they "live with Indian women, or take them as wives, . . . from no other motive than to be permitted to remain in the Indian country for the purpose of violating the Intercourse Law by introducing and vending ardent spirits."[48]

Alcohol helped exacerbate disorder in the Cherokee Nation. Until the ratification of a treaty among the Ross party, the Old Settlers, and the Treaty party in 1846, which subdued factionalism and general discord, the Cherokee people suffered uneasiness, confusion, political turmoil, and bloodshed. Chief Ross observed in 1842: "All these unhappy occurrences are to be traced to intemperance and the effects of smuggling ardent spirits into the Cherokee Country."[49] The *Cherokee Advocate* concluded in 1845 that the forced removal and the illegal liquor traffic had generated nationwide terrorism and lawlessness.[50]

Reinforcing its alcohol regulations, the National Council, on October 31, 1843, amended the prohibition of 1841 and granted the Cherokee sheriffs and officers the right to examine, under search warrants, houses suspected of concealing alcohol.[51] On December 11, the council empowered a special guard to maintain order around the council ground during its session. The council charged the guard to destroy any intoxicating liquors it could find and also "to arrest and confine until they become sober, any drunken persons or any others, who may behave disorderly."[52] The enforcement of these laws remained entirely another issue, however, and Chief Ross lamented in 1844 that Cherokee and U.S. officials as well as good citizens of the Nation "had not ... jointly taken some prompt and efficient steps to put it [alcohol] down in as much as the laws of both Countries prohibits its introduction and use in this Nation under the penalty of its being destroyed."[53]

The Cherokee-Arkansas border became a particular scene of drunken brawls and outrage. Evansville, Maysville, and Fort Smith, Arkansas, provided the Cherokees ample opportunities to obtain alcohol. Evansville seems to have been the most popular place for "run[ning] across the line."[54] Because town merchants often constructed their stores "immediately upon the line," in both the Cherokee Nation and Arkansas, these "line houses" enabled many outlaws to step across a "plank in the floor" and escape the jurisdiction of the country where they had committed their crimes.[55] Between 1844 and 1846, the *Cherokee Advocate* reported six murders caused by excessive drinking in Flint District of the Cherokee Nation, just across the border from the town.[56] In December 1844, the Evansville storekeepers made a "solemn resolution to sell no intoxicating liquors whatever, to any Indian, for two months."[57] Just a hundred days later, a drunken Cherokee became a victim of Evansville whiskey.[58] The *Advocate* asked what had become of the temperance pledge taken by those whiskey dealers who "some time since *pretended* to have ceased their vending to Indians."[59] The impact of the liquor traffic in border towns was so threatening that the Cherokee Council, on January 10, 1845, authorized Chief Ross to ask the governors of the states of Arkansas and Missouri to cooperate with him in blocking the business.[60]

The border towns were not the only sites of alcohol purchase and consumption. An active illicit liquor trade also took place within the boundaries of the Nation. Some Cherokee women obtained alcohol at the mouth of Bayou Menard and served it at their restaurants. For example, Sarah Coody's eating house and dance hall, located three and a half miles southeast of Fort Gibson, became a popular spot: "Sarah Coody's dinners and suppers were known far and wide." Many Cherokee townspeople came to Coody's to have "hilarious times," one recollected.[61] The most attractive spot, however, was Fort Gibson, where traders illegally transported whiskey by canoes and steamboats on the Arkansas River. U.S. soldiers garrisoned at the fort as well as Cherokees purchased this contraband.

An Arkansan who identified himself as "Dupleix" tried to defend the character of the soldiers at Fort Gibson. He maintained in a letter to the *Arkansas State Gazette* that Fort Gibson was "beyond the reach of the greater portion of whiskey sellers" and that "the military at this post, are in a great measure, preserved from the evil effects of a drunken soldiery."[62] Chief Ross disagreed: "The pernicious practice of trafficing and using intoxicating liquors about Fort Gibson and its vicinity, has for a long time been a source of much complaint and annoyance."[63] The disorderly conduct of the soldiers stationed at the fort as well as its presence within the Nation provoked a prolonged dispute. Ross expressed the Cherokees' sentiment on the fort: "The Military Posts established in the Nation are of no advantage to the Cherokees, if the object in their establishment is to afford protection to the Indians."[64]

In his 1843 annual report, Indian Agent Pierce M. Butler agreed with Ross that "so far as it regards the Indians, the garrison does not have a beneficial influence. On the contrary, they would be better off, if the garrison were one hundred miles distant from them."[65] Butler's observation instantly incurred the anger of the readers of the *Arkansas State Gazette* and resulted in a direct attack against him by the U.S. military man who wrote to the editor under the name of "Veritas." Branding the agent a man of "illiberal spirit," "Veritas" attempted to negate the "erroneous impressions" of Fort Gibson and the U.S. soldiers generated by the report. Whereas Butler contended that "ten quarts are consumed at the Garrison, where one is used among the Cherokees," "Veritas" provided his own estimation that "where ONE quart is consumed at the Garrison, FORTY quarts are used among the Cherokees." Believing that "[t]he Military at Fort Gibson, from their earliest occupation of the country, have exerted a salutary influence in checking the introduction and use of ardent spirits in the Nation," "Veritas" concluded that the Cherokees, despite the evidence to the contrary, would not agree with Agent Butler's statements.[66]

In reply to "Veritas," Butler countered the assertion "Veritas" made that the location of the fort placed it beyond the illegal liquor traffic: "A child six years old, in the whole range of the country, would not be so silly as to utter such a remark." Clearly, he contended, "the garrison is the attraction" for both American and Cherokee whiskey traders. The soldiers there had money to purchase the product while most of the Cherokees in the Nation did not. Having absolute confidence in the validity of his 1843 annual report, Butler challenged "Veritas" that "if in every one hundred inhabitants in the nation, ninety-five, yea ninety-nine, do not concur in the report, then s[h]all it be conceded that 'Veritas' is right and the report false."[67] Butler's accounts, rather than the accusation "Veritas" made against him, soon proved to be accurate when violence broke out between Cherokees and soldiers stationed at the fort.

According to the *Cherokee Advocate*, in December 1844 several U.S. soldiers took a jug of whiskey from the house of a Cherokee named Nelly Taylor. William Nicholson and an unnamed woman pursued the villains and came across several of them on their way back to Fort Gibson. Believing that they were the ones who had committed the robbery, Nicholson began whipping them. When Nicholson discovered that they were innocent, he released them immediately and did not see them again until several months later when they met at a frolic at the house of Polly Spaniard. A U.S. soldier called Wyankoop started a fight, and two others joined him. Fearing that they would attack him with sticks, Nicholson drew a knife and stabbed a soldier named Brown in the shoulder. He then attacked Wyankoop and "killed him instantly." When the third soldier attempted to prevent Nicholson's escape and wounded him in the arm with a stick, Nicholson dealt him a fatal blow to his side. Fleeing Spaniard's house, Nicholson escaped.[68]

Retaliation against Nicholson quickly followed. The *Cherokee Advocate* reported that "some eight or ten uniformed barbarians" raided Polly Spaniard's house at night. Far from fulfilling their duty "to preserve *peace* and protect the *weak and defenceless*," the soldiers attacked several women in the house. They assaulted one woman with an ax and beat an-

other with a club, stabbing her through the hand with a bay-
onet. Other women also had their hands and arms "more or
less 'hacked'" with knives. In the prairie, these agitated military men found yet another woman who fell victim to their
depravities, and they threw her down and injured her.[69]

This outrageous conduct by the U.S. soldiers posted at
Fort Gibson impressed the Cherokees with the dangerous
situation posed by the garrison and led to a public meeting in
Tahlequah on March 24, 1845. Those present agreed that Fort
Gibson was a hotbed of vice and that it had attracted whiskey peddlers, gamblers, and prostitutes. Furthermore, many
of the enlisted men who served there were immoral, they
stated. The Cherokees demanded "a speedy abandonment
of Fort Gibson, and the removal of the U.S. Troops without the limits of the Cherokee country."[70] As the *Cherokee
Advocate* pointed out, this resolution was not "the offspring
of groundless prejudice against the United States Military,"
but "the natural results of the flagrant wrongs that have been
perpetrated upon Cherokee citizens and property, . . . and the
vice and immorality that do, and always have existed, about
the reserve, diffusing their pernicious influences throughout
the country."[71] This meeting also signaled a new resolve by
Cherokee citizens to terminate domestic strife.

On August 13, 1846, Chief John Ross and the leader of
the Treaty party, Stand Watie, met face to face in the office of the commissioner of Indian affairs in Washington.
Agreeing to move beyond old animosities, both approved a
treaty ratified with amendments by the Senate that formally
ended several years of civil conflict. The Treaty of 1846 subdued the party rivalry that Chief Ross called "the bane of our
existence—the fountain of many bitter waters."[72] These two
leaders ultimately secured the integrity of the Nation and
saved it from dividing into two distinct political entities.[73]

During the time of trouble, an increasing number of Cherokees had sought unity and an end to the widespread violence in a reinvigorated temperance movement that promised to transcend political factionalism. On September 12, 1836, some western Cherokee people had gathered together and, assisted by American Board missionary Samuel A. Worcester, revived the Cherokee Temperance Society. Adopting the principle of total abstinence from "all that can possibly intoxicate," ninety-one people signed the pledge: "We hereby solemnly pledge themselves that we will never use, nor buy, nor sell, nor give, nor receive, AS A DRINK, any whiskey, brandy, gin, rum, wine, fermented cider, strong beer, or any kind of intoxicating liquor." The temperance pledge promised them "a perfect security, *so far as it is kept,* against all possibility of becoming or continuing a drunkard." Within two years of its formation, the society had won the support of 345 members, only 5 of whom were reported to have broken the pledge.[74] By 1846, the membership had increased to 3,373. The *Cherokee Advocate* triumphantly announced: "One-fifth, or very nearly that proportion, of the population of the Nation, now belongs to the Society!"[75]

The Cherokee Temperance Society actively recruited public officials of the Cherokee Nation. The society, for example, resolved on October 22, 1842, to "adjourn to meet at Tahlequah on the 17th of November next at three o'clock p.m., or as soon after that hour as the National Council shall adjourn" so that it could invite to its meeting the principal chief, councilmen, and "all the public functionaries of the Nation."[76] Attendance provided politicians with an opportunity to take a united public stand on this moral issue, thereby giving the Cherokee Temperance Society a quasi-political purpose. The National Council encouraged members to attend temperance gatherings, and the National Committee on October 16, 1845, adjourned at noon to send committee members to the annual national meeting of the Cherokee Temperance Society.[77]

The meeting opened with hymns and prayers. After a few remarks delivered by Pres. Walter S. Adair, the secretary read an annual report that contained accounts of success: "Many emphatically 'hard cases,' have renounced their cups, tapered off and become cold water men, in precept and practice."[78] Temperance reformers, preachers, and formerly intemperate men addressed the meeting either in English or in Cherokee. While people added their names to the pledge during the intermissions, numbers of the audience joined in temperance songs in the Cherokee and English languages. The Reverend Dr. Elizur Butler of Fairfield Mission presented to the audience full-color plates, or drawings, prepared by Dr. Thomas Sewall of Washington. Widely circulated in the 1840s as a "shock tactic" among mainstream American temperance societies, Dr. Sewall's plates vividly illustrated the great danger of alcohol to the human body.[79] At the request of the Cherokee Temperance Society, Butler lectured on these diagrams at many local temperance meetings. During his temperance lecture tour of 1846, the year in which political factions reached a truce, Butler assisted Cherokees in several districts to organize auxiliaries to the parent society. With the help of Native interpreters, he stimulated the interest of the general public in the cause and convinced many of the importance of taking the pledge of total abstinence.[80]

Offering hope for the future, on October 2, 1845, Cherokee children organized the Cherokee Cold Water Army in the public square of Tahlequah. Sixty-seven children under the age of sixteen signed the pledge of the Cherokee Temperance Society. Temperance reformers regarded the children as "the beauty and hope of our country" and maintained that "the shortest and most effectual way of working a reformation among a people, is to begin, with the rising generation among them."[81] While writing cold water songs that "would suit a child's step," the missionary Samuel A. Worcester taught his children and "all who came under his influence" that "they *could* do something and that they were expected to do their part."[82] Under the supervision of Marshal Stephen Foreman and Deputy Marshal William P. Ross, these Cherokee boys and girls sang, "Come and join us, one and all" as they marched in procession through Tahlequah under the banners of the Cold Water Army. One banner bore the image of a coiled rattlesnake in a bottle, "with his head out, and mouth wide open," together with the motto, "ALCOHOL. IT BITETH LIKE A SERPENT, AND STINGETH LIKE AN ADDER."[83] With "quite a Marshal appearance," the young Cherokee soldiers, even at an early age, waged war against "King Alcohol."[84]

The Cherokee Temperance Society systematized its reforming efforts by establishing auxiliaries in each district in the Nation. By the late 1840s, all the districts joined to advance the cause of temperance. The oldest auxiliary society in the Cherokee Nation was the one organized in Fort Gibson soon after the formation of the Cherokee Temperance Society in 1836. Observing the teetotal pledge in this active whiskey depot seems to have been extremely difficult, however, and more than 30 out of the 114 initial signers had violated the pledge by 1838.[85] Still, "the Christian Commander of the Post of Fort Gibson," Col. Gustavus Loomis, made a great effort to influence his military men, and, "ever alive to the calls of humanity," he often took a group of musicians and a choir stationed at the garrison to the Cherokees' temperance gatherings and furnished them with temperance music.[86]

Samuel A. Worcester's daughter Hannah visited "many

temperance meetings in different parts of the Nation—some in the woods on the banks of the beautiful clear-running streams—or near some one of the fine springs so plentiful in our Nation." Each of her siblings played a role in the crusade against alcohol: "My brothers made music when they were hardly taller than their violins. One brother spoke the first 'speech' he ever made (in public) at the age of sixteen, on Temperance."[87] Her sister, Ann Eliza, played the melodeon on these occasions.[88] Missionaries and their families, however, never played a central role in the Cherokee temperance movement. In attending district temperance sessions, they often found themselves and few of their church members and neighbors surrounded by several hundred Cherokee men, women, and children. The *Cherokee Advocate* reminded readers that "the Cherokees themselves sustain their Temperance meetings."[89]

Alcohol, therefore, did not overwhelm Cherokee citizens. Instead, an active reform movement developed, particularly in the Flint District, the area adjacent to Arkansas that had been "the theatre of more drunken outrages than any other part of the nation."[90] On July 3, 1845, about seven hundred men, women, and children met at Fairfield to form the Flint District Auxiliary Temperance Society. Many "were not able to obtain seats in the house." The meeting opened at noon with peals of the church bell. The most popular part of the meeting was a performance of temperance songs by a group of young Cherokee women. "Whether it was their personal *beauty*, their *unassuming and graceful deportment*, or their *sweet melodious voices*, or all *combined*, that so *attracted* my attention, I cannot say," one observer wrote the *Advocate*. Yet he admitted a "*particular partiality*" for the Cherokee ladies who "had in some measure learned to sing and were not ashamed to *open their mouths* and show what they could do." After several speeches delivered in Cherokee and English, the meeting went into recess at two o'clock, and a temperance picnic enabled people to come and enjoy *"sweet cold water"* as well as barbecued meat, bread, and potatoes. The site of Dr. Butler's missionary and temperance work, the Flint District Temperance Society hosted his lectures on Dr. Sewall's color plates and obtained many names to the abstinence pledge.[91] After the third annual meeting at Fairfield Mission on July 1, 1847, the society announced that it had 643 enrolled members.[92]

Through these efforts, Dr. Butler earned his reputation as a temperance lecturer. His fame even had crossed the border, and "some twenty-four citizens of Fort Smith" asked him to come and explain "the different stages of inebriety" with Dr. Sewall's vivid diagrams. One of his hosts admitted that "Fort Smith has not been exempt from the evils flowing from the distillery, and the picayune tippling shop."[93] Nevertheless, a "large . . . proportion of the 'youth and beauty,' of Fort Smith," as well as many of the men, came to listen to his lectures. Receiving "this cordial co-operation of the friends of temperance in the Indian country," a temperance society immediately organized in Fort Smith with more than one hundred teetotalers "to aid them in the promotion of the cause there."[94]

Spreading the gospel of total abstinence, the Cherokee Temperance Society, with the help of its auxiliaries, reached a large number of Cherokee citizens. With a solid base of support, temperance reformers began to politicize the question of alcohol. In the 1848 annual meeting, the Cherokee Temperance Society appointed Samuel A. Worcester, William P. Ross, and the Reverend Thomas Bertholf to write a petition on behalf of the society to the legislature of the state of Arkansas requesting assistance in curtailing the illegal liquor traffic into the Cherokee Nation.[95] Because of the strict tribal laws that made alcohol a contraband article, they wrote, "we are not aware of the existence of a single place in the nation, where ardent spirits are openly and publicly sold." Yet the illegal liquor trade continued to threaten the lives of the Cherokee citizens because "along the border of the nation, just within your jurisdiction, and beyond the reach of Cherokee legislation, . . . the nefarious traffic is carried on openly and without restraint." Thus, "the places of trade along your line are all fountains of deadly evil to the Indians on your border."[96]

The state of Arkansas did not seriously consider this petition. Pleading for "renewed attention," the Cherokee Temperance Society once again sent a memorial to the Arkansas legislature in 1850, this time on behalf of the Cherokee Nation: "The undersigned Citizens of the Cherokee Nation, respectfully and humbly, but most earnestly ask of your honorable body, the speedy enactment of efficient laws, for the suppression of the Sale of intoxicating drinks, by citizens of your state, to the citizens of Indian Nations on our border." The memorialists contended, "No intoxicating drink, is manufactured among us. It all comes from abroad, and chiefly from, or through the State of Arkansas." Although the document circulated among the friends of temperance in Arkansas for signatures, their support made little difference.[97] In 1851, the society had to announce that their endeavors, "after some discussion in the Arkansas legislature, were finally lost, for the present."[98]

If it failed to affect the laws of the adjoining state to remove "a continuous chain of grog shops" situated along the line "from Fort Smith and Van Buren to Maysville," the Cherokee Temperance Society did influence internal Cherokee politics and reinforce alcohol regulations.[99] Although the Cherokee

Nation had passed a series of prohibition laws in the early 1840s, all Cherokees did not necessarily approve these actions. Some violently obstructed officials in enforcing these liquor laws. When the sheriff of Flint District poured whiskey on the dance ground in 1846, for example, a number of hostile men "severely" beat him.[100] For the district sheriff to execute the tribal regulatory acts safely, Cherokee temperance reformers concluded, they had to broaden the appeal of their movement.

While it implanted the doctrine of total abstinence in the minds of many Cherokee citizens, the Cherokee Temperance Society also had to encourage sheriffs to enforce the law. One wrote the *Advocate* about his concerns: "If I hunt, find and spill some person's liquor, I'll lose a vote next election."[101] In 1848, the members of the Flint District Auxiliary Temperance Society agreed to assist the district sheriff in destroying any intoxicating liquors introduced into the Nation.[102] In 1851, the sheriff himself, in turn, asked the citizens of the district "to lend him their aid and indulgence in the execution of the laws and suppression of the *liquor trade*."[103] When the sheriff of Tahlequah destroyed forty-eight barrels of whiskey during the 1849 annual meeting of the Cherokee Temperance Society, citizens did not ostracize him; instead, they elected him a member of the National Committee.[104] By the early 1850s, the Cherokee Nation gained widespread support for more stringent enforcement of the laws.

In 1851, when Chief Ross recommended that the National Council adopt even more effective measures to suppress the flow of liquor into the Nation, the secretary of the Cherokee Temperance Society wrote: "The voice of this society may very possibly blend with that of our Executive in this desirable request."[105] Considering the difficulties that law enforcers had confronted, an amendment to the 1841 prohibitory act, passed on November 4, 1851, provided them a strong incentive. The sheriff who reported the violation of this act would receive one-fourth of the fine paid by the offender, the National Treasury would get half of the fine, and the final one-fourth would go to the informer. When the sheriff and solicitor failed to faithfully perform their duties, they paid a penalty of twenty-five dollars from their salaries.[106]

The action taken by the National Council once again convinced the Cherokee temperance reformers of the importance of broad popular support for the cause of temperance because "the sheriffs will not execute the laws, unless public opinion demands it, and upholds them in it." They maintained that "what is wanted is a healthier tone of public sentiment." In 1852, they resolved that "the members of this Society pledge themselves to support, at the ensuing election, no man for the office of Sheriff, but those known to be in favor of enforcing the existing laws in regard to the introduction and vending of ardent spirits."[107]

Using national politics, the Cherokee Temperance Society encouraged its members to defeat intemperate men in elections because if they failed to do so, "the nation must hasten to ruin." When the Nation continued to have "drunken Councils," citizens had to try harder to sustain temperance societies and exercise influence over immoral politicians. As the temperance reformers concluded, "Good laws, well executed, and voluntary societies, well sustained, *ought* to go hand in hand."[108]

The Cherokees had managed to reclaim their eastern legacy by linking legal and social reform, sovereignty, and morality. Political unification made the passage and enforcement of prohibition possible, and temperance societies enabled Cherokees to demonstrate their moral superiority. While the memory of removal long remained with Cherokees, it did not ultimately paralyze them because they drew upon their experiences with alcohol in the East to reassert legal and moral authority. Problems with alcohol transcended factions, and temperance permitted a national consensus that gradually expanded to other issues. Future trials awaited the Cherokees in July 1860 as the Cold Water Army held its last temperance parade, but for the moment, the Cherokees regained their sense of national purpose.[109]

5

A Nation under Siege

The American Civil War rekindled old animosities. Chief
John Ross's strong plea for neutrality could not offset bitter internal factionalism that ultimately forced him to ally
with the Confederate States in the treaty of October 7, 1861.
Barely a year had passed when Ross, following a majority of
his people who had repudiated the Confederate alliance, left
the Nation under federal guard. Until the Confederate surrender at Appomattox, the Cherokees fought their own civil
war. The Treaty of 1866 with the United States confronted the
Cherokees with several difficult issues. In particular, the land
grants for railroads, the emancipation and enfranchisement
of slaves, and the partial transference of legal jurisdiction to
the United States produced an influx of American citizens
into the Nation and caused dissension among Cherokees,
who feared that they were losing control of their Nation.[1]
Their inability to regulate alcohol epitomized the erosion of
Cherokee institutions, values, and sovereignty.

The Treaty of 1866 presumably placed further restrictions
on the sale of alcohol. Before the Civil War, when George M.
Murrell, a wealthy merchant who married a niece of Chief
John Ross, asked permission to bring a small quantity of intoxicating liquors to his house in Park Hill for his private
use, Commissioner of Indian Affairs James W. Denver rea-

soned that the Trade and Intercourse Acts did not prohibit "medicinal or domestic" use of alcohol "especially where the party using it is of character and standing such as you are said to possess."[2] The Treaty of 1866, however, limited the use of alcohol in the Nation to the U.S. military medical department, which obtained a small amount "for strictly medical purposes."[3] Soldiers stationed at Fort Gibson complained to Agent John N. Craig that the doctors furnished intoxicating liquors only for those who were in critical condition, even though "the climate makes the use of such liquors from time to time, almost . . . absolute physical necessity for the healthiest and most robust persons." Craig recognized that "such is the belief" among these soldiers, and he explained to Commisioner Ely S. Parker that the inaccessibility of alcohol at the fort caused them "an unnecessary inconvenience" and "a serious hardship."[4] On September 13, 1869, the Department of the Missouri at Fort Leavenworth, Kansas, issued General Orders No. 42, which under the written permission of the post commander, allowed post traders in the Indian territory to distribute alcohol to the officers who wanted it "for family use."[5]

In the summer of 1871, this policy encouraged a druggist at Fort Gibson to seek authorization to obtain and sell several types of liquor to treat Cherokee townspeople. An adopted citizen, Frank J. Nash had run a drugstore under U.S. and Cherokee licenses for seventeen years. The Trade and Intercourse Acts of the United States, however, provided him "no legitimate way to obtain Alcoholic Stimulants" in the Nation, and Nash felt frustrated when he could not properly fill a doctor's prescription. Although he used tinctures and other alcoholic preparations made by wholesale pharmacists, his longtime experience suggested that "all preparations put up by wholesale druggists are of uncertain strength, and should never be used in dispensing medicine." Because typhoid fever and pneumonia raged in the Nation, Nash continued, "many deaths occur for want of proper means to support the patient."[6]

Having in hand a memorial from physicians in the Nation, Agent John B. Jones concurred with Nash on the importance of providing more effective medical care for the Cherokees: "Notwithstanding my extreme temperance principles, both from conscientious and prudential motives, the necessity which calls forth this petition is so apparent that I cannot withhold my endorsement." Jones did not think it right that "physicians of the highest moral character cannot get the necessary stimulants to save the lives of their patients" while "[a] miserable set of bad men are constantly smuggling bad whiskey into this Nation . . . & do great harm" to the Cherokees.[7] On September 7, 1871, H. R. Clum, acting commissioner of Indian affairs, granted to Nash a license to sell spirituous liquors and wine "strictly and only for medicinal purposes" at Fort Gibson. Twelve days later, Nash signed a bond for five thousand dollars to ensure his compliance.[8]

This episode indicated to the Cherokees flexibility on the part of federal officials, and granting a license to permit the sale of spirituous liquors "on prescription of a *respectable physician*" became an acceptable practice within the Nation.[9] Some unscrupulous medical practitioners, however, abused this privilege of introducing intoxicating liquors among Cherokees, and Indian Agent S. W. Marston stated in 1876 that whiskey traders in the Nation consisted largely of the "parties holding a license to sell it from the United States Government."[10] A citizen of Vinita, moreover, reported to the *Cherokee Advocate* that "a man can, under peculiar circumstances, when he is sick or 'naturally wants it,' get a bottle of whiskey in Vinita, without incurring the danger of going to Fort Smith as a witness." Federally licensed, Dr. John R. Trott sold a quart of alcohol at the high price of a dollar and a half in this railroad town. Dr. Luther S. Arnold heard about "the prospects of a speedy fortune" and "made a bold dash" for the War Department where he successfully procured "the—Goose—that was to lay him the golden egg, in the shape of a license to sell fermented liquors, for medical purposes, in the town of Downingville." Arnold opened a drugstore in the name of his Cherokee wife in a town situated at the intersection of two rail lines, called both Vinita and Downingville, which were "two in *name* and in *law*" but, in fact, "one and the same place."[11] The entry of Arnold into the drug business in this town threatened the "monopoly of the medicated whisky" trade Trott enjoyed. At the request of Trott, who hoped that the U.S. officer would eliminate his competition, Lieut. Philip Sheridan investigated the case and revoked the licenses of both on March 15, 1878.[12]

Vinita/Downingville had acquired a reputation for lawlessness fueled by alcohol, and many Cherokees considered this town to be emblematic of the problems that railroads brought. Suspecting that the coming of railways into their country was part of a continuous attempt by the U.S. government to open up the area to American homesteaders, many citizens had opposed the granting of railroad rights-of-way in the Treaty of 1866. The Cherokee treaty delegation to Washington, however, felt compelled to agree to the construction of two railroads through the Nation.[13] Railroad interests were so strong that Congress issued four charters within a week of the agreement to this article although the Senate had not ratified the treaty with the Cherokees. On July 27, 1866, the Atlantic and Pacific Railway Company secured a land grant to build an east-west route across the Indian territory without competition. On June 6, 1870, the

Missouri, Kansas, and Texas Railway Company (popularly known as the "Katy") reached the northern edge of the Cherokee Nation and won the right-of-way southward.[14]

The construction of railroads in the Cherokee Nation brought bootleggers who sold liquor to company crews. Cherokee people protested the presence of such a "criminal element" in the Nation, but the vice president of the Katy explained to the acting secretary of the interior on October 6, 1870, that the company had sent only "responsible parties" to the construction site and that it had nothing to do with troublemakers who peddled whiskey to workers along the line "without our consent, or that of our agents."[15] Some evidence suggests that Cherokee entrepreneurs seized this economic opportunity, despite the fact that it was illegal, and the chief engineer of the Atlantic and Pacific accused Cherokees of having tempted his employees with cider and urged Chief Dennis W. Bushyhead to send tribal sheriffs to arrest these miscreants.[16]

Once the railroads came into the Nation, depots and the towns that grew up around them enticed purveyors and consumers of alcohol. Vinita, at the junction of the Katy and the Atlantic and Pacific, was, from the start, "occupied for the most part by whiskey peddlers and toughs." When the sale of townsite lots opened in February 1872, a considerable number of Americans began selling whiskey on their newly acquired property. An early history chronicled "[m]any thrilling stories and incidents of this period" in this railroad town: "Brawls and fights were frequent and now and then a man would be killed."[17]

In 1873, more upstanding citizens of Vinita petitioned Agent Jones to remove from the Nation "a man of questionable character" named Ranch. The memorialists claimed that Ranch had, for several months, sold whiskey at his tavern with his mistress, a Mrs. Clark, and "kept such a crowd of drunkards around." Although Agent Jones ordered Ranch to close his business and leave the Nation, he refused to do so. Intending to dispatch the U.S. military to deport Ranch, Jones went to Vinita to investigate only to find the culprit dead following an alcohol-related fight.[18]

According to Jones, Ranch served whiskey at his store to two Cherokees, Joseph Cochran and an unnamed man. They got drunk, and their friend, Morgan, disarmed them. Ranch asked Morgan to take the weapons out of his place, and while Morgan was gone, Ranch beat Joseph Cochran senseless with a club. William Cochran heard of his brother's misfortune, rushed into the tavern, and took Ranch into custody. Perceiving that his brother breathed his last, William shot and killed the storekeeper and avenged the murdered. The mistress immediately left the premises, and a mob set fire to the barn where Ranch had stored his whiskey, burning the barn to the ground. Ranch had "nobody to mourn his loss."[19]

The building of the railroads accelerated the influx of an American population into the country, but such an external factor was not the only cause of this rush. The Cherokees themselves also helped foreigners enter and reside legally in the Nation. On November 22, 1867, the National Council passed a law allowing citizens to obtain permits for Americans they wished to employ by paying small fees to district judges.[20] Since the Treaty of 1866 had affirmed the abolition of slavery in the Nation, wealthy Cherokee planters suffered a serious labor shortage: "Individual Cherokees are constantly applying for permits to hire white men as laborers, Mechanics, Clerks & c. This has always been done, to a limited extent. But now such applications are vastly multiplying."[21] These hired laborers, however, disappointed the

Cherokees and U.S. agents. Only a few demonstrated diligence in working for citizens. Most proved to be "unprincipled white men who take refuge in the territory to escape from just penalties for crimes committed in adjoining States, many of whom are engaged in the liquor traffic, others in circulating counterfeit money, and still others in fermenting troubles among the Indians."[22] While some of these men married Cherokees and became adopted citizens, many tenant farmers and sharecroppers brought their families with them and stayed on farms when their terms expired because they believed that Congress would soon pass a territorial bill and end common Indian title. Mechanics and store clerks who had immigrated to the Nation often entered into silent partnerships with Cherokees and continued their businesses within the Nation. Still others, by having their permits renewed, chose to stay on legally, but ultimately the Cherokees found that "many persons of the worst character assert a right of residence in the Territory."[23]

While the influx of American citizens increased lawlessness in the Nation, the Treaty of 1866 posed yet another question to the Cherokees. The U.S. government guaranteed the Cherokees' "exclusive jurisdiction in all civil and criminal cases arising within their country in which members of the nation, by nativity or adoption, shall be the only parties," but it granted to the U.S. Court for the Western District of Arkansas the authority to try criminal cases involving non-Cherokees in the Nation as well as violators of the Trade and Intercourse Acts prohibiting liquor trade in Indian country. Although the federal government promised to establish U.S. District Courts in the Indian Nations, it did not do so, and the Cherokee Nation surrendered much of its legal jurisdiction.[24] Arkansas quickly realized that it could manipulate the treaty stipulations to undermine Cherokee authority and encouraged deputy marshals associated with the U.S. District Court to patrol the Nation to find federal violators.

According to Agent Craig, these deputy marshals were "generally men of very indifferent character." Primarily seeking the rewards the Intercourse Acts guaranteed informers, they entered the Nation to search for whiskey, and in the process they repeatedly harassed Cherokees. Although none of the federal provisions allowed them to search the belongings of anyone in the Indian territory, the deputies, "without warrant or writ," raided stores and steamboats and assaulted travelers. Making every possible attempt "to fix upon individuals evidence of having violated the law forbidding the introduction of spirituous or malt liquors," these U.S. deputy marshals formed "a sort of monopoly of lodging the information" on illicit liquor trade in the Cherokee country.[25]

The National Council of the Cherokee Nation resented the "numerous depredations" committed by those who were "styling themselves as 'Deputy Marshalls'" of the U.S. District Court in Arkansas. On December 2, 1869, the council authorized Chief Lewis Downing to protest to Agent Craig against these deputy marshals and to beseech Pres. Ulysses S. Grant to provide protection for the Cherokees.[26] The deputy marshals escalated their oppressive and abusive raids, however, and people in the Nation regarded them as "being 'worse than the horse thieves.'"[27]

In "a pretended seizure" of goods from Cobb & Co. in Webbers Falls without a search warrant, for example, Deputy Joseph Peavy claimed that his appointment as deputy was "warrant enough." Agent Craig took Peavy into custody, but U.S. Marshal William A. Britton protested the intervention in his "orders to Deputies ... to arrest all parties found violating, or who have violated the law, whether they have writs for the Criminals or not even without the advice of an Indian

Agent who have heretofore been generally classed as great scoundrels." He threatened Craig: "I will undertake to arrest you for resisting an officer."[28] When they raided stores kept by intermarried Americans, the deputy marshals accused them of conducting businesses in the Nation without a U.S. license and forcibly arrested them. The deputies disregarded the Cherokees' longtime practice of granting citizenship to those who married Cherokees and infringed on the Cherokees' right to regulate internal commerce by their own laws. The fear of false arrests by the U.S. deputy marshals spread among adopted citizens, and some traders asked the agent for the same protections guaranteed Cherokee citizens under the treaty stipulations. Agent Craig began questioning the status of these adopted citizens himself. He made inquiries on July 2, 1870, into "whether the Indian Office regards the right of citizens of the United States, incorporated into the body of Cherokee citizens, to trade within the Cherokee territory, as unquestionable under United States laws" and whether or not the Indian agent was to extend to these intermarried traders the same protection that the treaties had assured to "Cherokee citizens."[29]

Meanwhile, Agent Craig inadvertently upheld the view of the U.S. District Court in Arkansas in a silent-partnership case involving a Cherokee adopted citizen. In the summer of 1870, Agent Craig learned that an American citizen, U.S. Postmaster Robert Cuthbertson of Marble Salt Springs, was operating a store without a U.S. license with Alexander Clapperton, formerly a pension agent at Fort Gibson. Several Cherokees as well as U.S. deputy marshals informed Craig that Cuthbertson purchased whiskey at Fort Smith and sold it to Indians. Establishing a silent partnership with John B. Wright, who married a Cherokee, Cuthbertson and Clapperton successfully "put [him] forward to cover illegal trading." Agent Craig, however, believed that this adopted citizen was "an irreclaimable drunkard, . . . entirely unfit for business of any kind." Cuthbertson and Clapperton had purchased the trading goods in the name of Wright and sold them at the store. Craig seized the merchandise Wright claimed to be his and forced Clapperton out of the Nation, but he could not remove Cuthbertson because he was a federal employee.[30]

This illegal scheme convinced Craig that "[c]itizens of the United States who come to the country as office-holders always engage in enterprises that induce complaint from the Indians," and he recommended that "competent Cherokee citizens be preferred for local offices."[31] U.S. District Attorney James H. Huckleberry's refusal to take action in this case deepened Craig's distrust of the U.S. District Court in Arkansas: "I have brought, and attempted to bring many important offenders to justice, but always without success, in consequence of carelessness on part of officials of the court, which comes from belief that no importance attaches to enforcement of law in the Indian country."[32] When he seized Wright's goods, however, Craig endorsed the view of the U.S. District Court concerning adopted citizens and helped reverse the long-established tacit agreement between the Cherokee Nation and the United States acknowledging the rights and privileges of Cherokee adopted citizens. Federal authorities finally responded to the situation by ruling that "whatever obligations a white man may have taken upon himself or whatever privileges he may have obtained by becoming a Cherokee by adoption, his responsibility to the laws of the United States remains unchanged and undiminished."[33] As far as federal officials were concerned, adopted citizens of the Cherokee Nation were, after all, "simply citizens of the United States," and "no such relation as that of adopted citizenship existed" in the Nation.[34]

To the Cherokees, however, these intermarried Americans were unquestionably Cherokee citizens, and they regarded it as absurd that adopted citizens had to obtain a U.S. license to trade with Cherokees because adoption was, within the context of Cherokee political culture, the same as naturalization. Just like naturalized citizens, adopted citizens enjoyed the same privileges of citizenship as those born into the Nation.[35] Even more offensive, deputy marshals arrested Cherokee citizens for crimes against intermarried Americans and dragged them to the U.S. District Court in Arkansas where they had little chance of fair trials. Several gunfights between Cherokee sheriffs and U.S. marshals arose from the contested jurisdiction over cases involving adopted citizens.[36] Chief Lewis Downing protested in 1872 that the Treaty of New Echota had assured the Nation of the exclusive jurisdiction over its own citizens and "*such persons as have connected themselves with them,*" who, the chief contended, were the "citizens of the United States who have connected themselves by lawful marriage with a Cherokee."[37] The Treaty of 1866 reaffirmed this privilege: "Where a citizen of the Cherokee Nation whether native or adoptive commits a crime against the person or property of an adopted citizen, . . . we alone have the sole right to try the offenders, and to punish them."[38] Chief Downing, therefore, believed that the Nation had "complete and absolute jurisdiction over its adopted citizens" and that "our jurisdiction must . . . not [be] divided between our courts, and the courts of the United States." Referring obliquely to *Worcester v. Georgia* (1832), the chief maintained that U.S. courts had been "a protection to us, and a blessing" until jurisdiction shifted to the district judges in Arkansas who became "really the aggressors, and we the sufferers."[39]

The whiskey hunts had proved to be the most abusive and oppressive acts of the deputy marshals. Downing observed that "having possession of any quantity, however small, in the Indian Country is *prima facie* evidence." Section 20 of the 1834 Intercourse Act and its amendments, Downing maintained, "never intended to include Indians even by implication." "In order to constitute the offence," he insisted, "there must be some person who is solely and exclusively under the jurisdiction of the United States, who must sell, exchange[,] give[,] or dispose of spirituous liquor or wine to an Indian, who by the consent of the United States, is not under the sole and exclusive jurisdiction of the U.S. government, but is the subject of the government[']s protection, and care." Unless an Indian superintendent, agent, subagent, or U.S. military officer "has reason to suspect or is informed that any *white person or Indian* is about to introduce, or has introduced any spirituous liquor or wine into the Indian Country," he believed, "the punishment were never intended to extend to Indians."[40]

In 1854, Congress amended an 1851 statute that established two judicial districts in Arkansas. Under the terms of the amendment, the U.S. Court for the Western District surrendered to the tribal courts jurisdiction over citizens of the Indian Nations charged with engaging in illicit liquor trade.[41] Section 3 of this amendment stated that the twentieth section of the 1834 Intercourse Act prohibiting liquor trade in Indian country did not apply to "any Indian committing said offences in the Indian Country, or to any Indian Committing any Offences in the Indian Country who has been punished by the local law of the tribe."[42] According to Downing, federal alcohol regulations did not apply to Indians in Indian country because this act establishing two U.S. District Courts in Arkansas had "repealed" anything in section 20 "that provided punishment for offences therein contained which extended to Indians." Instead, it granted

Indians a sovereign right to control the liquor trade within their Nations and punish violators as they wished. The "spys under the name of Deputies," as Downing described them, however, rendered the Cherokees' liquor laws "inoperative almost." These deputy marshals, "seldom having writs other than blanks, that they fill at their convenience," made forcible arrests "without regard to circumstances or the facts of the case, and without any of the forms of law." Finally, "the judge of the Court tunes up cases of every kind against an Indian without regard to treaty from the having in possession half a pint of mere whiskey to burrells [sic]" and banefully prosecuted "many without cause and for the value of a dollar worth of liquor."[43]

Agent Jones lamented that "this Court with its officers has become an outrageous machine for oppressing the Cherokee people."[44] He confirmed Downing's allegations: "It has become a very common occurrence for innocent men to be arrested by these marshals, and dragged to Fort Smith, Arkansas, a distance of perhaps fifty, one hundred, or even one hundred and fifty miles, and compelled to give bail in a city of strangers, of whose language they are ignorant; or in default of such bail to be incarcerated in the common jail, until the meeting of the court."[45] Chief Downing's strong protestation convinced Jones that "the extent to which this court can exercise jurisdiction over them should be properly defined by an authority which the said court will be bound to respect, & to which it must submit."[46]

In early 1874, Commissioner of Indian Affairs Edward P. Smith proposed to Congress, through the secretary of the interior, amendments to section 20 of the Intercourse Act prohibiting alcohol in Indian country. As Chief Downing effectively pointed out, the fundamental flaw in this provision was its ambiguity. It was never clear to whom the law applied when it stated "any person" and, therefore, whether and when Indians in Indian country were subject to federal alcohol regulations. Some U.S. courts construed this act to exempt Indian whiskey dealers from punishment and acquitted them. In his draft, Smith inserted the phrase "including Indians" in parentheses following the words "any person" so that both Americans and Indians in Indian country became liable under this proposed amendment.[47] Without prescribing a minimum penalty for its violation, moreover, "the law is not a terror to evil-doers, as it should be." Smith suggested imprisonment for "not less than sixty days nor exceeding two years" and a fine of "not less than one hundred dollars, nor more than three hundred dollars."[48] When Congress passed amendments to the Intercourse Act, however, none of Smith's proposals appeared on paper. Congress simply affirmed Chief Downing's position. Stating, "Every person, except an Indian, in the Indian country," the first amendment, then numbered section 2139 of the Revised Statutes, excluded an Indian from the penalty when he "sells, exchanges, gives, barters, or disposes of any spirituous liquors or wine to any Indian under the charge of any Indian superintendent or agent, or introduces or attempts to introduce any spirituous liquor or wine into the Indian country." This provision also failed to set a minimum penalty for its violation. The second amendment, section 2140, stipulated that Indians as well as American citizens were liable to search and seizure of the concealed liquor or wine they introduced into Indian country, thereby contradicting the first amendment, which exempted Indians in Indian country from arrest.[49]

The U.S. District Court in Arkansas ruled in 1876 that section 2139 of the Revised Statutes did indeed exempt Indians from penalty for introducing alcohol into Indian country, but this decision did not retard the deputy marshals' indiscriminate raids into the Cherokee Nation.[50] On the contrary, a year later the phrase "except an Indian, in the Indian country" was eliminated from this section, further accelerating and even legitimizing their aggressiveness.[51] Only professional whiskey peddlers seemed to have evaded their pursuit. Until the fall of 1883, for example, the U.S. marshal could not detain a notorious liquor trader, along with his less experienced partner, who had for more than ten years caused drunken brawls in Tahlequah.[52] More cunning was a man who expanded his whiskey business by rowing back and forth between the two sides of the Arkansas River. When the U.S. marshal ordered whiskey and attempted to arrest him, the peddler left six quarts of "Arkansas River water," rowed back to the opposite side, and deceived the marshal.[53]

The deputies cheated innocent people more frequently than they were cheated by professional smugglers in the Cherokee Nation. Their most notorious practice was "'planting' whiskey" in the wagons of travelers and settlers passing through the Nation.[54] James B. White, who spent his childhood in Fayetteville, Arkansas, recollected that when his father was traveling across the Cherokee country, a U.S. marshal ordered him and some others to stop their wagons so he could search for whiskey. His father replied, "You are welcome to do so, but there is no liquor in the wagons unless you put it there and if you find any I will shoot you." Officers examined their wagons, announced that they did not see any whiskey, and discharged the travelers. When the party camped for the night, White's father found a quart of whiskey that the marshals had hidden in his wagon with the intention of using it as a pretense to arrest him and seize his goods.[55] A Cherokee named William M. James also remembered that a traveler near Poteau in the Choctaw Nation shot three U.S. deputies with his rifle when they searched his wagon and pulled out the bottles they had concealed. James commented that "these murders helped to clean up the deputies and find a more honorable bunch of men."[56] Travelers in Indian country, however, were not always so fortunate. One former whiskey peddler, George Tanner, stated that he personally knew several innocent men who had fallen into this wicked trap and had been charged with "introduction."[57]

Once the U.S. deputy marshals of the district court in Arkansas snagged these federal law violators and dragged them to Fort Smith, they summoned witnesses from the Nation. One witness noted the length of the journey: "On a Saturday the summons was served by a bland little Deputy Marshal. On the next day the start was made. Over hill and dale, rock and ravine, creek and chuckhole—all of blessed Sunday and unblessed Monday was taken up in making the trip there. Tuesday morning found the witness in 'Garrison Avenue'" at Fort Smith.[58] The journey to Fort Smith was dangerous, and witnesses had to be alert at all times. At the Arkansas River, they took the ferry boat, *The George W. Mayo*, operated by the "enterprising Morgan family," where they encountered U.S. marshals and deputies with criminals as well as "those who were hunting after criminals," fugitives, horse thieves, gamblers, whiskey peddlers, and drunkards all on board.[59]

The trip to the U.S. District Court was costly. When an American named Ninnian Tannehill went to Fort Smith to testify against a boy who allegedly sold whiskey in the Indian territory, he received "10 cents per mile for going and $1.50 per day while there."[60] This did not cover necessary expenses, however, and because the U.S. District Court often detained witnesses for months before the trials, they also had to abandon their farms and businesses in the Cherokee Nation. Furthermore, "foreign parts represented by the thriving city of Fort Smith" overwhelmed them. Garrison Avenue, the city's main thoroughfare, provided "ways and means for the hundreds of witnesses who are compelled to stay here week after week, to drown their 'fond recollections of home.'" They found "many" whiskey stores "at the very place where the Indians are brought to be taught better." "There is," more surprisingly, "one inside of the Court house where a poor fellow who has sold some liquor a mile away across the line will receive his sentence of imprisonment and fine. There are a hundred just outside where liquor-selling is approved and fostered by law, and where the *other law* is practically laughed at and contemned."[61]

When they finally appeared at the court to testify, an overt aversion of Arkansas jurors toward Indians instilled in them a "dread of being taken to Fort Smith as a witness."[62] Indians could hardly have fair trials before the juries that usually regarded the accused as "another Territory desperado." Witnesses as well as criminals of the Indian territory learned that in the end, "the mere fact of residence in the Territory is a certificate of bad character to Arkansas jurymen."[63]

Convicted most often of selling liquor, many Cherokee criminals went to Little Rock or Detroit to serve their sentences. Alex Tehee, who spent more than 160 days at Little Rock, charged that officials treated Indians harshly and that "to whip a man until he couldn't walk was an every day occurrence." Because "sickness is no excuse so long as a person can drag themselves about," he had to work even when he was seriously ill.[64] The national prison in Detroit seems to have been a little better. Officers fed and treated prisoners well, taught them a trade, and helped them become "better fitted for life than when they entered except in one thing." In the very place where whiskey peddlers were to rehabilitate themselves, "you can let an Indian have whiskey to excess."

Others developed tuberculosis in confinement.[65] Having introduced one quart of whiskey into the Indian territory and received a jail sentence of two years—"the fullest extent of the Law"—a Cherokee named George Lowrey suffered "a very painful illness, Lung and Bronchial trouble," and died in the Detroit prison on December 4, 1882.[66]

Indian agents in the 1880s attempted to redress the abuse and oppression of Indians by the U.S. marshals and deputies and the U.S. district judges in Arkansas. They concluded that they could do so by establishing a U.S. District Court within the Indian territory, "as the treaty provides and the Indians desire."[67] As long as the U.S. District Court in Arkansas retained jurisdiction over the Indian territory, they argued, Indians would suffer injustice. Furthermore, many crimes remained unreported because a witness did not wish "to make three or four trips, 150 miles each way, across the country, . . . on horseback to tell what he knows about horse thief," which "punishes the witness almost as severely as it does the accused."[68] Criminals of the United States knew this, and they transformed the Cherokee Nation into "the refuge of thousands of evil-doers who have fled from their homes in the States and made this region a Botany Bay."[69]

The Cherokees sought to eliminate bootleggers from the Nation. Cherokee sheriffs, in particular, attempted to perform their duties faithfully, even at their peril. On Christmas Day of 1872, for example, Deputy Sheriff Frank Consene of Saline District, along with three guards, boldly fought back when George Lewis and his followers began shooting in order to protect their whiskey. Consene's matter-of-fact comment about the incident reflected his resolve: "There would have been no shooting had they given up their whiskey and not Commenced shooting, at us first."[70]

Once arrested and brought to the Cherokee courts, those

peddling whiskey were usually convicted in a jury trial and fined. Failure to pay the fine resulted in remand to the national prison where they served their sentence.[71] Despite this strict enforcement of the law against the sale of alcohol, provisions relating to drunkenness seem more lenient. The Cherokees did not make drunkenness a crime, and the law enabled juries to acquit individuals of murder if both the perpetrator and the victim had been drunk. As the law directed, "Such killing is excusable when done . . . by accident or misfortune, in the heat of passion, upon any sudden and sufficient provocation."[72]

Still, the Cherokees in the postbellum period well recognized that the illicit liquor trade, when intertwined with the practice of carrying deadly weapons, drastically increased the crime rate in the Nation. A communication of "Q" to the *Cherokee Advocate* described how these two agents for mischief incited each other:

> Dangerous weapons in the hands of drunken persons are always suggestive of violent deeds. Whiskey and sixshooters have become by association inseparable companions, either losing prestige in the absence of the other. Jointly they produce about all the deviltry and crimes among the people. Take away sixshooters, whiskey would be disarmed in a great measure of its criminal influences and power to do mischief. Take away whiskey, the preparation for desperate deeds, and the incentive to passion and recklessness, would be wanting, and sixshooters would become comparatively useless.[73]

Under the influence of alcohol, for example, Andrew Foreman shot the horse a female relative was riding with her escort; when he became sober the next morning, he apologized to them for his misconduct and paid for the dead horse.[74] Foreman and his victims were fortunate. The Nation had experienced many "accidental" deaths of innocent citizens caused by intoxicated armed Cherokees shooting guns "in the air" or "into the ground."[75]

In the early 1880s, Chief Dennis W. Bushyhead vigorously attempted to suppress "these twin brothers of all evil" among his people.[76] He asked the National Council to reinforce the laws against alcohol and concealed weapons.[77] He called upon the sheriffs of the districts in the Nation to faithfully and impartially execute these stringent laws to preserve peace and order.[78] The *Cherokee Advocate* implored citizens to "make a united strenuous effort" to keep themselves sober and disarmed.[79] The neglect of their duties as Cherokee citizens or officials was "very little less criminal than a breach of the law itself" and "gives us no enviable character abroad."[80]

Such pleas on the part of the Cherokee officials helped retain the reputation of the Cherokee Nation as a temperance pioneer. Those Americans who were planning to furnish prohibitory laws for their communities made inquiries into the Cherokees' liquor law operation. In the middle of the 1882 election campaign, for example, P. W. Reeder of Cedar Rapids, Iowa, requested Chief Bushyhead to come or to send a representative to his town to explain how effective alcohol regulations could be.[81] Bushyhead assured Reeder that "the law works well and is unquestionably successful in every way" among his people and promised to send Cherokee temperance speakers up north.[82]

The Cherokees continued to use their alcohol regulations as a means to protect their sovereignty and perseveringly attempted to publicize their success. Legal problems arising from the sale and consumption of alcohol, however, outweighed their efforts and plagued the postbellum Cherokee

Nation. The railroads brought in many scoundrels, and hired laborers from the neighboring states often ended up as lawless intruders. While the "Cherokees have been taught to regard treaty stipulations as the permanent law of the land," the U.S. marshals and deputies arbitrarily and illegally harassed them and threatened their lives.[83] The U.S. deputy marshals refused to respect Cherokee naturalization laws and claimed that adopted citizens of the Nation were citizens of the United States. Disdaining the Cherokees' stringent liquor laws, these deputy marshals indiscriminately arrested Cherokee citizens for introduction or possession of whiskey in the territory. Indian agents in the 1880s repeatedly urged the federal government to establish a U.S. District Court inside the Indian territory as "the promptest remedy" for crime among Indians.[84] In the minds of the Cherokees, a change in the location of the U.S. District Court from Arkansas to the Indian Nations would not provide a solution to the lawlessness.[85] The agents contended that the Cherokees' reluctance to go to Fort Smith to testify as a witness encouraged criminal elements in the Nation, but few Cherokees dared to surrender fellow citizens to the oppressive U.S. District Court in Arkansas. The Cherokees sought to punish offenders themselves in accordance with the laws of the Nation. The U.S. deputy marshals usurped the legal jurisdiction of the Cherokee Nation and the Cherokees' sovereign right to handle their own internal affairs. The U.S. District Court in Arkansas became a symbol of terror and the loss of Cherokee legal sovereignty. The United States seemed to be absorbing, little by little, the Cherokee Nation. Would the Cherokees' struggle against alcohol once again serve as a bastion against American encroachment as it had in the years before removal?

8

Cherokee Temperance, American Reform, and Oklahoma Statehood

Until the 1880s, the consumption and regulation of alcohol had been potent political issues in the Cherokee Nation in large part because they involved the broader question of sovereignty. As Cherokee women, who could not vote or hold public office, became more visible in the temperance movement, the emphasis shifted to the morality of drinking. When Ada Archer of the Cherokee Female Seminary became the first Cherokee woman to speak in public on temperance in 1884, she condemned Cherokee citizens for their unwillingness to observe U.S. laws designed to prevent liquor sales by American citizens to Indians. Harking back to the struggle over sovereignty between the U.S. and Cherokee governments that had been going on for decades, she expressed dismay that "[i]t is dreaded by many persons that the citizens of the Cherokee Nation are more or less imposed upon by the Intercourse laws, that their rights are unduly restrained, and that they are not only under no obligation to sustain those laws, but should resist them as far as possible." The refusal of Cherokees to obey federal alcohol regulations exacerbated the liquor traffic among her people. What was worse, she charged, fear of private revenge prevented Cherokees from reporting cases "either to our own courts or to the U.S. Court," and "public virtue carries a blind eye" to the illicit liquor trade. Standing before the Tahlequah Christian Temperance Union, "largely composed of officers of the Government, and comprising representatives from all the professions and stations in life," Archer in effect accused the Cherokee Nation of being incapable of coping with the problem: "Let us clearly understand the fact, . . . that we cannot enforce our own law for want of public sentiment, and moral courage among our citizens." She believed that the Cherokees needed "live moral force" to reinvigorate "the force of law."[1] Archer was not alone in her criticism of the Cherokee government. An independent Indian Nation seemed to many Americans to be an anachronistic obstacle to national economic development and progress. The arrival of railroads and the exploitation of natural resources within the Nation led many Cherokees to link the future of their people to the promise of the United States, and they too began to question the viability of Cherokee sovereignty. Just as railroads tied some Cherokees to American industrialists and politicians, temperance forged a bond between Cherokees and American reformers who increasingly saw Cherokee sovereignty as an impediment to moral uplift. Women took the lead in this movement after the early 1880s.

Cherokee women's involvement in temperance efforts coincided with the remarkable reform movement developed by "white-ribboners" of the Woman's Christian Temperance Union (WCTU). Excluded from institutionalized politics, women seized upon temperance as a moral issue in order to assert their influence in the public arena. The "Woman's Crusade" against alcohol dated back to Christmas Eve of

1873. On that day a group of women in Hillsboro, Ohio, marched into saloons and hotels and demanded that owners halt the sale of alcoholic beverages. "The Duty of Christian Women in the Cause of Temperance," the customary speech delivered by itinerant lecturer Diocletian Lewis one day earlier, had encouraged these women to enter places where they had never before been. Their action marked the dawn of the Woman's Crusade of 1873–1874. Sweeping the state of Ohio "like a prairie fire," the temperance cause soon spread beyond the state to more than nine hundred communities across the country. By praying and singing, female parties persuaded saloon keepers and hotel owners to sign the pledge to withhold alcohol, and within four months, more than one thousand saloons closed their doors, at least temporarily, indicating the coming age of the women's temperance movement in the United States.[2]

The Woman's Christian Temperance Union formally organized and held its first national meeting in Cleveland, Ohio, on November 18, 1874. Accepting male reformers as honorary members and guests only, the WCTU functioned as the first independent national female temperance organization in the United States.[3] Elected the second president of the WCTU in 1879, Frances E. Willard emerged as the union's leading figure. During her nineteen-year presidency (1879–1898), Willard established the basic policies of the WCTU and institutionalized the women's temperance movement under the motto "For God, and Home and Native Land." The badge the WCTU adopted was symbolic; just as white light reflected all the prismatic colors, the knot of white ribbon these temperance women wore represented "purity and peace" and "all the correlated reforms that center in the protection of the home."[4] Emphasizing both temperance and temperance-related causes, Willard enthusiastically committed herself and the union to contemporary social issues such as woman suffrage and labor exploitation. Embracing about two hundred thousand women during the 1880s, the WCTU expanded beyond moral authority to become an important political voice.[5]

Year after year, Willard conducted lecture tours to spread the cause while sending other national organizers to establish new unions and strengthen old ones throughout the country.[6] Sarah P. Morrison became the first white-ribboner to make her way into Indian territory. In the fall of 1879, Morrison accompanied Emeline H. Tuttle to her husband's mission station at the Quapaw Agency in the territory. During the six weeks of her stay, Morrison and the Tuttles attended the International Temperance Convention in Tahlequah, which organized a committee to ask the commissioner of Indian affairs to order rigid enforcement of the federal liquor laws in the territory. The committee claimed credit for the criminal convictions of at least six whiskey dealers. While holding temperance meetings throughout Indian territory, moreover, these non-Natives visited the Cherokee National Council, which was in session. They presented a letter from President Willard as well as an address authorized by the National WCTU, which later appeared in local Indian newspapers, the *Cherokee Advocate* and the *Indian Journal*, with Cherokee and Creek translations.[7] While she hoped for the more effective enforcement of the federal intercourse acts, Morrison applauded the Cherokees for their decision to enact their own prohibitory laws, under which their citizens "should be doubly protected." Her statement that Native involvement in the cause of temperance "modified previous impressions" she had had led to an official visit by the National WCTU president to the territory two years later.[8]

During her 1881 speaking tour to the southern states,

President Willard visited Indian territory with her private secretary, Anna Gordon. Her fame preceded her. In early May, Cherokee Chief Dennis W. Bushyhead received a letter from the vice president of the National WCTU, along with a reference from a minister who commended Willard for her "thorough knowledge of the subject, calm but deeply impressive tone, [and] a style of perfect finish."[9] Bushyhead requested L. Jane Stapler, together with several other women and clergymen, to form a committee to welcome this honorable guest to the capital of the Nation and to make her visit "pleasant and agreeable to herself, and profitable to our people."[10] Much to her surprise, perhaps, Willard encountered "Not a wigwam nor blanket nor warwhoop" during her visit to Indian territory.[11] Instead, she found a prosperous people engaged in farming, ranching, and commerce. Willard's hostess, Jane Stapler, was the daughter of a distinguished Cherokee leader, Elijah Hicks; niece of former Chief John Ross; wife of John W. Stapler, a Tahlequah merchant and former Chief Ross's brother-in-law; and superintendent of the Tahlequah Sabbath School.[12] Stapler soon emerged as a leading temperance reformer in Indian territory.

With Stapler at the helm, the cause of temperance gained ground among Cherokee citizens. Residents of Tahlequah, for example, felt that Chief Bushyhead's reforming efforts were not adequate, and they collected 112 signatures for a memorial to ask Bushyhead to exercise his authority more thoroughly to protect children in the town from the vice of alcohol.[13] The Tahlequah chapter of the WCTU was organized in the early 1880s while the men's Tahlequah Christian Temperance Union regularly held mass meetings and temperance lectures.[14] The *Cherokee Advocate* wrote: "The outlook now for a grand temperance boom is most auspicious."[15] The National Council encouraged temperance activities and granted a town lot in the capital to the business committee of the Tahlequah Christian Temperance Union to build a reading room and library to generate public support for temperance.[16]

Just as President Willard, in observing the Nation's prosperity, attributed it "to the absence of the drinking customs" among townspeople, the Cherokees' active involvement in temperance impressed WCTU organizers who had not yet visited the Nation.[17] J. Ellen Foster of Iowa, for example, requested Chief Bushyhead to send her a copy of the Cherokee liquor laws, along with his remark that the Cherokees successfully prohibited alcohol. She believed that "such a statement from you would carry conviction" in her upcoming lectures in the North.[18]

In November 1883, reformers invited a famous temperance lecturer, Emma Molloy, to Tahlequah.[19] At seven o'clock at night, the Reverend W. A. Duncan, president of the men's Tahlequah Christian Temperance Union, escorted Molloy to the Baptist church where "the clapping of hands and stamping of feet" awaited her. Molloy mesmerized her Cherokee listeners: "For two hours she held the attention of the audience, so completely that the falling of a pin to the floor could have been heard all over the house." The *Cherokee Advocate* announced that Molloy's visit to the Nation had "inaugurated, . . . a Temperance movement that must result in great good." At the close of her address, many signed the pledge of total abstinence, and she did not leave the lecture hall until about eleven o'clock.[20]

Having spent the Christmas holidays in her house in Illinois, Molloy returned to Indian territory in early January. When she arrived in Muskogee, she discovered that ice on the Arkansas River prevented the operation of the ferry that would take her to the Cherokee Nation. Refusing to be delayed, she crossed the river "by footing it over on the ice." She hailed a mail hack and reached Tahlequah, "cold and fatigued, but with zeal unabated." Although Jane Stapler and her husband privately welcomed Molloy to town, they could not keep her arrival secret for long: "The news of her return spread over the town rapidly; and in less than two hours the Baptist Church was warmed, lighted and made ready for an evening meeting." Her "informal and short" address was enough for an excited Cherokee audience, and "a general hand-shaking and interchange of friendly greetings" followed.[21]

The *Cherokee Advocate* praised Molloy when she presented another lecture series in Fort Gibson: "Interest in the community has grown, and the attendance increased, from night to night, until the Methodist church, which is the largest room in the village, is now scarcely able to accommodate the people."[22] After her address, however, "all but a few" left the church, ignoring her invitation to take the temperance pledge, and "she could not restrain her feelings any longer, and sat down and cried as if her heart would break."[23] An eyewitness to the Molloy Christian Temperance Union meetings, Elizabeth Ross, seems to have provided a clue to the disparity between the huge attendance and the apparent disinterest in temperance: "Women speakers were seldom seen and heard, and for the purpose of listening to a woman a number of persons, who otherwise probably would have remained at home, were present."[24]

The missionary Samuel A. Worcester's granddaughter, Emma Hicks, was more skeptical. She attended Molloy's address one night and wrote to her aunt that despite her "*wonderful* influence and power of persuasion" and "the good work she had done at Tahlequah," "I fear she will not" have any luck in Fort Gibson where "the people . . . are more hardened and *utterly indifferent* to every thing that is good, than any place in the Territory, or any where else."[25] Even the novelty of a woman lecturer was not likely to reform most of Fort Gibson's residents, who often squatted illegally on Indian land and used their anomalous legal position to engage in unscrupulous and even criminal behavior, including the importation, consumption, and sale of alcohol.

If it did not suppress drunkenness, Molloy's visit to the Nation was influential in reinvigorating the activities of the Tahlequah Woman's Christian Temperance Union. In February 1884, recording secretary Katie Ellett reported to the *Union Signal*, an official organ of the National WCTU: "God has wonderfully blessed us within the past three months. . . . [T]he whole country is stirred on the subjects of temperance and religion. Many drunkards have been reclaimed."[26] A temperance advocate at Fort Gibson who identified herself as "Cherokee" also wrote that "though she is gone, the spirit of her work is still with us."[27] Announcing in the *Cherokee Advocate* that the Tahlequah WCTU would meet in the Methodist church on March 29, "Cherokee" appealed to the conscience of women in the Nation: "Mothers, you are the very ones we need. Your presence even, will help us, . . . Sisters, can you sit quietly by and see your brothers enticed into that path that leads, step by step, down, down to destruction of both body and soul?" By reminding Cherokee women of how they could exercise their female influence on the issue of temperance, "Cherokee" continued her plea: "Not forcibly; but quietly as the snow over-spreads the earth; would we spread the pure white mantle of Temperance over our community, over this, our Indian Land."[28] Emma Molloy came back once again in May on another speaking tour to Tahlequah, Fort Gibson, and Vinita.[29] Meanwhile, the Tahlequah WCTU met regularly, continued to emphasize motherhood and the proper training of the young, and invited children of the cold water army, called the Band of Hope, to its official gathering.[30]

In the years following, Martha G. Tunstall replaced Emma Molloy as a WCTU organizer in the Cherokee Nation. On New Year's Eve of 1885, Tunstall wrote Frances Willard and pleaded with her to "give me the field ... with proper credentials." Claiming to be "forty-seven years old, of Cherokee descent," Tunstall assured Willard that "I could do a grand work among them; being one of them they would know I meant good and would not be suspicious of me as they are of white people."[31]

In November 1886, Tunstall, accompanied by her minister husband, who may have found the Indian territory a promising mission field, visited Tahlequah under the auspices of the National Woman's Christian Temperance Union and commenced a week of daily temperance meetings. While she encouraged Cherokees to sign the total abstinence pledge, Tunstall helped white-ribboners in the Nation pursue legislative solutions for intemperance. On November 24, the Tahlequah WCTU received an invitation from the council, the lower house of the Cherokee nation, then in session, to present whatever propositions it had in mind. Members of the union gathered at the Presbyterian church and prepared a memorial beseeching the Cherokee National Council to enact a tribal law to punish drunkenness. Col. DeWitt Clinton Duncan, whom Tunstall described as the "most courteous and hospitable to his well-wishers," introduced ten WCTU workers to the Cherokee National Council, and their spokeswoman, Miss Sweet, presented a petition.[32] The council passed the bill, but opposition from the president of the Cherokee Senate prevented the Nation from branding drunkenness a misdemeanor.[33]

By the end of 1887, Tunstall seems to have felt overwhelmed: "Mrs. Tunstall has worked almost entirely alone."[34] By attending the National WCTU annual meeting in November, Tunstall fulfilled her long-cherished wish "to 'see one woman's meeting before she died.'"[35] She retired from the organizing work for the territory, returned to Arkansas, and taught school in a border town.[36]

In correspondence to the *Union Signal*, Julia A. Rogers complained that the Indian territory was "a very discouraging field more so, because the leaders in every good work must come from among the missionaries, and they have so many cares connected with their church work." Rogers, however, also recognized that the National WCTU was partly responsible for the apparent Cherokee disinterest in the temperance movement: "The idea prevails that *any* one can do this work; but there are many quite cultivated people here—so many of them, that unless a speaker has true eloquence they are not impressed."[37] Perhaps in an effort to elevate the level of discussion, in May 1888 the National WCTU sent Mary E. Griffith of Kansas to the territory to encourage temperance among the Indians. Tahlequah white-ribboners explained to Griffith the long history of Cherokee temperance with "admirably enforced" prohibitory laws and contrasted that to the current failure of "our national, paternal government" to enact meaningful alcohol regulations. Griffith agreed: "Our government can never civilize the Indians by their present policy." During her six weeks' stay, Griffith spoke before Cherokee citizens several times. She reorganized the Band of Hope as a Loyal Temperance Legion for children, a move that the *Tahlequah Telephone* ridiculed by saying that "if we had kept a list of all the organizations that have been formed in Tahlequah, for temperance purposes and for good intentions, it would fill up the Telephone; and yet what has become of them all?"[38]

American temperance reformers and Cherokee towns-people both challenged the early attempts of WCTU workers in the Indian territory, but their critiques were not entirely accurate. Under the direction of Pres. Jane Stapler, the Tahlequah WCTU recruited many Cherokee women to join in "our effort to elevate the morals and unify the society of our town."[39] The Tahlequah WCTU became a major force for social reform in Indian territory. The union held monthly public meetings as well as entertainments.[40] Members visited the national prison regularly to teach Cherokee convicts the importance of a temperate life.[41] Helen R. Duncan of Iowa, who married Cherokee Colonel Duncan, introduced "scientific" temperance instruction in Indian schools.[42] The presence of Cherokee white-ribboners in the Nation also affected the Cherokee police force. Soon after his appointment as high sheriff of the Cherokee Nation on April 28, 1888, Jesse B. Mayes announced his intention to watch, as the law of the Nation directed, every corner of the town to find the illicit liquor trade.[43] Reminding them to "blame yourselves, not me for doing my duty," Mayes warned Cherokee citizens: "Now boys this is meant not only for whiskey peddlers but for all those who some times bring it [alcohol] in and deal it out to friends who after imbibing . . . cause guards great trouble and run risk of serious difficulties."[44] Jane Stapler visited Mayes in November to present to him a cake and a bouquet of flowers in token of her appreciation of his being "an efficient officer," and Mayes, in return, reassured the president that he would "do his level best to keep peace and order in Tahlequah."[45]

In June 1888 the Tahlequah WCTU hosted a lecture series by a national organizer, Sarah M. Perkins, of Cleveland, Ohio. Tennessee M. Fuller, the corresponding secretary, plotted the route so that Perkins could travel throughout the Cherokee,

Creek, and Choctaw Nations. On June 16, 1888, Perkins arrived at Vinita. The town failed to advertise her coming, however, and Perkins herself had to send announcements to ministers and place a notice at the post office. She delivered two temperance addresses on the following day and left for Tulsa where the hearty welcome of the Creek chief, his friends, and missionaries offset the initial disinterest. While she successfully organized unions in Choteau, Muskogee, and Webbers Falls, Perkins met with indifference at Fort Gibson, where, she observed, "there was not much interest in the work": people were fond of "a large Indian Council" and war dances, and "a temperance meeting seemed a small affair after all these festivities." In Tahlequah, the "most cultured and refined" Cherokee women, Jane Stapler and Tennessee M. Fuller, entertained her. On her way to Texas, Perkins stopped over in Eufaula, Atoka, and Caddo to organize more unions.[46] By becoming part of a national organization of the United States, Native women joined with American women for the common cause of temperance.

On July 18, 1888, women temperance reformers in Indian territory held a two-day, territory-wide Woman's Christian Temperance Union convention in Muskogee.[47] Sarah M. Perkins enlisted the assistance of the Texas State WCTU president, who returned with her to monitor the convention. The delegates elected Jane Stapler, president of the territorial WCTU; Tennessee M. Fuller, corresponding secretary; Ira Myatt of Eufaula in the Creek Nation, recording secretary; and Mrs. T. S. Brewer of Muskogee, treasurer. A group of African American women also attended the meeting, and they sought to organize as a union. The territorial WCTU resolved that it would appoint "a colored superintendent for work among that race." Perkins, who had campaigned for temperance in the Creek and Choctaw Nations as well as among the Cherokees, expressed her satisfaction and surprise: "I was astonished that the women, unaccustomed to public speaking, could express themselves so well in little impromptu speeches."[48]

On May 4, 1889, the Indian Territory WCTU celebrated its second anniversary at a meeting in Tahlequah. The capital of the Cherokee Nation once again received special guests from the National Woman's Christian Temperance Union. White-ribboners of Indian territory did not miss this opportunity to demonstrate to President Willard and her private secretary Anna Gordon how much they had accomplished as temperance workers since their last visit in 1881. The corresponding secretary announced in her report that "the W.C.T.U. has come to stay. The golden seed has been sown and the good women from all parts of our fair Territory are here to tell us that it is springing up to bring forth an abundant harvest for the future."[49]

In her annual address, President Stapler also encouraged fellow workers: "Sisters, the consciousness of ignorance and inexperience may weigh upon our souls. But hath not God chosen the foolish things of the world to confound the wise? Sisters, we are weak, but hath not God chosen the weak things of the world to confound the things which are mighty? Let us then, strong in faith, go forward in the glorious work of rescuing the perishing." She continued: "The most encouraging feature of our work is to be found in the determined spirit animating every Union."[50] In the spirit of the occasion, the Atoka Union of the Choctaw Nation invoked the number that southern Indians considered sacred: "We are seven—the magic number seven—hence we expect to succeed."[51]

On the following day, President Willard spoke in the morning before "a cultivated audience of Cherokees" at the

Presbyterian church and spent the afternoon visiting the national prison with I. B. Hitchcock who, as a WCTU representative, held Sunday school for Cherokee convicts. Anna Gordon addressed Sunday school children and the members of the Loyal Temperance Legion in Tahlequah who entertained her with marching songs. At night, Willard returned to the Methodist church and delivered another temperance lecture. The *Cherokee Advocate* praised these two speakers for possessing "the true orator's gift of saying clearly what is wanted to be said in the fewest words and plainest language." In Tahlequah, Willard and Gordon met Chief Joel B. Mayes, "who is, alas! a drinking man, as is painfully palpable," but they did not see any disturbing evidence of intemperance in the notorious Fort Gibson, and they ordered the *Union Signal* and some other temperance books for the reading room of the town.[52]

While the WCTU was having a major impact on the Cherokee Nation and its citizens, the growth of the temperance movement in Indian territory changed the image of Native people among temperance reformers. When a WCTU organizer, Barbara O'Brian, traveled in 1889, she reported that she stayed with "the charming president of the W.C.T.U. Indian Territory," Jane Stapler, and enjoyed the most "orderly" legislative session she had ever attended when she visited a Cherokee National Council meeting. She claimed that "this is the result of the labors of the W.C.T.U." National organizers who visited the Indian territory had all acquired a better understanding of Indian life, and they became defenders of Native people, especially Native women. O'Brian was no exception: "The expression 'as dirty as an Indian,' could not have had its birth among the Cherokees, for the full-blooded women could easily give lessons in neatness to many women in Kansas, Missouri and Texas; in fact, to women all over the United States."[53]

The presence of Indian Territory Woman's Christian Temperance Union president Jane Stapler at the 1890 annual convention of the National WCTU, held in Atlanta, Georgia, reinforced this enlightened view of Native American women. Anna Gordon's cordial invitation of Indian territory delegates to the national convention brought this Cherokee woman back to what was once Cherokee country.[54] Stapler spoke of her connection to the place and the cause: "You do not know, my sisters, what it means to me to come back after an interval of generations to the state where I was born and be welcomed so tenderly by my comrades of the white ribbon, who are fighting with me against the 'fire water,' that has been the curse of my race as well as of your own."[55]

Before the WCTU audience, Stapler deciphered a mechanism of Indian myth making. Although Indians, perhaps, had felt the woes of alcohol more keenly than others, "it does not necessarily imply that they have been the hardest drinkers." She recounted how unscrupulous Americans in the territory helped perpetuate this "drunken Indian" stereotype. They distributed alcohol among Indians, became intoxicated with them, and soon began fighting with them. When friends of both parties joined in the fray, "a rush to the frontier post with an alarm that 'The Indians are on the War-path' has caused a hasty parade of troops which has been met by an ambitious chief with his warriors," and a more deadly battle ensued.[56] The true cause of such "destruction and anguish," however, "when the weaker has been driven to the wall has not been written. Perhaps God in his wisdom has prevented their going on the pages of history to tarnish the glory of the greatest nation on earth." Although these alarming conditions led Congress to ban the sale and use of intoxicating liquors in Indian country, the federal liquor laws never entirely suppressed the traffic. The cooperation of the neighboring states in enforcing the law was crucial, she concluded, and "in saving the Indians from temptation thousands of whites will be less frequently tempted." Ultimately, "the war-whoop, white and red, [would] become a thing for historical allusion only."[57]

At the close of Stapler's speech, Zerelda G. Wallace of Indiana came forward to offer a testimonial: "Fifty years ago I saw Mrs. Stapler, though until now I did not know it was the same person." Wallace had met Stapler on board a steamboat when her father was taking her to school in New Jersey. Replying to Wallace's surprise that she was an Indian, Stapler said: "Oh, the white people think of Indians as having rings in our noses and bells on our toes; but give us a chance and time will show that the Indian is capable of as high civilization as the whites." Wallace now acknowledged that President Stapler had appeared at the Atlanta Convention "as the best exemplification of her own prophecy."[58] With her passionate address, Stapler had enlightened all white-ribboners present.

The wctu workers' reforming efforts in the territory continued, but they became increasingly disillusioned with elected officials. The *Cherokee Advocate* criticized Tahlequah city authorities for having "remained disgustingly silent" on the intemperate states of both young and old men "lying around on the side-walks like hogs in mud."[59] In 1891, when members of the Tahlequah wctu presented a temper-ance pledge to the Cherokee National Council for signa-tures, moreover, only twelve out of one hundred senators and councilors consented "to touch no intoxicants during that term of our Legislature."[60] The refusal marked a decline in moral standards among Cherokee statesmen.

Women reformers particularly objected to the practice of vote buying with whiskey. On August 3, 1891, an election day for chief and other officers of the Nation, sisters of the Tahlequah WCTU gathered "at the polls in full force." They set up a booth near the polling place and decorated it with white ribbons, banners, and a portrait of President Willard. They served nonalcoholic refreshments at their booth, and "by their presence," they hoped to prevent Cherokee rival parties from using alcohol to entice male citizens to vote for their candidates.[61] The adage, "The man who could pass out the most whiskey usually got the most votes," however, proved true.[62] A Cherokee named Degardunah Judge admitted that on the election day, a Downing party member, Silas Clork, together with his interpreter named Butterfly, gave Judge whiskey and a pair of shoes to vote for Joel Mayes, the Downing candidate for Cherokee chief. Despite his pro-National party sentiment, Judge attested, under the influence of alcohol, he cast a vote for Mayes.[63] Judge probably was not alone.

One of the issues temperance women in the early 1890s collectively tackled was the shipment of malt liquors by railroad and express companies into Indian territory. On September 18, 1889, the superintendent of the Wells-Fargo Express Company informed his agents that the company attorneys had interpreted section 2139 of the Revised Statutes, which prohibited the sale of "any spirituous liquors or wine" in the territory, to mean that it did not restrict the introduction of malt liquors, such as beer and ale, among Indian tribes.[64] Thereafter, the company began shipping these alcoholic beverages openly into Indian territory.[65] Meanwhile, the Pacific Express Company, which operated along the lines of the Missouri, Kansas, and Texas Railway and the Kansas and Arkansas Valley Railway, refused to permit the Indian police under the command of Agent Leo E. Bennett to examine packages and destroy concealed liquor. The company complained that the Indian police deputized outsiders to search its offices and seize alcohol. Furthermore, a crowd of people occasionally followed the police into the express offices to watch the indiscriminate search.[66]

Agent Bennett explained to the Pacific Express Company that Rule 26 of the Regulations of the Indian Department, which the secretary of the interior had approved on September 23, 1884, granted the Indian police the right to detain "the perpetrators of certain crimes and misdemeanors," which he believed included bootlegging and the possession of alcohol. He continued that "the Indian police have for many years passed exercised this authority unquestioned by express companies." In "check[ing] express packages for liquor," therefore, an Indian policeman "would hold them up to his ear and shake them and if his suspicions were aroused, he would smash the package." Bennett assured the company's assistant superintendent that in the future, the Indian police officers would examine packages only in the presence of railroad or express agents and that they would search only those they had reasonable grounds to suspect contained spirituous liquors. Bennett promised that he would remind the Indian police officers of their responsibility for damages incurred in falsely opening packages and clarified that intoxicants, as the Indian Office instructed in 1883 and reaffirmed in 1889, included not only spirituous liquors and wine but also cider, essences, patent medicines, and any other compounds that produced intoxication.[67]

Secretary of the Interior John W. Noble confirmed that Bennett's "present instructions are as moderate as the condition of the case will allow." Noble also extended to the Pacific Express any benefit of the doubt: "I am quick to believe that your company has no disposition to transport any forbidden articles into that Territory, and that whatever may thus be sent is contrary to your desires and interests."[68] The Pacific Express agreed to order its shipping agents throughout the country to refuse the shipment of liquor into the Indian territory and, in receiving packages, make certain that the ones addressed to the territory did not contain alcohol.[69] When the territorial WCTU petitioned the Missouri, Kansas, and Texas Railway for cooperation in the prevention of the liquor traffic, that company assured President Stapler that it also would make every effort to stop the flow.[70]

In the summer of 1891, however, Judge David M. Bryant of the U.S. Court for the Eastern District of Texas ruled that the introduction and sale of malt liquors in the Indian territory did not violate federal laws. Agent Bennett stated that Judge Bryant's "unfortunate encouragement" immediately "opened up the breweries the most profitable field they have ever delighted in debauching" and sanctioned "numerous lager-beer dives all over the Chickasaw nation," which lay between the Cherokee and Creek Nations and Texas. Agent Bennett lamented: "Year by year the Territory seems to become a more inviting field to the avaricious venders of the various kinds of intoxicating beverages." On August 22, Commissioner of Indian Affairs T. J. Morgan telegraphed Bennett that the secretary of the interior had authorized him to seize packages containing beer shipped into the territory and hand them over to the U.S. marshal.[71] The *Cherokee Advocate* applauded the secretary's decision as "eminently proper" and added that "with the toleration of this beer or hop tea or by what other name it may be called, will come other and more pernicious stuff and the result will be, blood shed and riotous conduct followed by sorrow, shame and grief in many house holds."[72] When Agent Bennett seized a carload of beer in Lehigh, Choctaw Nation, however, the U.S. marshal refused to hold it for him. What was worse, the attorney general concurred with the decision of the U.S. District Court in Texas and declined to "take any steps which might render the marshal responsible on his bond."[73]

Tennessee M. Fuller, corresponding secretary of the Indian Territory WCTU, reported to the national headquarters in 1892: "The special work of our Unions this year has been against beer, the sale of which Judge Bryant . . . declared was not illegal." White-ribboners in the territory petitioned local authorities to prevent the sale of beer and hop tea, and they circulated for signatures a memorial addressed to Pres. Benjamin Harrison appealing for a ban on the sale of malt liquors among Indians. Meanwhile, Pres. Jane Stapler asked a lawyer in Washington to lobby for a prohibition bill in Congress.[74]

When Judge Isaac C. Parker of the U.S. District Court in Fort Smith finally called a halt to the beer business in Indian territory, "the beer venders were brought to realize that perhaps, after all, they were not to be allowed to violate the laws with impunity."[75] On July 23, 1892, Congress passed an amendment to section 2139 of the Revised Statutes that specifically provided, "No ardent spirits, ale, beer, wine, or intoxicating liquor or liquors of whatever kind shall be introduced, under any pretense, into the Indian country."[76] In rejoicing, the women of the Tahlequah WCTU rang all the church bells in the town.[77]

Well before these express and railroad companies, along with the U.S. District Court in Texas, overtly challenged the authority of the federal government, bootleggers had invented "a variety of guises to escape detection" in the Indian territory.[78] Although the *Cherokee Advocate* wrote in 1889 that "we are not sure that it is not a legal crime to sell it even to cure anybody," the Nation had, for several years, legalized the consumption of alcohol with prescriptions of licensed physicians.[79] This encouraged illicit dealers to open drugstores and distribute alcoholic patent medicines freely within the Nation; many Cherokee young men seem to have obtained their first drink in one of these drugstores. A Cherokee named Wallace Thornton of Vian, for example, recollected that his rite of passage into adulthood was by gulping "Prickly Ash Bitters" at a store in Webbers Falls: The "boss bought some of this bitters and passed it around and, of course, when the bottle came to me, I took a big drink—but one drink was enough."[80]

In the fall of 1892, Chief C. J. Harris attempted to expel from the Nation "quack" doctors who practiced medicine without a Cherokee license and endangered "the lives of innocent and often ignorant people."[81] Harris found their presence problematic especially because they sold their patients "some nostrum which they claim will cure anything" but, most likely, contained a high percentage of alcohol.[82] White-ribboners of the Indian territory, moreover, considered the marketing of Jamaica ginger, which was 90 percent alcohol, particularly alarming because it was readily available at drugstores.[83] It was, however, an extremely difficult task for the temperance women to find these self-styled professionals because customers, knowing that they themselves would be charged with the possession of intoxicants, protected them.[84] In order to prosecute Jamaica ginger dealers, President Stapler solicited state WCTUs for contributions, and Tahlequah white-ribboners used these donations to post a one-hundred-dollar reward for information on those who were distributing Jamaica ginger and other alcoholic medicines among Cherokees.[85] With financial assistance from various state unions, the Tahlequah WCTU succeeded in forcing a number of druggists in the Nation to refrain from selling patent medicines that produced intoxication.[86]

White-ribboners of the Indian territory worked for the cause of temperance in an organization established exclusively for women, but male citizens also assisted their reforming efforts. Local clergymen, in particular, provided moral support and encouragement. The Reverend W. R. King was a regular lecturer for the Tahlequah wctu. Emphasizing the importance of female influence and education in the work of temperance, King proclaimed that "public opinion is the creative power." He reminded the white-ribboners that "*as members of society we are responsible for the morality of the community.*" Contending that they could not "expect temperance so long as it is *respectable* to be intemperate," King insisted that temperance reformers work to transform the "moral sentiment of individuals."[87]

King conveyed to these white-ribboners in Tahlequah another powerful message: "The hope for temperance in America is not legislation but education along temperance lines." He attempted to rectify the prevailing idea among temperance workers that "intemperance is an evil that can be put down once and forever." He contended that "intemperance is here to stay just as long as men are human, and the heart is sinful" and reminded them that "every generation must do" the work "for itself" and that women had a special task in achieving this goal. King had more than moral influence in mind. Temperance, he believed, began in the kitchen: "Bad cooking is a continual temptation to drink." Then, the reforming efforts "must continue into the parlor. Our homes must be reformed." He charged mothers and wives to make their homes attractive, pleasant, and comfortable for their husbands and sons so that they would stay home rather than spend their evenings at a saloon or billiard hall.[88] Although he challenged Cherokee temperance women to reform the domestic realm, King also praised these reformers for their unrelenting efforts to educate Cherokee citizens and encouraged them to continue: "You will meet with rebuffs and discouragements, you may have things to dishearten you, but don't give up."[89]

The Dawes General Allotment Act of 1887 authorized the president to allot land to individual Indians and grant U.S. citizenship to those who received the allotments, but it exempted the southern tribes of eastern Oklahoma. The adoption of this general policy did not lead to the immediate dissolution of Cherokee government and absorption of Cherokee citizens into the United States. In 1893, Congress created the Commission to the Five Civilized Tribes, commonly called the Dawes Commission, and charged it to negotiate allotment agreements with the tribes. On June 28, 1898, Congress enacted the Curtis Act providing the allotment of Cherokee land by the Dawes Commission upon completion of the tribal rolls and the abolition of the judicial functions of the Cherokee Nation. Congress allowed the state of Arkansas to extend its jurisdiction over Indian territory and enforce all state laws except the one legalizing the liquor traffic within the state boundaries.[90] On August 7, 1902, Cherokees themselves consented to a dissolution of tribal government as of March 4, 1906, but many Indians opposed the absorption by Oklahoma of the Indian territory and insisted that they have a state of their own, independent of Oklahoma, if the United States wished to integrate them into its society.[91]

American temperance reformers did not share such sentiment with Native people, and they took action well before the citizens of the Indian territory began organizing themselves to secure self-government in a newly established state. When the federal government attempted to complete its assimilation policy by dissolving tribal governments at the turn of the twentieth century, the National wctu began publicizing alcohol-related lawlessness of the Indian territory. In 1899, the *Union Signal* reiterated the data presented by U.S. agent Leo E. Bennett a decade earlier: "95 per cent of all criminal cases heard by that body [the U.S. District Court in Fort Smith] were *directly* traceable to intoxicants." Agent Bennett believed whiskey manufacturers and distributors to be tempters and Indians to be victims, and Judge Isaac C. Parker, from his nineteen-year experience at Fort Smith, provided a proof in 1894 that "the great number of crimes in the Indian country have been committed by people who are citizens of the United States," but such observations did not affect the ardent advocates of temperance in mainstream American society.[92] The National wctu concluded that the Native people were to blame because "it was difficult to control their thirst for fire-water." The American white-ribboners found the stereotype of "drunken Indians" to be a powerful weapon to promote their own cause, and this image dominated the descriptions of Native people in the *Union Signal*: "A sober Indian may be made into a good citizen, but drunk, his savage instincts and passions convert him into a demon."[93] Dorothy J. Cleveland, the national superintendent of Work Among Indians, reminded her comrades in 1902 that prohibition did not work at all in the Indian territory "because the Indian has a STRONG appetite for stimulants—an inheritance of generations" although she also lamented that "his white brother has NO RESPECT for the LAW" controlling the liquor trade among the Indians.[94]

The question of prohibition and that of statehood further challenged the Native people of the Indian territory, and the resurgence of the "drunken Indian" stereotype among American white-ribboners exacerbated the matter. At the 1901 National wctu annual convention, a longtime Baptist missionary among the Choctaws, Joseph Samuel Murrow, asserted that "the W.C.T.U. need not concern itself with the question of single or double statehood for Indian Territory and Oklahoma, but that it could not afford to lose one inch of prohibition territory."[95] Concurring with Murrow, the national union promptly telegraphed Pres. Theodore Roosevelt to retain prohibitory laws among the Indians "because it is well known that the Indian race has a peculiar and most powerful appetite for intoxicating liquors," which, it feared, would "very speedily" destroy the entire Native population if the federal government legalized drinking among the Indian tribes.[96] For American temperance reformers, securing prohibitory laws in a new state was the top priority; whether or not Indians in the Indian territory retained self-government in a state separate from Oklahoma was secondary. After all, Cherokee sovereignty, in their view, was not as compelling a moral issue as prohibition. They understood that the merging of Indian territory with Oklahoma without its consent might well violate the treaty stipulations that guaranteed the Indians the right of self-government as well as the rigid enforcement of federal liquor laws. In an attempt to take the Natives' sentiments into consideration, on March 4, 1904, the National WCTU presented to Congress a memorial "remonstrating against . . . the union and admission of Indian Territory and Oklahoma Territory as one state unless the sale of intoxicants therein is prohibited." Still, the national union believed that the Native people would eventually agree to unite with citizens of Oklahoma for joint statehood if they could obtain prohibition in a new state; Indians abhorred joint statehood essentially because "it means the extension over Indian Territory of laws admitting intoxicants, which will be peculiarly disastrous and ruinous to the Indian people."[97]

American temperance reformers were correct. White-ribboners of the Indian territory indeed objected to the integration of their domain into the adjacent territory because "we have enough open saloons in our drug stores" and could not tolerate more liberal liquor laws.[98] They reported to the national annual convention in 1902: "We have been working to hold our Prohibitory Law by not being annexed to Oklahoma."[99] In the early 1900s, the Indian Territory WCTU repeatedly petitioned the president of the United States and Congress to preserve prohibitory laws among Indians and to oppose the annexation of the Indian territory to an Oklahoma rife with saloons.[100]

Missionaries also joined in the prohibition statehood movement. Believing that this was "the matter of the greatest concern to the people of the Indian Territory, Indians and whites alike," they insisted that the federal government insert in enabling legislation a provision that prohibited the sale and manufacture of intoxicating liquors not solely among the Indians. The Muskogee Ministers' Association proclaimed in 1904: "Let us avoid taking any position on the question of single or separate statehood. We want PROHIBITION STATEHOOD whether single or separate."[101]

To many citizens of the Indian territory, the loss of autonomy after the dissolution of their tribal governments was of prime importance, and their leaders worked vigorously to retain Indians' right to control their own lives. Leaders advocated prohibition, and they did so because they thought that a proposal of prohibition would help them secure separate statehood, which they believed provided them and their people the last vestige of tribal sovereignty. When he received a letter from white-ribboner Mrs. James Samuel Murrow of Atoka in March 1903, therefore, Choctaw Chief Green McCurtain recognized her and her temperance organization to be "of much assistance to our plan of separate statehood." Referring to the action taken by Natives to attain separate statehood, Murrow stated: "This is certainly just the thing to do." She also mentioned the importance of pursuing prohibition with statehood because "there is very little hope of a continuance of the Indian race unless intoxicating liquors is kept from them." Although he believed that Native people of the Indian territory should advocate prohibition "for the preservation of the Indian race together with his vast estate" and thus did not entirely agree with Murrow, Chief McCurtain urged the leaders of other Indian tribes including Cherokee Chief T. M. Buffington to write her that they upheld prohibition.[102] The delegates of the Five Tribes confirmed this once again in a convention held in Eufaula two months later, resolving that their councils would send memorials to various temperance and religious organizations and obtain assistance in their attempt to secure a state government separate from Oklahoma.[103]

The Campaign Committee of the Constitutional Convention for independent statehood for the Indian territory convened in Muskogee on August 21, 1905. Delegates proclaimed that "All people naturally desire self government" and that the integration of the Indian territory into Oklahoma against its will would also "offend . . . the feelings of the people of Oklahoma." A code of laws the people in Oklahoma had enacted were not "agreeable or suitable to the people of Indian Territory in a vast number of particulars." The most objectionable provision permitted saloons in Oklahoma. Under the treaty stipulations, the United States had granted Indians the right to govern themselves, and "the people of Indian Territory not only do not wish to be united with Oklahoma, but they are violently opposed to it."[104]

The *Cherokee Advocate* was more explicit: "We want to

govern ourselves in our own way [*sic*], with our own means, and by our own people, without the interference of any other community in the world. We have had enough of the assistance of outside friends in governing us, and that is the very thing of which we are thoroug[h]ly sick." It continued: "We want separate statehood because our Indian people are our friends and neighbors, whom we well understand and with whom we are glad to be on terms of social equality. This spirit does not exist in Oklahoma."[105] Indeed, a sympathizer in Philadelphia agreed: "Oklahoma boldly proclaims that she will not have prohibition. By this very disregard of the wishes and rights of her proposed mate she shows herself unfit for Statehood."[106]

Advocates of separate statehood for the Indian territory named their prospective state the State of Sequoyah, and except for "medicinal, mechanical, and scientific purposes," the proposed constitution declared the use of alcohol unlawful: "The manufacture, sale, barter, or giving away of intoxicating liquors or spirits of any kind within this State is forever prohibited." The governor of the state would appoint three "Enforcement commissioners" to effectively implement this prohibitory law among its citizens.[107]

Although the territorial WCTU president in her 1904 annual address declared that "we are in favor of prohibition statehood regardless of boundaries," her comrades did not unanimously approve of this statement.[108] The disparity within the territorial WCTU became apparent at the national annual convention the following year. Sensing that joint statehood with Oklahoma was inevitable, Pres. Mabel R. Sutherland implored the national union to assist in extending prohibition over "the state formed from Oklahoma and Indian Territory."[109] The report prepared by Corresponding Secretary Lucy Belle Davis for that convention clearly stated, however, that "the W.C.T.U. have advocated separate statehood with prohibition."[110] The Oklahoma Enabling Act of 1906 prohibited the sale of alcohol in the Indian territory part of the new state for twenty-one years after statehood, but Congress gave the Oklahoma side the right to decide what it would do with the liquor trade.[111] After Indian territory lost the battle for separate statehood, the Oklahoma Territory wctu began fighting to secure a "uniform constitution for the whole state."[112] In the 1906 annual convention, the National wctu proudly announced that "we have good reason to believe that forty thousand square miles will be added to the prohibition territory when in a few months the people of Oklahoma declare in the Constitutional Convention, or by the votes of their people, that their state shall be free from the legalized saloon."[113] The ratification of the new state's constitution was scheduled for September 17, 1907. Indian Territory wctu president Mabel R. Sutherland solicited assistance among her territorial white-ribboners: "Do your best to get temperance men from Indian Territory elected to the constitutional convention so a prohibition clause may be inserted in the state constitution."[114] Indeed, the Oklahoma state constitution prohibited alcohol.[115]

Suggested by both National wctu president Lillian M. N. Stevens and Territorial president Sutherland, the 1906 territorial executive committee proposed "call[ing] new W.C.T.U. work Sequoyah" when the Indian territory and Oklahoma amalgamated.[116] In the territorial annual convention of that year, however, white-ribboners of the Indian territory concluded that they would remain a separate union and, after Oklahoma statehood in 1907, would change the name of the organization to the Eastern Oklahoma Woman's Christian Temperance Union.[117] When Pres. Abbie B. Hillerman of the Oklahoma wctu attended the Indian Territory wctu's annual meeting the following year and invited the group to unite with the Oklahoma union, the territorial union declined her offer and elected its own officers.[118] Hillerman was not entirely discouraged: "The white women were unanimously in favor of it, but some of the Indian women felt that the time had not yet come for Union. I am sure the two organizations will be united in their efforts to eradicate the saloon and all its evils."[119] While the Oklahoma WCTU celebrated its victory in the statewide prohibition campaign, the National WCTU Executive Committee resolved in November 1907:

Inasmuch as former Indian Territory is now a part of the State of Oklahoma, and as the National W.C.T.U. can recognize but one State Union (except in states having colored organizations, or where geographical conditions make it necessary) your Committee recom-[m]end that plans be made by the Presidents of Indian Territory and Oklahoma looking toward the union of the two organizations, said plans to be submitted to the General Officers of the National Woman[']s Christian Temperance Union who shall have power to ratify, amend or reject the same. We further recommend that one year be given to make all needed changes.[120]

On September 11, 1908, white-ribboners of the former Indian Territory WCTU gathered together and commemorated its last annual convention in Muskogee where a group of temperance women had commenced their reform movement in 1888 as an auxiliary to the National Woman's Christian Temperance Union. Pres. Lilah D. Lindsey spoke: "The Indian Territory Woman[']s Christian Temperance Union has reached its majority as does a voting citizen of the United States at the age of twenty one. . . . How little our pioneers realized at that time what their efforts would bring forth with that small membership." On this memorable day, Lindsey announced to her comrades that the national union had beseeched her "organization of several hundred members" to merge with the one in Oklahoma to work together for the cause of temperance.[121] Four days later, President Lindsey and other Indian territory delegates left for Oklahoma City where, in a day, the "white wedding bells for the union of the two states" welcomed them. In a symbolic "wedding of unions," the Indian Territory and Oklahoma WCTUs both formally dissolved on September 18, 1908, and their members united in the formation of the "Greater Oklahoma State Woman's Christian Temperance Union."[122]

The temperance movement had united Cherokee women with the women of the other Five Tribes, all of which also had the WCTUs, and non-Indian women in the common goal of prohibition. For these women, temperance initially took precedence over political affairs, in which they had no voice. Temperance was a moral issue, they believed, and they often despaired over the failure of male Cherokee political leaders to embrace their cause. Cherokee officials' rather cavalier attitude toward alcohol consumption even at polling places led some of these women to question the value of Cherokee sovereignty. When allotment and statehood threatened that sovereignty, however, the Native women who advocated temperance found themselves increasingly disheartened by their American comrades who expressed the biased views about Native people, and they felt reluctant to make a concerted effort to attain prohibition statehood in accordance with their national organization. In the last decisive battle for tribal sovereignty and survival, these Native temperance women could not work effectively with their WCTU comrades nor with the citizens of the Indian territory. Just as their leaders differed over the question of statehood, Indian territory white-ribboners were no longer united, and they did not unanimously raise their voices or exert their substantial influence to protect the Cherokee Nation along with Native male leaders. While Indian men attempted once again to embody the Cherokee tradition of resorting to sobriety to secure sovereignty, their female temperance counterparts realized that they could not pursue even their cause without a solid tribal political entity. In the end, the loss of sovereignty and the creation of Oklahoma brought the uniquely Cherokee temperance movement to an end.

CONCLUSION

As the Cherokee experience demonstrates, the story of Native Americans and their relationship with alcohol is a complicated one. Taking the long view—across two centuries—suggests that a single analytical model or a deeply held moral conviction cannot adequately explain the role of alcohol in Native societies. At specific times, alcohol created problems in Cherokee society, but at other times, Cherokees managed to regulate consumption in ways that asserted their sovereignty and demonstrated their morality. That is, among the Cherokees, alcohol in and of itself does not seem to have been an omnipresent, debilitating problem. The construction of alcohol as a problem by politicians, reformers, and scholars, however, has played an important role in Cherokee history, and this study has attempted to distinguish those constructions from the actual history of alcohol among the Cherokees. The history of alcohol in turn reflects the history of the Cherokee people.

Like many goods acquired from Europeans, Cherokees found ways to integrate alcohol into their culture. Gifts to warriors, especially from the British, generally included guns and ammunition, paint, and rum. Cherokees, therefore, came to regard alcohol as one of the accoutrements of war. They used it as a powerful war medicine, drank to excess, and sobered up to engage their enemies with confidence. Until the mid-eighteenth century, chiefs controlled the alcohol trade, but the British invasions of the Seven Years' War and the postwar restructuring of the trade compromised the authority of chiefs. Cherokee men, in particular, began to drink in other contexts. The drunkenness that became widespread must be understood in terms of the loss of Cherokee land, the demise of the deerskin trade, the destruction of villages, and the inability of traditional political structures to deal with these devastating changes. It was only one aspect of the broad disruption to Cherokee lives.

The ability of the Cherokees to pull themselves together after a half century of war, invasion, and defeat and to construct a society that became the model that missionaries and U.S. officials hoped other societies would follow is well-known. Taking control of the alcohol problem is a part of that story. Cherokee efforts to regulate the sale and consumption of liquor became a bone of contention between the Cherokee Nation and the United States long before the Supreme Court recognized Cherokee sovereignty in *Worcester v. Georgia*. Laws concerning alcohol and temperance societies became points of national pride for Cherokees and, when removal loomed, gave them the moral high ground as they struggled to preserve their national existence as well as their homeland in the East. Once again, however, individual Cherokees faltered as whiskey traders flooded their country where their own laws were suspended, and critics pointed to an increase in drunkenness as evidence of the moral failings of the Indian race. It was a claim that the Cherokees would hear again after their expulsion from the Southeast and resettlement in Indian territory.

After removal, the Cherokees defied their critics, reconstructed their Nation, and enacted new laws to regulate alco-

hol. They reinvigorated their temperance societies, and following the Civil War, Cherokee women became particularly
active in the Woman's Christian Temperance Union. Just as
in the East, however, avaricious non-Indians on the margins
of their Nation, where Cherokee law did not reach, preyed on
individuals. Economic development brought into the Nation
hordes of non-Indians who were not subject to Cherokee law,
and drunkenness and other forms of lawlessness increased.
Reformers in the United States looked askance at the situation, but instead of advocating the universal enforcement
of Cherokee law within the Nation's boundaries, they urged
the allotment of Cherokee land, the dissolution of tribal
government, the incorporation of the Cherokee Nation
into the state of Oklahoma, and the assimilation of Indian
people into American society. Drunkenness was part of the
"Indian problem," and the way to solve the problem, the reformers believed, was to do away culturally with the Indians.
Those Cherokee women who joined the temperance crusade
tended to support this view, and they were among the first to
appreciate fully its implications. When Oklahoma joined the
Union, the temperance societies these Native women had
established were folded into those organized by American
women, and Indians ceased to be visible participants. Indians
became the objects of reform, not the activists in firm control
of their own affairs.

A focus on alcohol as simply a problem threatens to ob-
jectify the Cherokee people who consumed it, incorporated
it, abused it, regulated it, and opposed it. The Cherokees'
use of alcohol has many dimensions, some of which may be
sociological, psychological, or physiological, but by historiciz-
ing that use, we can recognize the agency of the Cherokees
themselves. We can avoid essentialist arguments and the air
of inevitability that those arguments assume. Cherokees ini-

tially acquired alcohol from Europeans, but what they subsequently did with it reflected their own culture and history. They were most successful at controlling alcohol abuse when they were able to exercise their sovereignty; they were least successful when confronted with the power of the United States and the avarice of its citizens. At the beginning of the twenty-first century, some Cherokees drink, many do not, and their tribal governments encourage sobriety in a number of ways. And excessive drinking is not a uniquely Cherokee or exclusively Indian problem: it plagues many communities, ethnic groups, and classes across the United States and around the world. Tracing the history of alcohol among the Cherokees, however, can help us understand the process by which Indian drunkenness became emblematic of powerlessness and defeat. More important, it enables us to appreciate the unrelenting struggle of the Cherokee Nation to exercise its sovereignty, to promote the welfare of its people, and to chart its course in a world full of challenges borne by the civilized tree.

NOTES

INTRODUCTION

1. Native Americans in the southwestern United States and the northwestern part of Mexico produced intoxicating drinks well before Spanish conquest. They incorporated intoxicants into their ceremonies and rituals while others consumed alcoholic beverages for social and more secular purposes. Waddell, "The Use of Intoxicating Beverages," in Waddell and Everett, *Drinking Behavior Among Southwestern Indians*, 1–32.

2. Westermeyer, "'The Drunken Indian,'" 29. In his important work on alcohol regulation, historian William E. Unrau forcefully makes this point: "It is worth remembering . . . that national prohibition applied only to Indians in the nineteenth century, and here, perhaps, may be found a key for understanding the origins and full flowering of the 'drunken Indian/sober white' stereotype that continues to this day." Unrau, *White Man's Wicked Water*, 122–23.

3. Leland, "Native American Alcohol Use," in Mail and McDonald, *Tulapai to Tokay*, 22–23.

4. Lemert, *Alcohol and the Northwest Coast Indians*, 323–24, 333–35, 336–39.

5. Lemert, *Alcohol and the Northwest Coast Indians*, 358.

6. Lemert, *Alcohol and the Northwest Coast Indians*, 333–34, 353–55, 365.

7. Leland, "Native American Alcohol Use," in Mail and McDonald, *Tulapai to Tokay*, 23.

8. Hamer, "Acculturation Stress," 285–86, 294–97, 300–301.

9. Hamer, "Acculturation Stress," 301.

10. Dozier, "Problem Drinking," 80–81.

11. Dozier, "Problem Drinking," 74.

12. MacAndrew and Edgerton, *Drunken Comportment*, particularly chaps. 4 and 7.

13. Lurie, "The World's Oldest On-Going Protest Demonstration," 311–32.

14. Lurie, "The World's Oldest On-Going Protest Demonstration," 314–15, 316–17, 325.

15. Levy and Kunitz, *Indian Drinking*, 12, 148, 150.

16. Levy and Kunitz, *Indian Drinking*, 18–19.

17. Levy and Kunitz, *Indian Drinking*, 24, 61–82. Observing the ease with which the Navajos gave up drinking, Levy and Kunitz maintained that those Navajos who exhibited deviant drinking behaviors and were labeled as alcoholic were not addicted to alcohol after all, for which their follow-up study provided additional support. Levy and Kunitz, *Indian Drinking*, 148, 150; Kunitz and Levy, *Drinking Careers*, 2–3, 226, 227. Kunitz and Levy, however, were not ignoring Navajo drinkers who were at high risk for becoming alcohol dependent. To seek effective preventive measures for the Navajos, they examined whether alcoholism and conduct disorder before age fifteen, seemingly a strong indicator of alcohol dependence, were associated. Kunitz and Levy, *Drinking, Conduct Disorder, and Social Change*.

18. Levy and Kunitz, *Indian Drinking*, 181–84.

19. Leland, *Firewater Myths*, 4–5.

20. Leland, *Firewater Myths*, 14–15.

21. Leland, *Firewater Myths*, 5.

22. Leland's subsequent bibliographical guide, "Native American Alcohol Use," appears in Mail and McDonald, *Tulapai to Tokay*, 1–49. For a more updated literature review, see Mancall, "A Note on Sources," in *Deadly Medicine*, 245–59.

23. Room, "Alcohol and Ethnography," 170, 176.

24. Jacek Moskalewicz, "Comments," in Room, "Alcohol and Ethnography," 184.

25. Waddell, "Malhiot's Journal," 246–68.

26. Axtell, "Imagining the Other," in *Beyond 1492*, 35.

27. Mancall, *Deadly Medicine*, particularly chaps. 2, 4, and 7.

28. Hatley, *The Dividing Paths*, 49; Reid, *A Better Kind of Hatchet*, 137.

29. Hatley, *The Dividing Paths*, 48–50.

30. McLoughlin, "Cherokee Anomie, 1794–1810," in *The Cherokee Ghost Dance*, 29–33.

31. McLoughlin, "Cherokee Anomie," in *The Cherokee Ghost Dance*, 3–4.

32. See Wallace, *The Death and Rebirth of the Seneca*, particularly 277–85, 303–10.

33. White, *The Roots of Dependency*, 1–146.

34. See McLoughlin, *Cherokee Renascence in the New Republic*.

35. For an in-depth study of slavery among the Cherokees, see Perdue, *Slavery and the Evolution of Cherokee Society, 1540–1866*.

36. Cherokee delegation to John C. Calhoun, 11 February 1824, Letters Received by the Office of Indian Affairs, 1824–1881, RG 75, National Archives, Washington DC, M-234, Roll 71, #0018. Hereafter documents from this archive will be cited as M-234 with date and roll and frame numbers.

37. Prucha, *American Indian Policy in the Formative Years*, 102–38 (page references are to reprint edition). For discussion of federal alcohol regulations in nineteenth-century Indian country, see also Unrau, *White Man's Wicked Water*.

38. Foreman, *The Five Civilized Tribes*, 378–89.

39. Wardell, *A Political History of the Cherokee Nation, 1838–1907*, 264.

40. See McLoughlin, *After the Trail of Tears*.

1. ALCOHOL ARRIVES

1. De Brahm, *De Brahm's Report of the General Survey*, 108.

2. Hudson, *The Southeastern Indians*, 122–28.

3. See Carson, *Searching for the Bright Path*, 14, 22–25.

4. Fairbanks, "The Function of Black Drink among the Creeks," 131–34; Merrill, "The Beloved Tree," 72–73. Caffeine stimulates the central nervous system and helps make one clearheaded and less susceptible to fatigue. Its diuretic effect also promotes perspiration. Hudson, introduction to *Black Drink*, 5.

5. Merrill, "The Beloved Tree," 40, 55, 56–58. During his extensive

trip to the Southeast in the 1770s, William Bartram discovered yaupon among the Cherokees at Jore in present-day North Carolina, but he stated that it "was the only place I had seen it grown in the Cherokee country." Waselkov and Braund, *William Bartram on the Southeastern Indians*, 82. See also Merrill, "The Beloved Tree," 42, map 1.

6. Black drink–related Cherokee documents are never as thorough nor informative as the ones on the Creeks. Yet as anthropologist Charles Hudson has noted, black drink became "one of their defining cultural traits" among the southeastern tribes. Hudson, introduction to *Black Drink*, 2; Merrill, "The Beloved Tree," 41, 57. On the use of black drink and its cultural significance to the southeastern Indian tribes, see also Fairbanks, "The Function of Black Drink among the Creeks," 120–49, and Hudson, *The Southeastern Indians*, 226–29.

7. For example, the Green Corn Medicine the Cherokees consumed in their annual Green Corn Ceremony consisted of bearded wheat grass, Adam's needle, spiny amaranth, and at least one of the following: volunteer corn, wild lettuce, jewelweed, gourd, green amaranth, ragweed, and wild comfrey. Witthoft, "The Cherokee Green Corn Medicine," 213n2, 216.

8. Timberlake, *Lieut. Henry Timberlake's Memoirs, 1756–1765*, 100–101 (page references are to reprint edition). Although some European observers witnessed Indians vomiting after consuming black drink, Timberlake did not experience this emetic effect. Evidently, the tea itself did not induce such emetic action; the purgative vomiting was a culturally learned behavior among the southeastern Indian tribes. See also Waselkov and Braund, *William Bartram on the Southeastern Indians*, 248n70.

9. A Cherokee myth specifically defines cedar, pine, spruce, holly, and laurel as "evergreens." Mooney, *James Mooney's History*, 240.

10. Mooney, *James Mooney's History*, 240; Hudson, *The Southeastern Indians*, 121, 134, 144.

11. Hudson, *The Southeastern Indians*, 411; Longe, "A Small Postscript," 44 (original transcript appears on page 45).

12. Longe, "A Small Postscript," 16 (original transcript appears on page 17).

13. Hudson, *The Southeastern Indians*, 226–29; Merrill, "The Beloved Tree," 56–57.

14. Alice W. Oliver, who had lived in Texas from childhood and become intimately acquainted with the Karankawa Indians on the Gulf Coast, recognized that the tribe substituted alcohol for its traditional ceremonial beverages. She noted in 1888 that when whiskey was available, the Indians used it "instead of the youpon tea [black drink]" on the following day of religious ceremonies. Oliver, "Notes on the Carancahua Indians," 30 October 1888, 18–19. Scholars have presented different interpretations of the meaning of drinking to the Creeks. See Saunt, *A New Order of Things*, 146n36, 147, and Braund, *Deerskins and Duffels*, 125–26. While Saunt observes the ceremonial aspect of alcohol in colonial Creek society, Braund argues that "Creeks did not drink alcohol in a ceremonial context" and that they did so "to enjoy themselves." See also Saunt, *A New Order of Things*, 147n42.

15. Adair, *Adair's History*, 327 (page references are to reprint edition).

16. Minutes of 12 June 1718, William L. McDowell, ed., *Colonial Records of South Carolina: Journals of the Commissioners of the Indian Trade, September 20, 1710–August 29, 1718* (Columbia: South Carolina Archives Department, 1955), 287. Hereafter documents from this archive will be cited as *CRSC Journals* with date and page number. See also Minutes of 2 December 1717, *CRSC Journals*, 236; Commissioners of the Indian Trade to William Hatton, 11 June 1718, *CRSC Journals*, 291; Minutes of 23 January 1716/17, *CRSC Journals*, 150.

17. Adair, *Adair's History*, 365.

18. Reid, *A Better Kind of Hatchet*, 35.

19. See Carson, *Searching for the Bright Path*, 13–14, 27, 28–29.

20. Cooper, *The Statutes at Large of South Carolina*, 2:309–10.

21. Cooper, *The Statutes at Large of South Carolina* 2:677–80. The complete text of this act appears in *CRSC Journals*, 325–29.

22. Hatley, *The Dividing Paths*, 17–18, 20–22, 32–33, 34; Reid, *A Better Kind of Hatchet*, 36–37.

23. Commissioners of the Indian Trade to Theophilus Hastings, 23 July 1716, *CRSC Journals*, 84–85. On July 22, 1718, the lords proprietors repealed the 1716 regulatory act, but the general assembly managed to reestablish the government trade operation the following March, which continued until 1721. Cooper, *The Statutes at Large of South*

Carolina, 2:680; 3:86–96, 141–46; Smith, *South Carolina as a Royal Province 1719–1776*, 214–15 (page references are to reprint edition).

24. Reid, *A Better Kind of Hatchet*, 82; Corry, *Indian Affairs in Georgia, 1732–1756*, 32; Mereness, *Travels in the American Colonies*, 95.

25. Minutes of 10 July 1716, CRSC *Journals*, 73; Commissioners of the Indian Trade to Theophilus Hastings, 23 July 1716, CRSC *Journals*, 84; Reid, *A Better Kind of Hatchet*, 77. Despite this agreement, the garrison at the Congarees was not built until 1718. Mereness, *Travels in the American Colonies*, 95.

26. Commissioners of the Indian Trade to Theophilus Hastings, 23 July 1716, CRSC *Journals*, 84. The commissioners specifically noted that rum "shall be sold there [Savannah Town], and not sent up to you [Cherokee factor Theophilus Hastings] for Sale."

27. Reid, *A Better Kind of Hatchet*, 137.

28. Minutes of 7 November 1716, CRSC *Journals*, 123.

29. Commissioners of the Indian Trade to Charlesworth Glover, 9 August 1716, CRSC *Journals*, 102.

30. Minutes of 10 September 1717, CRSC *Journals*, 205.

31. Minutes of 23 November 1717, CRSC *Journals*, 231.

32. Instructions for John Coleman, 12 June 1718, CRSC *Journals*, 291–92; Reid, *A Better Kind of Hatchet*, 100–101.

33. Cooper, *The Statutes at Large of South Carolina*, 3:231.

34. Cooper, *The Statutes at Large of South Carolina*, 3:230–31.

35. George Chicken to the President [of the Council of South Carolina, Arthur Middleton], 30 August 1725, Chicken, "Journal of Colonel George Chicken's Mission," 136–37.

36. Meriwether, *The Expansion of South Carolina, 1729–1765*, 191.

37. Scheme for Regulating the Indian Trade, n.d., William L. McDowell, ed., *Colonial Records of South Carolina: Documents Relating to Indian Affairs, May 21, 1750–August 7, 1754* (Colombia: South Carolina Archives Department, 1958), 87. Hereafter documents from this archive will be cited as CRSC *Indian Affairs, 1750–1754* with date and page number.

38. For Euro-Americans' alcohol consumption in colonial America, see Rorabaugh, *The Alcoholic Republic*, 25–35.

39. Brown, *Old Frontiers*, 123n23.

40. See MacAndrew and Edgerton, *Drunken Comportment*, particularly chap. 7.

41. Adair, *Adair's History*, 122–23, 394.

42. Adair, *Adair's History*, 6, 180.

43. Adair, *Adair's History*, 372–73. In cases where the spelling of colonial Cherokee town names vary from document to document, I follow Betty Anderson Smith's spellings in "Distribution of Eighteenth-Century Cherokee Settlements," 46–60.

44. Affidavit of David Dowey, 25 [23] May 1751, CRSC *Indian Affairs, 1750–1754*, 57.

45. "The Talk of Cukaaouskassatte (which signifies the dreadful King) Emperor of the Cherokee Nation, to His excellency James Glen, Esq.; Governor, and c. of his Majesty's Province of South Carolina," 29 April 1745, *South-Carolina Gazette*, 18 May 1745.

46. George Cadogan to Governor Glen, 19 March 1750, CRSC *Indian Affairs, 1750–1754*, 11; Deposition of Stephen Creagh, 22 March 1750, CRSC *Indian Affairs, 1750–1754*, 13–14.

47. Affidavit of Herman Geiger, 11 May 1751, CRSC *Indian Affairs, 1750–1754*, 113–14; Affidavit of Charles Banks, 1 June 1751, CRSC *Indian Affairs, 1750–1754*, 23.

48. Affidavit of John Williams, 21 May 1751, CRSC *Indian Affairs, 1750–1754*, 19–20; Talk of Governor Glen to the Cherokees Concerning their Treaty, 26 November 1751, CRSC *Indian Affairs, 1750–1754*, 189; William L. McDowell, ed., introduction to *Colonial Records of South Carolina: Documents Relating to Indian Affairs, 1754–1765* (Columbia: University of South Carolina Press, 1970), xv–xvi. Hereafter documents from this archive will be cited as CRSC *Indian Affairs, 1754–1765* with date and page number.

49. Talk of the Cherokee Towns to Governor Glen, 6 May 1751, CRSC *Indian Affairs, 1750–1754*, 173.

50. The Head Men and Warriors of the Lower Cherokees to Governor Glen, 10 May 1751, CRSC *Indian Affairs, 1750–1754*, 62.

51. McDowell, introduction to CRSC *Indian Affairs, 1754–1765*, xvi; Governor Glen to the Committee on Indian Affairs, n.d., CRSC *Indian Affairs, 1750–1754*, 52–55; Governor Glen to the Traders of the Cherokee Nation, n.d., CRSC *Indian Affairs, 1750–1754*, 66–67; Governor Glen to the Cherokee Emperor, 8 June 1751, CRSC *Indian Affairs, 1750–1754*, 173.

52. Governor Glen to the Ranger Captains, 15 June 1751, CRSC *Indian Affairs, 1750–1754*, 168–70.

53. Governor Glen to Tacite of Hywasse, n.d., CRSC *Indian Affairs, 1750–1754*, 67–68; Governor Glen to Henry Parker, 9 September 1751, CRSC *Indian Affairs, 1750–1754*, 120.

54. Governor Glen to the President and Council of Georgia, 15 June 1751, CRSC *Indian Affairs, 1750–1754*, 171–72; Governor Glen to Henry Parker, 9 September 1751, CRSC *Indian Affairs, 1750–1754*, 120–21.

55. Lieutenant Governor Burwell to Governor Glen, 26 October 1751, CRSC *Indian Affairs, 1750–1754*, 159–61.

56. Captain Fairchild to Governor Glen, 24 August 1751, CRSC *Indian Affairs, 1750–1754*, 121–22.

57. Talk of Governor Glen to the Cherokees Concerning their Treaty, 26 November 1751, CRSC *Indian Affairs, 1750–1754*, 187–96.

58. *South-Carolina Gazette*, 6 May 1745.

59. Ordinance for Regulating the Cherokee Trade, 3 December 1751, CRSC *Indian Affairs, 1750–1754*, 198–200. See also Regulations for Indian Affairs, [31 August 1751], CRSC *Indian Affairs, 1750–1754*, 134–37.

60. Lud. Grant to Governor Glen, 4 March 1752, CRSC *Indian Affairs, 1750–1754*, 222–24.

61. Meriwether, *The Expansion of South Carolina*, 192.

62. Cooper, *The Statutes at Large of South Carolina*, 3:767.

63. Anthony Dean to Governor Glen, 13 April 1752, CRSC *Indian Affairs, 1750–1754*, 259.

64. Corry, *Indian Affairs in Georgia*, 26.

65. Ludwick Grant to Governor Glen, 8 February 1753, CRSC *Indian Affairs, 1750–1754*, 367.

66. Proceedings of the Council Concerning Indian Affairs, 6 July 1753, CRSC *Indian Affairs, 1750–1754*, 448.

67. Jacobs, *Indians of the Southern Colonial Frontier*, 25–27.

68. Jacobs, *Indians of the Southern Colonial Frontier*, 35.

69. Jacobs, *Indians of the Southern Colonial Frontier*, 35–36.

70. Jacobs, *Indians of the Southern Colonial Frontier*, 87, 88.

71. Jacobs, *Indians of the Southern Colonial Frontier*, 88–89.

72. Jacobs, *Indians of the Southern Colonial Frontier*, vii, xvi. Although the Indian superintendency system retained its political capacity, the colonies regained the power to regulate the Indian trade in 1768. Prucha, *American Indian Policy in the Formative Years*, 11–25.

73. Captain Rayd. Demere to Governor Lyttelton, 26 October 1756, *CRSC Indian Affairs, 1754–1765*, 229.

74. James Beamer to Governor Glen, 21 February 1756, *CRSC Indian Affairs, 1754–1765*, 105.

75. James Beamer to Governor Glen, 21 February 1756, *CRSC Indian Affairs, 1754–1765*, 106.

76. Captain Raymond Demere to Governor Lyttelton, 25 July 1756, *CRSC Indian Affairs, 1754–1765*, 149; Captain Rayd. Demere to Governor Lyttelton, 8 August 1756, *CRSC Indian Affairs, 1754–1765*, 160–61.

77. Captain Rayd. Demere to Governor Lyttelton, 8 August 1756, *CRSC Indian Affairs, 1754–1765*, 160.

78. Captain Rayd. Demere to Governor Lyttelton, 29 August 1756, *CRSC Indian Affairs, 1754–1765*, 171.

79. Later this husband proved to be a nephew of Cherokee headman Old Hop. Captain Rayd. Demere to Governor Lyttelton, 7 November 1756, *CRSC Indian Affairs, 1754–1765*, 242.

80. Captain Rayd. Demere to Governor Lyttelton, 26 October 1756, *CRSC Indian Affairs, 1754–1765*, 231.

81. Captain Rayd. Demere to Governor Lyttelton, 11 December 1756, *CRSC Indian Affairs, 1754–1765*, 267.

82. Captain Rayd. Demere to Governor Lyttelton, 1 March 1757, *CRSC Indian Affairs, 1754–1765*, 346.

83. Fort Loudoun was, at the time, short of corn. John Chevillette to Governor Lyttelton, 9 February 1757, *CRSC Indian Affairs, 1754–1765*, 337.

84. Captain Raymond Demere to Governor Lyttelton, 26 March 1757, *CRSC Indian Affairs, 1754–1765*, 348–49.

85. Captain Rayd. Demere to Governor Lyttelton, 1 April 1757, *CRSC Indian Affairs, 1754–1765*, 358–59.

86. Captain Rayd. Demere to Governor Lyttelton, 2 April 1757, *CRSC Indian Affairs, 1754–1765*, 360–61.

87. Peter C. Mancall has pointed out that British officials were never reluctant to furnish alcohol for their Native allies in order to maintain their allegiance. Mancall, *Deadly Medicine*, 47–49.

88. Headmen of the Lower Creeks to Governor Reynolds, 17 September 1756, *CRSC Indian Affairs, 1754–1765*, 192. See also Lower

Creeks to Governor Reynolds, 13 October 1756, *CRSC Indian Affairs, 1754–1765*, 239.

89. On the play-off politics of the eighteenth century among the Choctaws, see Carson, *Searching for the Bright Path*, chap. 2.

90. Talk of the Blind Slave Catcher of Chatuga, 2 January 1757, *CRSC Indian Affairs, 1754–1765*, 305–6.

91. Captain Rayd. Demere to Governor Lyttelton, 6 January 1757, *CRSC Indian Affairs, 1754–1765*, 309.

92. The Mankiller of Tellico to Captain Rayd. Demere, 25 January 1757, *CRSC Indian Affairs, 1754–1765*, 329.

93. Captain Rayd. Demere to Ostossity of Great Tellico, 26 January 1757, *CRSC Indian Affairs, 1754–1765*, 329.

94. Danll. Pepper to Governor Lyttelton, 28 June 1757, *CRSC Indian Affairs, 1754–1765*, 388.

95. Hatley, *The Dividing Paths*, part 3.

96. The Mankiller of Tellico to Captain Rayd. Demere, 25 January 1757, *CRSC Indian Affairs, 1754–1765*, 329.

97. Captain Rayd. Demere to Ostossity of Great Tellico, 26 January 1757, *CRSC Indian Affairs, 1754–1765*, 329–330.

98. Hudson, *The Southeastern Indians*, 243–44.

99. Information by Richard Finnelson, in *American State Papers: Indian Affairs* 1:290. Historian Tom Hatley has observed that the preparation for war among the Cherokees required "the consumption of both ritual potions and alcohol." Hatley, *The Dividing Paths*, 49. Other southeastern tribes also consumed alcohol in preparation for warfare. William Bartram observed a group of about forty Seminole warriors preparing for an expedition to the Choctaw country at a trading post on the St. Johns River in the summer of 1774. With "the continence and fortitude to withstand the temptation of even tasting a drop of it until their arrival here," these Seminoles brought with them twenty kegs of spirituous liquors they had purchased in St. Augustine. Once they arrived at a trading post, they consumed alcohol and soon "exhibited one of the most ludicrous bachanalian scenes" while their sober headmen monitored their actions. These headmen held a council with traders when their warriors became sober, and they managed to acquire shirts, blankets, and paint half on credit and departed for war. Waselkov and Braund, *William Bartram on the Southeastern Indians*, 65–71.

100. Captain Raymond Demere to Governor Lyttelton, 25 July 1756, CRSC *Indian Affairs, 1754–1765*, 147–48.

101. Saunt, *A New Order of Things*, 145–46, 146n36.

102. Jacobs, *Indians of the Southern Colonial Frontier*, 26. The excusing character of drunkenness can be found in many other Indian communities. MacAndrew and Edgerton, *Drunken Comportment*, 149–52.

103. Waselkov and Braund, *William Bartram on the Southeastern Indians*, 65–66.

104. Captain Rayd. Demere to Governor Lyttelton, 23 June 1756, CRSC *Indian Affairs, 1754–1765*, 125–26.

105. Perdue, *Cherokee Women*, 78.

106. Fairbanks, "The Function of Black Drink," 138, 140–41.

107. McLoughlin, "Cherokee Anomie," in *The Cherokee Ghost Dance*, particularly 29–33.

108. Schneider, "Bro. Martin Schneider's Report," 247, 252–53.

109. White, *The Roots of Dependency*, 1–146.

2. A STRUGGLE FOR SOVEREIGNTY

1. *U.S. Statutes at Large*, 1:137–38, 329–32, 469–74, 743–49. Historian Peter C. Mancall observed that "[i]n the colonial period, no single official had the authority to ban the trade; even the superintendents of Indian Affairs lacked sufficient power to do so. In the early national period, the Constitution's provision granting Congress the power to regulate trade with Indians gave the government the authority to stop the trade if federal officials believed it necessary." Mancall, "Men, Women, and Alcohol," 427.

2. Jefferson to Congress, 27 January 1802, in Richardson, *A Compilation of the Messages and Papers of the Presidents, 1789–1897*, 1:334–35.

3. Perdue, *Cherokee Women*, particularly part 3.

4. Sheehan, *Seeds of Extinction*, 232–42 (page references are to reprint edition). Educated Americans also believed that non-Indian drunkards could not become contributing members of American society or function effectively as rational voters. Rorabaugh, *The Alcoholic Republic*, 35–57.

5. *U.S. Statutes at Large*, 2:146.

6. Henry Dearborn to Benjamin Hawkins and others, 14 Septem-

ber 1802, Letters Sent by the Secretary of War Relating to Indian Affairs, 1800–1824, RG 75, National Archives, Washington DC, M-15, Roll 1, 276.

7. Prucha, *American Indian Policy in the Formative Years*, chap. 6. See also Unrau, *White Man's Wicked Water*, and Mancall, "Men, Women, and Alcohol."

8. Lipscomb, *The Writings of Thomas Jefferson*, 12:223–24.

9. Prucha, *American Indian Policy in the Formative Years*, 103–9.

10. On the Cherokee chiefs' eagerness to make money and get rich, see Perdue, "The Conflict Within," 55–74.

11. "Memorandum of an agreement between Tollentuskee & Tho. N. Clark," 11 May 1803, Records of the Cherokee Indian Agency in Tennessee, 1801–1835, RG 75, National Archives, Washington DC, M-208, Roll 2. Hereafter documents from this archive will be cited as M-208 with date and roll number.

12. "Regulating Houses of Entertainment on [the] Cumberland Road," 22 July 1803, M-208, Roll 2.

13. "Agreements entered into between Double Head and William Tharp Concerning the Ferry at the Junction of the Tennessee and Clinch Rivers," 20 October 1803, M-208, Roll 2; Return J. Meigs to [?], 24 October 1803, M-208, Roll 2; Return J. Meigs to Sampson Williams, 11 November 1803, M-208, Roll 2; "Conditions on which Double head disposing the stands on [the] Cumberland Road," 11 November 1803, M-208, Roll 2; Affidavit of William Tharp, 13 November 1803, M-208, Roll 2.

14. Return J. Meigs to Sampson Williams, 29 July 1803, M-208, Roll 2; Return J. Meigs to Secretary of War [Henry Dearborn], 25 October 1803, M-208, Roll 2; "Opening the road," Return J. Meigs to Secretary of War [Henry Dearborn], 25 October 1803, M-208, Roll 2.

15. Marston Mead to Return J. Meigs, 20 November 1816, M-208, Roll 7.

16. This shift in the use and meaning of alcohol can be found in communities where Native people produced alcoholic beverages of their own. According to historian William B. Taylor, Indian peasant villagers in central and southern Mexico consumed a fermented drink called pulque on ceremonial occasions well before Spanish conquest. The consumption of alcohol increased in the sixteenth

century because of the growing production of pulque for sale and the establishment of taverns and inns on the main colonial thorough-fares. By the early seventeenth century, taxes on alcoholic beverages had become a major source of revenue, and the colonial government further encouraged the liquor trade and the production of pulque. Taylor observed that although Indian peasants continued to drink ritually after the conquest, they shifted their "emphasis on rituals with secular rather than religious meaning" in the early colonial pe-riod. Taylor, *Drinking, Homicide and Rebellion*, 28–72.

17. Norton, *The Journal of Major John Norton, 1816*, 63–65. Norton claimed Cherokee descent through his father, but some scholars consider this statement doubtful. Fogelson, "Major John Norton as Ethno-ethnologist," 251.

18. J. P. Evans, "Sketches of Cherokee Character, Customs, and Manners," John Howard Payne Papers, Edward E. Ayer Collection, Newberry Library, Chicago, 6:215–17, 224, Microcopy (hereafter cited as Payne Papers).

19. James Vann to Return J. Meigs, 3 May 1802, M-208, Roll 1; Return J. Meigs to James Vann, 17 June 1802, M-208, Roll 1; "Journal of Occurrences in the Cherokee Agency in 1802," M-208, Roll 2.

20. "Journal of Occurrences in the Cherokee Agency in 1802," M-208, Roll 2; "Examination respecting the Death of an Indian who was Killed by another Indian on the night after the 21st December 1801 [*sic*] at So. W. Point," 22 December 1802, M-208, Roll 1; W. Whitson to John Sevier, 20 January 1804, M-208, Roll 2; John Lowrey to the Agent [Return J. Meigs], 6 February 1813, M-208, Roll 6; Return J. Meigs to John Fally, 15 March 1813, M-208, Roll 6.

21. Return J. Meigs to Henry Dearborn, 10 March 1807, M-208, Roll 3; Return J. Meigs to Henry Dearborn, 1 May 1807, M-208, Roll 3; Receipt, 4 October 1810, M-208, Roll 12.

22. Return J. Meigs to Henry Dearborn, 1 May 1807, M-208, Roll 3.

23. James Lusk to Governor [John] Sevier, 9 December 1807, M-208, Roll 3.

24. John D. Chishalnor to [Return J. Meigs], 15 January 1808, M-208, Roll 4; Deposition of Tkiuka, 15 January 1808, M-208, Roll 4.

25. Richard Brown to [Return J. Meigs], 12 August 1816, M-208, Roll 7; Goard and others to Return J. Meigs, 15 August 1816, M-208,

Roll 7; Goard to Return J. Meigs with the list of the American suspects, 15 [16] August 1816, M-208, Roll 7; Luther Morgan to John Lowrey, 17 August 1816, M-208, Roll 7; Return J. Meigs to Richard Brown and John Lowrey, 18 August 1816, M-208, Roll 7; John Lowrey to Return J. Meigs, 23 August 1816, M-208, Roll 7; [Return J. Meigs] to Lewis [*sic*] Winston, 25 August 1816, M-208, Roll 7; Louis Winston to Return J. Meigs, 29 August 1816, M-208, Roll 7.

26. Cherokee delegation to John C. Calhoun, 11 February 1824, M-234, Roll 71, #0019.

27. *Laws of the Cherokee Nation*, 6–7 (page references are to reprint edition). On November 2, Cherokee chiefs informed Agent Meigs that the council had passed this law and asked him to assist them in enforcing it. Pathkiller and Charles Hicks to Return J. Meigs, 2 November 1819, M-208, Roll 8.

28. See Perdue, "The Conflict Within," 64–66.

29. [Return J. Meigs] to Charles Hicks, 27 February 1821, M-208, Roll 9.

30. Return J. Meigs to John C. Calhoun, 22 September 1822, M-208, Roll 9. Although he did not criticize the Cherokee chiefs by name, Meigs seemed to refer particularly to such Cherokee leaders as Joseph Vann and Lewis Ross as "Speculating individuals." Vann and Ross were both men of wealth. Joseph Vann acquired his wealth largely from his father's estate in 1809. Lewis Ross, as a rich planter, owned numerous slaves and accumulated his wealth also by operating stores, ferries, and a mill. Perdue, "The Conflict Within," 62–63; Moulton, *The Papers of Chief John Ross*, 2:734, 738.

31. Return J. Meigs to John Floyd, 11 September 1822, M-208, Roll 9.

32. William A. Bowles to Secretary of War [Henry Dearborn], 29 April 1803, M-208, Roll 2.

33. Cherokee delegation to John C. Calhoun, 25 February 1824, M-234, Roll 71, #0039–43.

34. "Judge White[']s Opinion, on the right of the Cherokee Nation to impose a Tax on Traders," 27 May 1823, M-234, Roll 71, #0044–46. Emphasis in original. Considering the fact that he "was a brother-in-law of Governor Willie Blount and, at that time, a close friend of Andrew Jackson (though he later quarreled with and opposed him),"

William G. McLoughlin argued that "White was probably paid a fee for his services" when he made this pro-Cherokee observation. If McLoughlin is correct, the Cherokee chiefs, by the early 1820s, had become tactical diplomats. McLoughlin, *Cherokee Renascence in the New Republic*, 320.

35. Jacob Scudder, Gideon Morgan and Michael Huffacre, and John S. McCarty and John McGhee declined to pay taxes. For the list of traders in 1823–1824 in the Cherokee Nation, see Joseph McMinn to John C. Calhoun, 5 November 1824, M-234, Roll 71, #0363. McLoughlin examines the details of these traders' challenge to the Cherokee tribal right to internal taxation. See McLoughlin, *Cherokee Renascence in the New Republic*, 319–24.

36. Cherokee delegation to John C. Calhoun, 25 February 1824, M-234, Roll 71, #0039–43.

37. In the early 1830s, William Wirt, as a lawyer for the Nation, defended Cherokee sovereignty before the Supreme Court.

38. In *McCulloch v. Maryland*, Chief Justice of the U.S. Supreme Court John Marshall upheld the constitutionality of federal incorporation and the superiority of federal authority over state law. Gunther, *John Marshall's Defense of "McCulloch v. Maryland,"* 23–51.

39. William Wirt to John C. Calhoun, 2 April 1824, M-234, Roll 71, #0441–50. Emphasis in original.

40. Pathkiller, Major Ridge, and John Ross to Joseph McMinn, 5 November 1824, M-234, Roll 71, #0474–75; John L. McCarty to James G. Williams, 15 December 1824, M-234, Roll 71, #0478; James G. Williams to John C. Calhoun, 16 December 1824, M-234, Roll 71, #0466–68.

41. Thomas L. McKenney to Cherokee delegation, 22 February 1825, Letters Sent by the Office of Indian Affairs, 1824–1881, RG 75, National Archives, Washington DC, M-21, Roll 1, #0364–65. Hereafter documents from this archive will be cited as M-21 with date and roll and frame numbers; Receipt, M-234, Roll 71, #0179.

42. Thomas L. McKenney to Cherokee delegation, 1 March 1825, M-21, Roll 1, #0380–81. See also Cherokee delegation to Thomas L. McKenney, 28 February 1825, M-234, Roll 71, #0496–504.

43. Pathkiller, Major Ridge, and John Ross to Joseph McMinn, 5 November 1824, M-234, Roll 71, #0474–75; Cherokee delegation to

the House of Representatives, 10 February 1829, *Cherokee Phoenix*, 3 June 1829.

44. *U.S. Statutes at Large*, 3:682–83. John C. Calhoun, informing Meigs of the amendment to the Intercourse Act of 1802, wrote that it "contains several new & important provisions, to which your attention is particularly called." In his correspondence, however, Calhoun did not mention the regulation of spirituous liquors among the Indian tribes. John C. Calhoun to Return J. Meigs, 3 June 1822, M-208, Roll 9.

45. *Laws of the Cherokee Nation*, 26–27; *Cherokee Phoenix*, 10 April 1828.

46. The National Council passed the law on January 27, 1824. *Laws of the Cherokee Nation*, 36. See also "Intemperance," *Cherokee Phoenix*, 18 June 1828.

47. *Laws of the Cherokee Nation*, 39–40; *Cherokee Phoenix*, 24 April 1828.

48. *Laws of the Cherokee Nation*, 49.

49. Depositions of James Reid and Samuel Reid, and Alfred Denton, 25 February 1826, M-234, Roll 72, #0072–74; Charles Hicks to Hugh Montgomery, 22 April 1826, M-208, Roll 10; Depositions taken before the Agent in the case of James & S. Reid vs[.] the Cherokee Nation, 11 September 1826, M-234, Roll 72, #0076–77.

50. Hugh Montgomery to Charles Hicks and the National Committee and Council of the Cherokee Nation, 26 September 1826, M-208, Roll 10; Hugh Montgomery to Charles Hicks and the National Committee and Council of the Cherokee Nation, 23 October 1826, M-234, Roll 72, #0078–81; Hugh Montgomery to James Barbour, 18 December 1826, M-234, Roll 72, #0206–8; Charles Hicks and John Ross to Hugh Montgomery, 11 December 1826, M-234, Roll 72, #0044. See also "Treaty with the Cherokee, 1785" and "Treaty with the Cherokee, 1791," in Kappler, *Indian Affairs*, 2:10, 30.

51. Charles Hicks and John Ross to Hugh Montgomery, 11 December 1826, M-234, Roll 72, #0043–48.

52 Charles Hicks and John Ross to Hugh Montgomery, 11 December 1826, M-234, Roll 72, #0048–49. See also "Treaty with the Cherokee, 1791," in Kappler, *Indian Affairs*, 2:30–31.

53. J. C. Mitchell to Peter B. Porter, 15 December 1828, M-234, Roll 72, #0693–99; Thomas L. McKenney to Peter B. Porter, 17 Decem-

ber 1828, M-234, Roll 72, #0700–3; Thomas L. McKenney to [Peter B. Porter], 18 December 1828, M-234, Roll 72, #0704; Receipt, 1 May 1829, M-208, Roll 12. The Cherokees struggled to have this money returned. Even a year later, on November 27, 1829, Principal Chief John Ross authorized a delegation of Cherokee leaders to present to Congress a memorial that requested a refund of the money deducted from their annuity. Cherokee delegation to Peter B. Porter, 16 February 1829, M-234, Roll 73, #0014–18; Cherokee delegation to John H. Eaton, 14 April 1829, M-234, Roll 73, #0029–33; John Ross to George Lowrey and others, 27 November 1829, in Moulton, *The Papers of Chief John Ross*, 1:177–79.

54. *Acts of the General Assembly*, 98–101.

55. "Post Office Reform," *Cherokee Phoenix*, 28 May 1831; "High Handed Oppression," appeared originally in *Cincinnatti* [sic] *American* in *Cherokee Phoenix*, 23 July 1831; Cherokee Memorial to the Senate and House of Representatives of the United States of America, 9 January 1832, *Cherokee Phoenix*, 24 March 1832. For discussion on the Indian Removal Bill and the Georgians' harassment, see McLoughlin, *Cherokee Renascence in the New Republic*, 428–47, and Wilkins, *Cherokee Tragedy*, 202–53.

56. *Acts Passed at the Thirteenth Annual Session of the General Assembly*, 7–8.

57. McLoughlin, *Cherokee Renascence in the New Republic*, 277.

58. United States Congressional Serial Set, U.S. House, *Removal of Indians*, 21st Cong., 1st sess., 1830, H. Rept. 227, serial 200, 21.

3. THE MORAL HIGH GROUND

1. "Philanthropist" to the Editor [Elias Boudinot], *Cherokee Phoenix*, 22 April 1829.

2. *Cherokee Phoenix*, 22 April 1829.

3. Tyrrell, *Sobering Up*, particularly chaps. 3–6.

4. Tyrrell, *Sobering Up*, 16–32; Rorabaugh, *The Alcoholic Republic*, 5–21.

5. Tyrrell, *Sobering Up*, 33–53, 55.

6. Tyrrell, *Sobering Up*, 54–86.

7. Tyrrell, *Sobering Up*, 59; See also Andrew, *From Revivals to Removal*, 57–61, 83–84.

8. Prucha, *American Indian Policy in the Formative Years*, 219.

9. William Potter, "Station of Creek Path," *Missionary Herald* 18 (October 1822): 309; William Chamberlain, "Cherokee Mission," *Missionary Herald* 20 (November 1824): 348; William Chamberl[a] in to J. Evarts, 30 July 1824, Papers of the American Board of Commissioners for Foreign Missions, Houghton Library, Department of Manuscripts, Harvard University, Cambridge MA, ABC 18.3.1 v. 4, Microcopy, Roll 739, #0098–99. Hereafter documents from this archive will be cited by the notation beginning with ABC with date and volume, roll, and frame numbers. Used with permission of Wider Church Ministries of the United Church of Christ and the Houghton Library, Harvard University; "Carmel," *Missionary Herald* 23 (January 1827): 8; "Willstown," *Missionary Herald* 23 (January 1827): 8–9.

10. 8 February 1823, *Missionary Herald* 19 (June 1823): 171.

11. "Supposed Thirst of Indians for Spirits," 24 September 1821, *Missionary Herald* 18 (January 1822): 14; Brainerd Mission Journal, 24 September 1821, ABC 18.3.1 v. 2, Roll 737, #0171–72.

12. "W" to Elias Boudinot, *Cherokee Phoenix*, 27 May 1829; Samuel A. Worcester to Jeremiah Evarts, 27 May [1829], ABC 18.3.1 v. 5 pt. 2, Roll 739, #0643–44; William Chamberl[a]in, "General Notices respecting the Station [Willstown]," 7 September 1829, *Missionary Herald* 25 (December 1829): 374–75.

13. "Candy's Creek," *Missionary Herald* 25 (February 1829): 59. See also John C. Elsworth, "Brainerd," 8 August 1829, *Missionary Herald* 25 (October 1829): 318; John Thompson, "Carmel," 12 August 1829, *Missionary Herald* 25 (October 1829): 319.

14. William Holland, "Candy's Creek," 20 August 1829, *Missionary Herald* 25 (November 1829): 345–46.

15. The article on the Cherokee Temperance Society appeared in the *Cherokee Phoenix* dated Wednesday, November 4, 1829. It reported that "a respectable number of Gentlemen from various parts of the nation convened in the Council Room, on last Thursday evening, for the purpose of forming and organizing a general temperance society." Although the date of the editorial should correspond with that of the paper, the editorial was dated Wednesday, September 4, 1829. Thus, it was not clear exactly when the Cherokee

Temperance Society organized. "Temperance," 4 September 1829, *Cherokee Phoenix*, 4 November 1829.

16. James J. Trott was a Methodist missionary who married a Cherokee woman, Sally Adair, in 1828. McLoughlin, *Cherokees and Missionaries, 1789–1839*, 175.

17. George Lowrey (1770?–1852) entered Cherokee politics in 1809 as a member of the Standing Committee and served thirteen years. In 1826, he translated the Nation's laws into the Cherokee language. After attending the Constitutional Convention of 1827, he served from the following year as assistant principal chief. When the Cherokee National Temperance Society organized in 1833, he became its vice president. Moulton, *The Papers of Chief John Ross*, 2:726.

18. Richard Taylor (1788–1853) served as agency interpreter in 1816 and 1828. His frequent appointment as a delegate indicated his active participation in Cherokee politics. He was a member of the Constitutional Convention in 1827. In removal, he conducted one of the thirteen Cherokee detachments to the West. Moulton, *The Papers of Chief John Ross*, 2:736.

19. "Temperance," 4 September 1829, *Cherokee Phoenix*, 4 November 1829. The society appointed William Rogers as secretary and Walter S. Adair, Edward Gunter, John Huss, Elias Boudinot, and George M. Waters as members of the executive committee. See also "Improvement among the people," *Missionary Herald* 26 (January 1830): 10.

20. Marcus Palmer to Jeremiah Evarts, 15 July 1830, ABC 18.3.1 v. 6, Roll 740, #0239–41. Missionary journals edited and carried this correspondence, which also appeared in the *Cherokee Phoenix*. "Cherokees of the Arkansas," 15 July 1830, quoted from *Journal of Humanity* in *Cherokee Phoenix*, 5 December 1830; Marcus Palmer, "Progress in Religion and Morals," 15 July 1830, *Missionary Herald* 26 (November 1830): 352. See also "Constitution of the Arkansas Cherokee Temperance Society," *Cherokee Phoenix*, 27 August 1831.

21. David Brown was prominent among the Arkansas Cherokees. He served as a judge and a councilor of the Cherokee Nation West. Marcus Palmer, "Temperance—Religious Attention among the People," 25 August 1831, *Missionary Herald* 27 (December 1831): 386.

22. Cephas Washburn, "Measures Favorable to Temperance," 22 December 1830, *Missionary Herald* 27 (April 1831): 123–24; Palmer, "Temperance—Religious Attention among the People," 25 August 1831, *Missionary Herald* 27 (December 1831): 385–86.

23. Marcus Palmer to Jeremiah Evarts, 15 July 1830, ABC 18.3.1 v. 6, Roll 740, #0241.

24. Marcus Palmer, "Meeting of the Society for Promoting Temperance," 15 February 1831, *Missionary Herald* 27 (July 1831): 211–12.

25. Peggy Whiteman Killer to the Editor of the *Philadelphian*, "Report of a Cherokee Society," 24 October 1831, appeared originally in *Philadelphian* in *Cherokee Phoenix*, 31 December 1831.

26. *Laws of the Cherokee Nation*, 120, 121.

27. *Cherokee Phoenix*, 17 September 1828. See also *Cherokee Phoenix* 17, 24 April 1828.

28. *Cherokee Phoenix*, 24 April 1828.

29. "A Letter from a Cherokee to His Brother," 8 March 1828, *Cherokee Phoenix*, 11 February 1829.

30. *Cherokee Phoenix*, 12 March 1831.

31. "Confessions of a Prisoner," quoted from *Journal of Humanity* in *Cherokee Phoenix*, 8 July 1829.

32. "Confessions of a Prisoner," quoted from *Journal of Humanity* in *Cherokee Phoenix*, 8 July 1829.

33. Charles Sprague, "Intemperance," *Cherokee Phoenix*, 21 July 1828. For anecdotes about a drunken husband, see also "End of a Drundard [*sic*]," appeared originally in *Amherst, Ms. Inquirer* in *Cherokee Phoenix*, 28 February 1828; "Warning to Drunkards," appeared originally in *Eliz. Journal* in *Cherokee Phoenix*, 20 March 1828; "Philanthropist," "To the Ladies," *Cherokee Phoenix*, 26 August 1829; "A Drunkard's Death," appeared originally in *Journal of Humanity* in *Cherokee Phoenix*, 12 May 1832; "Beware of a Drunken Husband," *Cherokee Phoenix*, 4 August 1832; "Moderate Drinking Preacher," appeared originally in *Philadelphian* in *Cherokee Phoenix*, 29 September 1832; "Brother Johnathon's wife's advice to her daughter on the day of her marriage," appeared originally in *New England Farmer* in *Cherokee Phoenix*, 10 August 1833.

34. For mainstream American temperance societies, see "Intemperance," appeared originally in *Prov. Investigater* in *Cherokee*

Phoenix, 10 December 1828; "American Society for the Promotion of Temperance," appeared originally in *Boston Recorder* in *Cherokee Phoenix*, 25 March 1829; *Cherokee Phoenix*, 8, 15 April 1829; R. D. Mussey, "An address on Ardent Spirit," 5 June 1827, *Cherokee Phoenix*, 24 June; 1 July 1829; Isaac Parker, "Intemperance," 25 May 1828, *Cherokee Phoenix*, 15 July 1829; "American Temperance Society," November 1832, *Cherokee Phoenix*, 20 April 1833; "Extract of an Essay on the evils of Intemperance," 26 February 1833, *Cherokee Phoenix*, 6 September 1833. On the trials of the temperance movement in mainstream American society, see "A Good Law," appeared originally in *New York Oh.* in *Cherokee Phoenix*, 6 March 1828; "Temperance," appeared originally in *Hampshire Gazette* in *Cherokee Phoenix*, 20 March 1828; "Hot Coffee," "Hot Coffee vs. Rum," appeared originally in *New York Observer* in *Cherokee Phoenix*, 3 September 1828; "Declaration of Independence," *Cherokee Phoenix*, 25 March 1829; "Coercion," appeared originally in *We[s]tern Intelligencer* in *Cherokee Phoenix*, 10 June 1829; "Boarding Houses," appeared originally in *N.Y. Spectator* in *Cherokee Phoenix*, 15 July 1829; "Temperance," appeared originally in *N.Y. Courier* in *Cherokee Phoenix*, 28 September 1833.

35. "A traveller" to the Editor of the *Connecticut Observer*, quoted from *Connecticut Observer* in *Cherokee Phoenix*, 27 November 1830. Emphasis in original. See also John C. Elsworth, "Brainerd," 8 August 1829, *Missionary Herald* 25 (October 1829): 318.

36. *Cherokee Phoenix*, 21 April 1830. Emphasis in original.

37. Prucha, *American Indian Policy in the Formative Years*, 187.

38. "The Indians," quoted from *Journal of Communication* in *Cherokee Phoenix*, 31 March 1832. Emphasis in original. The American Board missionary Daniel S. Butrick must have been the author of this article. The original writing can be found in his journal entry for January 11, 1832. Journal of Daniel S. Butrick, 11 January 1832, ABC 18.3.3 v. 4, Roll 754, #0159–61.

39. See Satz, *American Indian Policy in the Jacksonian Era*.

40. A series of removal crises in the Nation resulted in the Cherokees' awareness of their self-identification. They came to define their distinct tribal identity by their ancestral land in the East. After the first removal crisis of 1806–1809, the Cherokees regarded those who emigrated to the West as "expatriates" because these people gave up

fighting to retain their homeland in the East. The second removal crisis of 1817–1819 reinforced this idea, and the western Cherokees were branded "traitors." When the Nation wrote a constitution in 1827, any citizens who moved to Arkansas forfeited "all their rights and privileges as citizens of this Nation." McLoughlin, *Cherokee Renascence in the New Republic*, 109–67, 206–46, 397–98; *Laws of the Cherokee Nation*, 119.

41. [Jeremiah Evarts], "Memorial of the American Board of Commissioners for Foreign Missions," 26 January 1831, in Prucha, *Cherokee Removal*, 304.

42. [Evarts], "Memorial," in Prucha, *Cherokee Removal*, 290–305.

43. *Cherokee Phoenix*, 20 April 1833.

44. "State and Prospects of the People," *Missionary Herald* 29 (December 1833): 460.

45. Sophia Sawyer to David Greene, 24 December 1833, ABC 18.3.1 v. 8, Roll 742, #0523–25; Daniel S. Butrick to David Greene, 15 January 1832, ABC 18.3.1 v. 7, Roll 741, #0033–35; Daniel S. Butrick to David Greene, 30 December 1831, ABC 18.3.1 v.7, Roll 741, #0035–36; Daniel S. Butrick, "State of the People in the neighborhood of Carmel," 9 August 1832, *Missionary Herald* 28 (December 1832): 400–401; Sophia Sawyer, "School at New Echota," 26 December 1832, *Missionary Herald* 29 (March 1833): 96–97.

46. William Chamberl[a]in at Willstown, 7 February 1832, *Missionary Herald* 28 (June 1832): 191.

47. Hugh Montgomery to Elbert Herring, 2 October 1833, M-208, Roll 10.

48. John Ross, Annual Message, 15 October 1833, *Cherokee Phoenix*, 23 November 1833.

49. Elbert Herring to Hugh Montgomery, 16 October 1833, M-208, Roll 10.

50. Perdue and Green, *The Cherokee Removal*, 82–85; Wilkins, *Cherokee Tragedy*, 240–42.

51. William Rogers to the Editor [Elijah Hicks], *Cherokee Phoenix*, 7 December 1833.

52. Perdue, *Cherokee Editor*, 25–33. See also Perdue, "The Conflict Within," 55–74.

53. James J. Trott to John Ross, 6 January 1836, in Moulton, *The Papers of Chief John Ross*, 1:379–80. Emphasis in original.

54. Perdue, *Cherokee Editor*, 198.

55. Perdue, *Cherokee Editor*, 222–25.

56. United States Congressional Serial Set, U.S. House, *The Committee of Claims, to whom was referred the bill from the Senate (No. 192) entitled "An act for the relief of George W. Paschall" report*, 24 April 1840, 26th Cong., 1st sess., H. Rept. 448, serial 371.

57. United States Congressional Serial Set, U.S. Senate, *Memorial of the Legislature of Alabama*, 8 February 1836, 24th Cong., 1st sess., S. Doc. 132, serial 280.

58. *American State Papers: Military Affairs* 7:532–41, 545.

59. Webster, "Letters from a Lonely Soldier," 28 June 1838, 155.

60. Journal of Daniel S. Butrick, 29 June 1838, Payne Papers, 9:81–82; Journal of Daniel S. Butrick, 1 July 1838, ABC 18.3.3 v. 4, Roll 754, #0280–81.

61. Cherokee Chiefs to Cherokee Agency, 1 August 1838, M-234, Roll 115, #0235.

62. En route, the leaders of the detachments wrote Chief Ross, informing him that they reached certain places and inquiring what they should do with such difficulties as lack of protection, frauds of American contractors, a shortage of rations, sickness, and death. See J. Powell to John Ross, 16 October 1838; Jesse Bushyhead to John Ross, 21 October 1838; Elijah Hicks to John Ross, 24 October 1838; Jesse Bushyhead and J. Powell to John Ross, 26 October 1838; Evan Jones to John Ross, 27 October 1838; George Hicks to John Ross, 4 November 1838; Thomas N. Clark Jr. to John Ross, 28 December 1838, 10 January 1839, in Moulton, *The Papers of Chief John Ross*, 1:682–86, 687–88, 696–97; and Evan Jones, "Letters, May–December 1838," in Perdue and Green, *The Cherokee Removal*, 164–68.

63. Contemporaries often used the term *Indian Territory* colloquially, but Congress never organized such a territory. This book, therefore, uses the term *Indian territory*.

64. Journal of Daniel S. Butrick, 4 October 1838, ABC 18.3.3 v. 4, Roll 754, #0351; Journal of Daniel S. Butrick, [5] October 1838, ABC 18.3.3 v. 4, Roll 754, #0351–52.

65. Journal of Daniel S. Butrick, October 1838, ABC 18.3.3 v. 4, Roll 754, #0358.

66. Journal of Daniel S. Butrick, October 1838, ABC 18.3.3 v. 4, Roll

754, #0358–60; November 1838, ABC 18.3.3 v. 4, Roll 754, #0363–64, 0365, 0366–67, 0369; January 1839, ABC 18.3.3 v. 4, Roll 754, #0396.

67. Journal of Daniel S. Butrick, October 1838, ABC 18.3.3 v. 4, Roll 754, #0360.

68. Journal of Daniel S. Butrick, November 1838, ABC 18.3.3 v. 4, Roll 754, #0366–67.

69. Journal of Daniel S. Butrick, 4 October 1838, ABC 18.3.3 v. 4, Roll 754, #0351.

4 · ALCOHOL AND DISLOCATION

1. Zillah Haynie Brandon, "Memoir, 1830–1838," in Perdue and Green, *The Cherokee Removal*, 85–91.

2. Brandon, "Memoir," in Perdue and Green, *The Cherokee Removal*, 89–91.

3. Lillybridge, "Journey," 3 March 1837, 233–34.

4. Lillybridge, "Journey," 6 March 1837, 234–35.

5. Lillybridge, "Journey," 11 March 1837, 238.

6. Lillybridge, "Journey," 18, 22 March 1837, 240, 242.

7. Cannon, "An Overland Journey," 166–73.

8. Cannon, "An Overland Journey," 21 November 1837, 170.

9. Deas, "Emigrating to the West," 1 May 1838, 163.

10. Deas, "Emigrating to the West," 158–63.

11. Deas, "Emigrating to the West," 1 May 1838, 163. See also Foreman, *Indian Removal*, 273–78, 280–83, 284–85.

12. Scott, "Address," 10 May 1838, 145.

13. Foreman, *Indian Removal*, 290–93.

14. Cephas Washburn to Jeremiah Evarts, 5 July 1830, ABC 18.3.1 v. 6, Roll 740, #0199. Emphasis in original. The *Missionary Herald* edited and carried this correspondence, part of which appeared in the *Cherokee Phoenix*. Cephas Washburn, "Cherokees of the Arkansas," 5 July 1830, *Missionary Herald* 26 (September 1830): 299; Cephas Washburn to the Editors of the *Missionary Herald*, 4 July 1830, appeared originally in *Missionary Herald* in *Cherokee Phoenix*, 1 October 1830.

15. C. Washburn to Thos. L. McKenney, 2 February 1830, M-234, Roll 77, #0659–62; Cephas Washburn to Jeremiah Evarts, 3 July 1828, ABC 18.3.1 v.6, Roll 740, #0159–60.

16. Cephas Washburn, "Cherokees of the Arkansas," 5 July 1830, *Missionary Herald* 26 (September 1830): 299; Cephas Washburn to Jeremiah Evarts, 5 July 1830, ABC 18.3.1 v. 6, Roll 740, #0199–201; C. Washburn to Thos. L. McKenney, 2 February 1830, M-234, Roll 77, #0659–62.

17. Prucha, *American Indian Policy in the Formative Years*, 120–26.

18. Ger. Vashon to J. H. Eaton, 12 April 1831, M-234, Roll 77, #0719–20.

19. Geo. Vashon to DuVal and Carnes, 9 April 1831, M-234, Roll 77, #0722; Ger. Vashon to J. H. Eaton, 12 April 1831, M-234, Roll 77, #0719. In May 1829, Col. Matthew Arbuckle, the commanding officer at Fort Gibson, confiscated the goods and liquor from the trading firm of DuVal and Carnes, which produced a prolonged dispute among Arbuckle, the traders, and the federal government. Prucha, *American Indian Policy in the Formative Years*, 121–25.

20. *U.S. Statutes at Large,* 4:564.

21. John Rogers and Glass to George Vashon, 18 October 1832, M-234, Roll 78, #0226.

22. George Vashon, "Abstract of the Seizures of Whiskey," 19 November 1832, M-234, Roll 78, #0227.

23. Geo. Vashon to Lewis Cass, 20 November 1832, M-234, Roll 78, #0223–24; John Drew to Lewis Cass, 6 March 1833, M-234, Roll 78, #0339, 0341.

24. Geo. Vashon to Lewis Cass, 20 November 1832, M-234, Roll 78, #0224; M. Stokes to [?], 26 August 1836, M-234, Roll 79, #0626; Geo. Vashon to Samuel Mackey, 5 May 1835, M-234, Roll 79, #0630. Charles Rogers's father, John Rogers, had distilled whiskey on the banks of the Tennessee River until 1817 when he emigrated to Arkansas with his family. Charles must have learned from his father how to make whiskey and decided to enter this lucrative business in the West. Foreman, *Advancing the Frontier, 1830–1860,* 27–28.

25. John Drew to Lewis Cass, 6 March 1833, M-234, Roll 78, #0339–41.

26. F. W. Armstrong to Elbert Herring, 3 May 1835, M-234, Roll 79, #0356; Geo. Vashon to Elbert Herring, 28 April 1835, M-234, Roll 79, #0357. Unlike many intermarried citizens who managed to take advantage of their dual citizenship status in the Cherokee Nation,

Harper found himself under the jurisdiction of the United States. See Geo. Vashon to Elbert Herring, 12 October 1833, M-234, Roll 78, #0466–70.

27. Geo. Vashon to Elbert Herring, 16 April 1833, M-234, Roll 78, #0444–46.

28. Geo. Vashon to Lewis Cass, 20 November 1832, M-234, Roll 78, #0224; Elbert Herring to George Vashon, 18 January 1833, M-21, Roll 9, #0236–37; Geo. Vashon to Elbert Herring, 16 April 1833, M-234, Roll 78, #0444–46; Geo. Vashon to Elbert Herring, 15 October 1833, M-234, Roll 78, #0472–75.

29. Geo. Vashon to Elbert Herring, 15 October 1833, M-234, Roll 78, #0472–75; Geo. Vashon to Elbert Herring, 4 March 1834, M-234, Roll 79, #0255–56; Geo. Vashon to Elbert Herring, 27 April 1835, M-234, Roll 79, #0403–4; E. Rector to Geo. Vashon, 30 May 1834, M-234, Roll 79, #0405; E. Rector to Geo. Vashon, 30 May 1834, M-234, Roll 79, #0406; Elias Rector to R. C. Byrd, 7 February 1834, M-234, Roll 79, #0407; M. Stokes to Elbert Herring, 19 July 1836, M-234, Roll 79, #0594. As late as 1846, Cherokee distiller Charles Rogers was petitioning federal officials for prompt remuneration. Thirteen years of struggle had brought him only about half of his estimated loss of $3,943. M. Stokes to [?], 26 August 1836, M-234, Roll 79, #0626; Geo. Vashon to Samuel Mackey, 20 March 1835 [?], M-234, Roll 79, #0627; F. W. Armstrong to Geo. Vashon, 21 April 1835, M-234, Roll 79, #0629; Geo. Vashon to Samuel Mackey, 5 May 1835, M-234, Roll 79, #0630; Samuel Mackey and William A. Keys to George Vashon, 26 September 1835, M-234, Roll 79, #0631–34; John Jolly and Joseph Vann to M. Stokes, 22 August 1836, M-234, Roll 79, #0638; M. Stokes to C. A. Harris, 26 August 1836, M-234, Roll 79, #0625; M. Stokes to C. A. Harris, 28 August 1836, M-234, Roll 79, #0636–37; S. C. Stambaugh to the Commissioner of Indian Affairs [William Medill], 15 May 1846, M-234, Roll 90, #0731.

30. John Stuart to Lewis Cass, 23 July 1833, M-234, Roll 78, #0399.

31. John Stuart to Lewis Cass, 12 August 1833, M-234, Roll 78, #0407–12.

32. "Cherokee Temperance Society," *Cherokee Almanac, 1838,* 19; "Cherokee Temperance Society," *Cherokee Almanac, 1847,* 27.

33. Elbert Herring to Superintendents and Agents of Indian Affairs, circular, 6 May 1833, M-21, Roll 10, #0151–52.

34. *U.S. Statutes at Large,* 4:732–33.

35. *U.S. Statutes at Large,* 4:732; John Stuart to R. Jones, 9 June 1838, Copies of Manuscripts in the Office of the Commissioner of Indian Affairs Washington DC (Western Superintendency: Miscellaneous and Schools) Compiled from original records selected by Grant Foreman, 1930, 154–55. Typescript. Oklahoma Historical Society, Archives and Manuscripts Division, Oklahoma City OK (hereafter cited as OHS, Foreman, Copies of Manuscripts [Western Superintendency]).

36. S. [?] Wood to Commissioner of Indian Affairs [Carey Allen Harris], 21 March 1838, M-234, Roll 82, #0664.

37. *U.S. Statutes at Large,* 4:729; M. Stokes to Wm. Armstrong, 26 September 1837, M-234, Roll 82, #0008. Emphasis in original.

38. Wm. Armstrong to C. A. Harris, 12 December 1837, M-234, Roll 82, #0003–4; Wm. Armstrong to M. Stokes, 9 September 1837, M-234, Roll 82, #0005–6.

39. William Armstrong to Wood and Harris, 12 December 1837, M-234, Roll 82, #0007; Wood and Harris to [?], 13 January 1838, M-234, Roll 82, #0615–18.

40. John Stuart to R. Jones, 25 April 1838, M-234, Roll 82, #0501–2; John Stuart, Special Order No. 1, 20 April 1838, M-234, Roll 82, #0504; Henry McKavett to John Stuart, 23 April 1838, M-234, Roll 82, #0504–5; Invoice of goods taken by Lieut. H. McKavett, 21 April 1838, M-234, Roll 82, #0507–15.

41. Wm. Armstrong to P. M. Butler, 20 December 1841, M-234, Roll 86, #0137–38; McLoughlin, *After the Trail of Tears,* 97.

42. Journal of Daniel S. Butrick, 30 November [1839], ABC 18.3.3 v. 4, Roll 754, #0451.

43. *The Constitution and Laws of the Cherokee Nation,* 32.

44. *The Constitution and Laws of the Cherokee Nation,* 57–58.

45. Hitchcock's Journal, 6 December [1841], in Foreman, *A Traveler in Indian Territory,* 48–49.

46. Hitchcock's Journal, 8 December [1841], in Foreman, *A Traveler in Indian Territory,* 55. See also E. A. Hitchcock to J. C. Spencer, 21 December 1841, in Foreman, *A Traveler in Indian Territory,* 241.

47. Hitchcock's Journal, 7 December [1841], in Foreman, *A Traveler in Indian Territory*, 52–53. The National Council passed a law on September 28, 1839, to legalize intermarriage and grant citizenship to non-Cherokees who lawfully married Cherokee women. *The Constitution and Laws of the Cherokee Nation*, 32–33.

48. M. Arbuckle to William Armstrong, 13 March 1838, OHS, Foreman, Copies of Manuscripts (Western Superintendency), 116–17.

49. John Ross to Lucy A. Butler, 20 July 1842, in Moulton, *The Papers of Chief John Ross*, 2:144. Agent Pierce M. Butler concurred with Chief Ross. P. M. Butler to J. C. Spencer, 4 May 1842, M-234, Roll 87, #0254–55.

50. *Cherokee Advocate*, 1 May 1845.

51. *The Constitution and Laws of the Cherokee Nation*, 86.

52. *The Constitution and Laws of the Cherokee Nation*, 100.

53. John Ross to Pierce M. Butler, 14 February 1844, in Moulton, *The Papers of Chief John Ross*, 2:196.

54. "Two More Murders," *Cherokee Advocate*, 21 November 1844.

55. Works Progress Administration, Project s-149, Indian-Pioneer History Collection, James Ewing Chandler, Vol. 19, 385, Typescript, Oklahoma Historical Society, Archives and Manuscripts Division, Oklahoma City OK. Hereafter documents from this collection will be cited as IPH, OHS, with interviewee's name and volume and page numbers; IPH, OHS, James P. Neal, Vol. 7, 414.

56. "The Drunkards End," *Cherokee Advocate*, 19 October, 1844; "Two More Murders," *Cherokee Advocate*, 21 November 1844; "Another Murder at Evansville," *Cherokee Advocate*, 28 November 1844; *Cherokee Advocate*, 5 December 1844; *Cherokee Advocate*, 19 December 1844; "Murder," *Cherokee Advocate*, 20 March 1845; "The Late Murder," *Cherokee Advocate*, 27 March 1845; "Evansville Again!" *Cherokee Advocate*, 28 August 1845. See also "Another Outrage," *Cherokee Advocate*, 1 May 1845; *Cherokee Advocate*, 8 May 1845.

57. "Evansville," *Cherokee Advocate*, 12 December 1844.

58. "Murder," *Cherokee Advocate*, 20 March 1845.

59. "The Late Murder," *Cherokee Advocate*, 27 March 1845. Emphasis in original.

60. *The Constitution and Laws of the Cherokee Nation*, 121.

61. IPH, OHS, John M. Adair, Vol. 1, 39–46; IPH, OHS, Breland

Adams, Vol. 99, 30–31. The Gold Rush fever induced Sarah Coody to sell her estate to John Lafeyette Adair and go to California, where she later died from complications of alcoholism.

62. "Dupleix," "Our Frontier," *Arkansas State Gazette*, 8 November 1843.

63. John Ross to Pierce M. Butler, 14 February 1844, in Moulton, *The Papers of Chief John Ross*, 2:196.

64. John Ross and others to John C. Spencer, 14 June 1842, in Moulton, *The Papers of Chief John Ross*, 2:134.

65. "Copy of a Report Made by P. M. Butler," 30 September 1843, *Cherokee Advocate*, 5 October 1844.

66. "Veritas" to the Editor [Benjamin J. Borden], *Arkansas State Gazette*, 28 February 1844; "Copy of a Report Made by P. M. Butler," 30 September 1843, *Cherokee Advocate*, 5 October 1844.

67. Pierce M. Butler to the Editor [Benjamin J. Borden], *Arkansas State Gazette*, 3 April 1844.

68. "The Affray at Fort Gibson—Infamous Outrages by U.S. Soldiers," *Cherokee Advocate*, 20 March 1845; "Bloody Affair near Fort Gibson," *Cherokee Advocate*, 13 March 1845.

69. "The Affray at Fort Gibson—Infamous Outrages by U.S. Soldiers," *Cherokee Advocate*, 20 March 1845. Emphasis in original. For the counterargument against the accounts of the incidents provided by editor William P. Ross and Ross's response to this, see "Officer of the Army" to W. P. Ross, 22 March 1845, appeared originally in *Arkansas Intelligencer* in *Cherokee Advocate*, 15 May 1845; The Editor [William P. Ross] to Capt. S. Wood, *Cherokee Advocate*, 15 May 1845.

70. "Public Meeting—The Military," *Cherokee Advocate*, 3 April 1845. See also "Fort Gibson," *Cherokee Advocate*, 17 April 1845.

71. "Public Meeting," *Cherokee Advocate*, 27 March 1845.

72. John Ross, Annual Message, 12 November 1846, in Moulton, *The Papers of Chief John Ross*, 2:317; *U.S. Statutes at Large*, 9:871–77.

73. McLoughlin, *After the Trail of Tears*, 55–59; Wardell, *A Political History of the Cherokee Nation*, 69–75, 353–54.

74. "Cherokee Temperance Society," *Cherokee Almanac, 1838*, 19; "Cherokee Temperance Society," *Cherokee Almanac, 1847*, 27. Emphasis in original.

75. "The Temperance Celebration," *Cherokee Advocate*, 23 July 1846.

76. S. A. Worcester to John Ross, 10 November 1842. Alice Mary Robertson Papers, Series II, Box 23, Folder 6, McFarlin Library, Department of Special Collections, University of Tulsa, Tulsa OK (hereafter cited as Robertson Papers).

77. "The National Committee," 16 October [1845], *Cherokee Advocate*, 23 October 1845.

78. "The Cherokee Temperance Society," *Cherokee Advocate*, 23 October 1845.

79. Tyrrell, *Sobering Up*, 90.

80. "The Cherokee Temperance Society," *Cherokee Advocate*, 23 October 1845; "The Temperance Celebration," *Cherokee Advocate*, 23 July 1846; "Temperance Lectures," *Cherokee Advocate*, 22 January 1846; "D." to [William P.] Ross, 9 February 1846, *Cherokee Advocate*, 19 February 1846; S. W. B. to Wm. P. Ross, *Cherokee Advocate*, 26 March 1846; "Progress of Temperance," *Cherokee Advocate*, 14 May 1846; D. D. Hitchcock to [William P.] Ross, *Cherokee Advocate*, 20 November 1845.

81. "Cold Water Army," *Cherokee Almanac, 1846*, 29; "The Cherokee Temperance Society," *Cherokee Advocate*, 23 October 1845; "Children's Temperance Meeting," *Cherokee Advocate*, 9 October 1845.

82. S. A. Worcester to David Greene, 18 July 1844, ABC 18.3.1 v.10, Roll 744, #0532–33; Letter of Mrs. Hannah Hitchcock, S. A. Worcester and Family, Grant Foreman Collection 83.229, Box 42, Folder 17, Oklahoma Historical Society, Archives and Manuscripts Division, Oklahoma City OK (hereafter cited as Worcester, Foreman Collection). Emphasis in original.

83. S. A. Worcester to David Greene, 12 August 1847, ABC 18.3.1 v. 13, Roll 747, #0577–78; "Cherokee Cold Water Army," *Cherokee Almanac, 1849*, 31.

84. *Cherokee Advocate*, 6 August 1849.

85. "Cherokee Temperance Society," *Cherokee Almanac, 1838*, 19.

86. Letter of Mrs. Hannah Hitchcock, Worcester, Foreman Collection; *Cherokee Advocate*, 4 March 1847.

87. Letter of Mrs. Hannah Hitchcock, Worcester, Foreman Collection.

88. Mrs. Edith Hicks Walker, The Cherokee Temperance Society, Worcester, Foreman Collection.

89. "Cherokees and Temperance," *Cherokee Advocate*, 16 April 1846.

90. D. D. Hitchcock to the Editor [William P. Ross], *Cherokee Advocate*, 5 June 1845.

91. "Dick" to the Editor [William P. Ross], 9 July 1845, *Cherokee Advocate*, 17 July 1845. Emphasis in original; J. C. to [William P.] Ross, 5 July 1845, *Cherokee Advocate*, 10 July 1845; "The Temperance Meeting," *Cherokee Advocate*, 10 July 1845.

92. Geo. W. Adair to the Editor [William P. Ross], *Cherokee Advocate*, 8 July 1847.

93. "See Here," *Cherokee Advocate*, 25 March 1847.

94. "L." to the Editor [William P. Ross], *Cherokee Advocate*, 29 April 1847; *Cherokee Advocate*, 27 May 1847; Elizur Butler to Wm. P. Ross, 15 May 1847, *Cherokee Advocate*, 27 May 1847.

95. D. H. Ross, 1 September 1848, *Cherokee Advocate*, 4 September 1848.

96. Memorial to the Senate and House of Representatives of the State of Arkansas, 11 December 1848, in "The Annual Meeting of the Cherokee Temperance Society," *Cherokee Advocate*, 5 November 1849.

97. Danl. H. Ross, "Annual Meeting of the Cherokee Temperance Society," 20 October 1850, *Cherokee Advocate*, 29 October 1850; Memorial of the Cherokee People to the Honorable, the Senate and House of Representatives, of the State of Arkansas, *Cherokee Advocate*, 5 November 1850.

98. D. H. Ross to [James Shepherd] Vann, "Meeting of the Cherokee Temperance Society," *Cherokee Advocate*, 4 November 1851.

99. D. H. Ross to [James Shepherd] Vann, "Meeting of the Cherokee Temperance Society," *Cherokee Advocate*, 4 November 1851.

100. "Maltreated," *Cherokee Advocate*, 17 September 1846.

101. *Cherokee Advocate*, 16 March 1852.

102. Geo. W. Adair, "Temperance Meeting," 8 January 1848, *Cherokee Advocate*, 24 January 1848.

103. *Cherokee Advocate*, 21 October 1851. Emphasis in original.

104. "Cherokee Temperance Society," *Cherokee Almanac, 1850*, 29.

105. D. H. Ross to [James Shepherd] Vann, "Meeting of the Cherokee Temperance Society," *Cherokee Advocate*, 4 November 1851.

106. *The Constitution and Laws of the Cherokee Nation*, 227. The law must have been enacted on November 4, 1851, not a year before as the original document was dated.

107. "The Maine Law," *Cherokee Almanac, 1853*, 29, 31. See also D. H. Ross, "Annual Meeting of the Cherokee Temperance Society," 27 October [1852], *Cherokee Advocate*, 24 November 1852.

108. "Cherokee Temperance Society," *Cherokee Almanac, 1859*, 29, 31. Emphasis in original.

109. Letter of Mrs. Hannah Hitchcock, Worcester, Foreman Collection.

5. A NATION UNDER SIEGE

1. For the federal government's attempts to destroy the institutional autonomy of the Five Tribes in Indian territory, particularly through its courts, see Burton, *Indian Territory and the United States, 1866–1906.*

2. J. W. Denver to George Murrell, 9 February 1859, M-234, Roll 102, #0459–60. When he requested another permit in the winter of 1868–1869, however, Secretary of the Interior Orville H. Browning repealed the previous action and forbade Murrell to bring whiskey into the Nation. O. Bleellcox [?] to the Secretary of the Interior [Orville H. Browning] or Indian Commissioner [Nathaniel G. Taylor], 23 November [?] 1868, M-234, Roll 102, #0460; Geo. M. Murrell to the Secretary of the Interior [Orville H. Browning], 10 February 1869, M-234, Roll 102, #0451; O. H. Browning to N. G. Taylor, 20 February 1869, M-234, Roll 102, #0456–57. See also N. G. Taylor to Geo. M. Murrell, 3 March 1869, M-21, Roll 89, #0120–21; W. F. Cady to Albert Pike, 24 September 1870, M-21, Roll 98, #0066.

3. "Treaty with the Cherokee, 1866," in Kappler, *Indian Affairs,* 2:949.

4. Jno. N. Craig to the Commissioner of Indian Affairs [Ely S. Parker], 12 October 1869, M-234, Roll 102, #0174–76.

5. W. G. Mitchell, General Orders No. 42, 13 September 1869, M-234, Roll 102, #0177.

6. Frank J. Nash to John B. Jones, 31 May 1871, M-234, Roll 104, #0960–91; Frank J. Nash to the Secretary of War [William W. Belknap], 28 August 1871, M-234, Roll 104, #0108–10.

7. W. A. Reese and others to J. B. Jones, 31 May 1871, M-234, Roll 104, #0958–59; John B. Jones to the Commissioner of Indian Affairs, 26 August 1871, M-234, Roll 104, #0956–57.

8. John B. Jones to F. W. Walker, 26 February 1872, M-234, Roll 105, #0296; Bond for Frank J. Nash, 19 September 1871, M-234, Roll 105, #0297–98.

9. University of Oklahoma Libraries, Western History Collections, Cherokee Nation Papers Microfilm Edition, Roll 43, Folder 5559, Correspondence from J. M. Bell to E. S. Erving regarding J. R. Trott, 5 February 1878. Emphasis in original. Hereafter documents from this microfilm edition will be cited as Cherokee Nation Papers with roll and folder numbers and description and date of the documents.

10. "United States Courts," in S. W. Marston to the Commissioner of Indian Affairs [John Q. Smith], 31 August 1876, *Report of the Secretary of the Interior*, 44th Cong., 2nd sess., serial 1749, 467.

11. On the creation of the Vinita/Downingville townsite, see Self, "The Building of the Railroads," 194–95.

12. G. A. M. to the Editor [George W. Johnson], 25 February 1878, *Cherokee Advocate*, 9 March 1878; Cherokee Nation Papers, Roll 43, Folder 5559, Correspondence from J. M. Bell to E. S. Erving regarding J. R. Trott, 5 February 1878. Emphasis in original; "No More Whiskey Traffic," Special Orders No. 20, 8 March 1878, *Cherokee Advocate*, 16 March 1878.

13. "Treaty with the Cherokee, 1866," in Kappler, *Indian Affairs*, 2:945; Wardell, *A Political History of the Cherokee Nation, 1838–1907*, 257–58; Self, "The Building of the Railroads," 183–84, 202.

14. Self, "The Building of the Railroads," 182–83, 185–88, 192.

15. Self, "The Building of the Railroads," 202; Geo. Denison to W. T. Otto, 6 October 1870, M-234, Roll 103, #0811–13.

16. Cherokee Nation Papers, Roll 36, Folder 3585, Correspondence from John E. Thomes to Principal Chief D. W. Bushyhead regarding the sale of cider, 30 May 1882.

17. "From *The Indian Chieftain*," 337.

18. Bird Chopper to the Editor [W. P. Boudinot], 22 April 1873, *Cherokee Advocate*, 3 May 1873. Cherokee—Vices, Grant Foreman Collection 83.229, Box 8, Folder 7, Oklahoma Historical Society,

Archives and Manuscripts Division, Oklahoma City OK (hereafter cited as Cherokee—Vices, Foreman Collection); [John B. Jones] to E. P. Smith, 6 May 1873, M-234, Roll 106, #0379–81.

19. [John B. Jones] to E. P. Smith, 6 May 1873, M-234, Roll 106, #0379–81; Bird Chopper to the Editor [W. P. Boudinot], 22 April 1873, *Cherokee Advocate*, 3 May 1873. Cherokee—Vices, Foreman Collection. See also "From *The Indian Chieftain*," 337, 339.

20. *Laws of the Cherokee Nation, Passed during the Years 1839–1867*, 148–49.

21. "Treaty with the Cherokee, 1866," in Kappler, *Indian Affairs*, 2:944; John B. Jones to F. A. Walker, 1 June 1872, M-234, Roll 105, #0495. In February 1863, the "Loyal" National Council passed an emancipation act that prescribed the end of slavery as of June 25, 1863. Wardell, *A Political History of the Cherokee Nation, 1838–1907*, 173–74.

22. G. W. Ingalls to E. P. Smith, 8 January 1875, M-234, Roll 108, #0478–79.

23. Jno. N. Craig to Ely S. Parker, September 1869, *Report of the Secretary of the Interior*, 41st Cong., 2nd sess., serial 1414, 845–46; John B. Jones to F. A. Walker, 1 June 1872, M-234, Roll 105, #0495–96; Jno. N. Craig to the Commissioner of Indian Affairs [Ely S. Parker], 30 September 1870, *Report of the Secretary of the Interior*, 41st Cong., 3rd sess., serial 1449, 748; McLoughlin, *After the Trail of Tears*, 241–42.

24. "Treaty with the Cherokee, 1866," in Kappler, *Indian Affairs*, 2:944, 946. The U.S. Court for the Western District of Arkansas was located initially in Van Buren and transferred in 1871 to Fort Smith. Wardell, *A Political History of the Cherokee Nation, 1838–1907*, 308.

25. Jno. N. Craig to Ely S. Parker, September 1869, *Report of the Secretary of the Interior*, 41st Cong., 2nd sess., serial 1414, 847–48.

26. "An Act of the National Council, requiring the Principal Chief, to call upon the United States Agent for the Cherokees to protest against the unlawful Acts of Pretended or real U.S. Marshals or their Deputies," 2 December 1869, M-234, Roll 103, #0220–22.

27. John N. Craig to the Commissioner of Indian Affairs [Ely S. Parker], 9 March 1870, M-234, Roll 103, #0211.

28. John N. Craig to the Commissioner of Indian Affairs [Ely S. Parker], 9 March 1870, M-234, Roll 103, #0210–14; S. S. Cobb,

Affidavit, 11 November 1869, M-234, Roll 103, #0223–24; William A. Britton to John Craig, 20 October 1869, M-234, Roll 103, #0218–19.

29. John Craig to the Commissioner of Indian Affairs [Ely S. Parker], 2 July 1870, M-234, Roll 103, #0289–90.

30. John N. Craig to the Commissioner of Indian Affairs [Ely S. Parker], 30 October 1870, M-234, Roll 103, #0446–47; John N. Craig to the Commissioner of Indian Affairs [Ely S. Parker], 16 February 1871, M-234, Roll 104, #0242–46.

31. Jno. N. Craig to the Commissioner of Indian Affairs [Ely S. Parker], 30 September 1870, *Report of the Secretary of the Interior*, 41st Cong., 3rd sess., serial 1449, 747.

32. John N. Craig to the Commissioner of Indian Affairs [Ely S. Parker], 16 February 1871, M-234, Roll 104, #0246–50.

33. "Reply to office letter, relative to Agent Craig's seizure of goods of Wright and others," 17 August 1870, M-234, Roll 103, #0788–91.

34. "United States district court," in John B. Jones to F. A. Walker, 1 September 1872, *Report of the Secretary of the Interior*, 42nd Cong., 3rd sess., serial 1560, 619.

35. John B. Jones to E. S. Parker, 30 June 1871, M-234, Roll 104, #0859–60. In this letter, Jones asked Commissioner Parker if federal authorities had any intention "to abrogate the present regulation requiring *adopted* citizens of the Cherokee Nation, to obtain a U.S. license [to] trade with the Cherokees." Emphasis in original.

36. One of the bloodiest gun battles between U.S. marshals and Cherokees was the Going Snake Tragedy of 1872. On April 25, the Going Snake District Court was trying a Cherokee named Ezekiel Proctor who had killed another Cherokee, Polly Chesterton, when she stepped in between Proctor and her husband, who were quarreling. Polly's husband, William Chesterton, was an intermarried American. When Polly's relatives feared that the Cherokee court would acquit Proctor on the ground that he had killed her accidentally, William swore out a warrant in the U.S. District Court in Arkansas as an American citizen for Proctor's arrest. Although this did not negate the Cherokees' right to try Proctor by their own laws, the U.S. marshal took fifteen or twenty deputies to the Going Snake District Court while the trial of the Proctor case was in progress. Presenting the warrant for Proctor's arrest, the marshal asked the court to hand

him over to the federal side. The Cherokee judge refused to surrender him. U.S. deputy marshal Sut Beck shot at Proctor and wounded him, and Cherokee deputies and others in the courthouse fired back. A terrible gunfight ensued and ended in the loss of many lives on both sides. Having obtained arrest warrants for those who were still alive, the federal marshal and his deputies soon came back to the Cherokee Nation. They arrested the Cherokee judge and several others, put them in jail at Fort Smith, and did not release them until the early summer of 1873. McLoughlin, *Champions of the Cherokees*, 463–64; McLoughlin, *After the Trail of Tears*, 299–300; John B. Jones to H. R. Clum, 29 October 1873, M-234, Roll 106, #0575–83.

37. See "Treaty with the Cherokee, 1835," in Kappler, *Indian Affairs*, 2:442.

38. See "Treaty with the Cherokee, 1866," in Kappler, *Indian Affairs*, 2:946.

39. Lewis Downing to J. B. Jones, 19 July 1872, M-234, Roll 105, #0624–31. Emphasis in original.

40. See *U.S. Statutes at Large*, 4:732; 12:338–39; 13:29.

41. Downing mistakenly stated that the original statute passed on March 3, 1851, contained this provision. See *U.S. Statutes at Large*, 9:594–95.

42. See *U.S. Statutes at Large*, 10:269–70.

43. Lewis Downing to J. B. Jones, 19 July 1872, M-234, Roll 105, #0634–45. Emphasis in original.

44. John B. Jones to F. A. Walker, 27 July 1872, M-234, Roll 105, #0607–8.

45. "United States district court," in John B. Jones to F. A. Walker, 1 September 1872, *Report of the Secretary of the Interior*, 42nd Cong., 3rd sess., serial 1560, 618.

46. John B. Jones to F. A. Walker, 27 July 1872, M-234, Roll 105, #0606–11.

47. United States Congressional Serial Set, U.S. House, *Intercourse with Indian Tribes*, 43rd Cong., 1st sess. 1874, H. Doc. 108, serial 1607.

48. United States Congressional Serial Set, U.S. House, *Penalty for Selling Liquor to Indians*, 43rd Cong., 1st sess., 1874, H. Doc. 177, serial 1610.

49. *Revised Statutes of the United States*, 18, pt. 1:375.

50. United States Congressional Serial Set, U.S. Senate, *Letter from the Acting Secretary of War*, 44th Cong., 1st sess., 1876, S. Doc. 34, serial 1664.

51. *U.S. Statutes at Large,* 19:244.

52. James R. Hendricks to W. H. Clayton, October 1883, James R. Hendricks Papers, Box H-31, Folder 13, University of Oklahoma Libraries, Western History Collections, University of Oklahoma, Norman OK.

53. IPH, OHS, Emory O. McGuire, Vol. 7, 53–54.

54. IPH, OHS, William M. James, Vol. 62, 353.

55. IPH, OHS, James B. White, Vol. 67, 217–18.

56. IPH, OHS, William M. James, Vol. 62, 353–54.

57. IPH, OHS, George Tanner, Vol. 46, 196.

58. "Old Injin" to the Editor [E. C. Boudinot], 10 September 1887, *Cherokee Advocate*, 28 September 1887.

59. IPH, OHS, Mrs. C. A. Fleetwood, Mrs. Roy Bradshaw, and Mrs. Eblen Hart, Vol. 91, 279–80; "Our Senators," *Cherokee Advocate*, 5 February 1886.

60. IPH, OHS, Ninnian Tannehill, Vol. 112, 35.

61. "Old Injin" to the Editor [E. C. Boudinot], 10 September 1887, *Cherokee Advocate*, 28 September 1887. Emphasis in original.

62. "United States Courts," in John Q. Tufts to the Commissioner of Indian Affairs [Hiram Price], 30 September 1881, *Executive Documents*, 47th Cong., 1st sess., serial 2018, 162.

63. "United States Court," in Robt. L. Owen to the Commissioner of Indian Affairs, 27 August 1888, *House Executive Documents*, 50th Cong., 2nd sess., serial 2637, 136.

64. *Cherokee Advocate*, 4 December 1889.

65. IPH, OHS, Mrs. Susanna Adair Davis, Vol. 2, 456–57.

66. R. B. Harris to the Editor [D. H. Ross], 9 December 1882, *Cherokee Advocate*, 15 December 1882; Jas. Nicholson to R. B. Harris, 5 December 1882, *Cherokee Advocate*, 15 December 1882.

67. "United States Court," in John Q. Tufts to the Commissioner of Indian Affairs [Hiram Price], [1883], *Executive Documents*, 48th Cong., 1st sess., serial 2191, 146.

68. "U.S. Court in the Indian Territory," *Report of the Secretary of the Interior*, 1 November 1886, *Executive Documents*, 49th Cong., 2nd

sess., serial 2467, 92; "United States Court," in Robt. L. Owen to the Commissioner of Indian Affairs, 27 August 1888, *House Executive Documents*, 50th Cong., 2nd sess., serial 2637, 135.

69. "U.S. Court in the Indian Territory," *Report of the Secretary of the Interior*, 1 November 1886, *Executive Documents*, 49th Cong., 2nd sess., serial 2467, 91.

70. Cherokee National Records, affidavit of Frank Consene, 19 January 1875, CHN45, Vol. 160, 52, Microcopy, Oklahoma Historical Society, Archives and Manuscripts Division, Oklahoma City OK. Hereafter documents from this archive will be cited as CHN with date and volume and page numbers.

71. *Compiled Laws of the Cherokee Nation*, 161–62.

72. *Compiled Laws of the Cherokee Nation*, 146; McLoughlin, *After the Trail of Tears*, 304–5; Burton, *Indian Territory and the United States*, 87–88.

73 "Q." "The Executive Order," *Cherokee Advocate*, 15 September 1882.

74. "Whiskey and Revolvers in Going Snake," *Cherokee Advocate*, 1 September 1882.

75. Mrs. Nan French to the Editor [E. C. Boudinot], 22 September 1887, *Cherokee Advocate*, 28 September 1887; Cherokee Nation Papers, Roll 32, Folder 3073, Pardon document for George Butler to J. B. Mayes and Members of Executors Council of Cherokee Nation, 22 October 1891.

76. "Whiskey and Revolvers in Going Snake," *Cherokee Advocate*, 1 September 1882.

77. Third Annual Message of D. W. Bushyhead, 9 November 1881, *Cherokee Advocate*, 9 November 1881. Papers of Principal Chief D. W. Bushyhead, Box B-56, Folder 164, University of Oklahoma Libraries, Western History Collections, University of Oklahoma, Norman OK; D. W. Bushyhead, Appendix to Message, "Carrying Dangerous Weapons," *Cherokee Advocate*, 17 November 1882. See also *Compiled Laws of the Cherokee Nation*, 161–62, 283–85.

78. D. W. Bushyhead, "Executive Order to Sheriffs," *Cherokee Advocate*, 15 September 1882.

79. "Whiskey and Revolvers in Going Snake," *Cherokee Advocate*, 1 September 1882.

80. "Carrying Concealed Weapons," *Cherokee Advocate*, 4 April 1874.

81. P. W. Reeder to D. W. Bushyhead, February 1882, CHN115, Cherokee (Tahlequah)-*Whiskey Traffic & Gambling Suppression*.

82. D. W. Bushyhead to P. W. Reeder, 20 February 1882, CHN121, Vol. 715E, 149–50.

83. "United States district court," in John B. Jones to F. A. Walker, 1 September 1872, *Report of the Secretary of the Interior*, 42nd Cong., 3rd sess., serial 1560, 619.

84. "U.S. Court in the Indian Territory," *Report of the Secretary of the Interior*, 1 November 1886, *Executive Documents*, 49th Cong., 2nd sess., serial 2467, 93.

85. "The Attempt," *Cherokee Advocate*, 20 January 1892.

6. CHEROKEE TEMPERANCE, AMERICAN REFORM, AND OKLAHOMA STATEHOOD

1. "Temperance Lecture," *Cherokee Advocate*, 25 January 1884; *Cherokee Advocate*, 2 May 1884.

2. Bordin, *Woman and Temperance*, 15–33; Epstein, *The Politics of Domesticity*, 95–100; Blocker, *"Give to the Winds Thy Fears."*

3. Bordin, *Woman and Temperance*, 34–51; National Woman's Christian Temperance Union, *Statement of Principles W.C.T.U. Catechism and Constitution* (The Temple, Chicago: [Woman's Christian Temperance Publication Association?], 1897), 8. Lilah D. Lindsey Collection, Series III, Box 3, Folder 9, McFarlin Library, Department of Special Collections, University of Tulsa, Tulsa, OK (hereafter cited as Lindsey Collection).

4. National Woman's Christian Temperance Union, *Statement of Principles*, 9.

5. Bordin, *Woman and Temperance*, 95–123; Epstein, *The Politics of Domesticity*, 115–46. See also Bordin, *Frances Willard*.

6. Bordin, *Woman and Temperance*, 50, 72–76.

7. "Report of the Corresponding Secretary, Indian Territory," *Minutes of the Woman's National Christian Temperance Union, at the Seventh Annual Meeting, in Boston, October 27th to 30th, 1880 with Reports and Constitution*. (New York: The National Temperance Society and Publication House, 1880), 92. Woman's Christian Temperance

Union National Headquarters Historical Files (joint Ohio Historical Society–Michigan Historical Collections–Woman's Christian Temperance Union microfilm edition, Woman's Christian Temperance Union series, Roll 1). Hereafter documents from this series will be cited as WCTU. Historical Files with roll and folder numbers, when available. See also Willard, *Woman and Temperance*, 504–10.

8. Sarah P. Morrison, "Report of Committee on Work among the Indians, Chinese, and Colored People," *Minutes of the Woman's National Christian Temperance Union Annual Meeting, 1880*, 61–62.

9. J. L. Patterson to the "Governor of the Cherokees," 7 May 1881; "Temperance," *Cherokee Advocate*, 11 May 1881; W. M. Wightman, 21 March 1881, *Cherokee Advocate*, 11 May 1881.

10. D. W. Bushyhead to L. J. Stapler, 18 May 1881. WCTU Historical Files, Roll 12, Folder 12.

11. Frances E. Willard Journal, 19 May 1881, Typescript, Frances E. Willard Memorial Library, Evanston IL.

12. For Jane Stapler's biographical sketch, see IPH, OHS, Mrs. Roy Bradshaw, Vol. 104, 132–44. See also *Cherokee Advocate*, 7 September 1872.

13. John S. Adair, Allen Ross, Wm. Johnston, and others to D. W. Bushyhead, n.d., CHN115, Cherokee (Tahlequah)-*Whiskey Traffic & Gambling Suppression*.

14. *Minutes of the Woman's National Christian Temperance Union Annual Meeting, 1880*, 132.

15. *Cherokee Advocate*, 21 September 1883.

16. *Laws and Joint Resolutions of the Cherokee Nation*, , 153–54 (page references are to reprint edition).

17. J. Ellen Foster to D. W. Bushyhead, 18 February 1882, CHN 115, Cherokee (Tahlequah)-*Whiskey Traffic & Gambling Suppression*.

18. Mrs. J. Ellen Foster to D. W. Bushyhead, 31 January 1882, CHN 115, Cherokee (Tahlequah)-*Whiskey Traffic & Gambling Suppression*.

19. The *Cherokee Advocate* consistently called her "Emily" Molloy although her real name was Emma Molloy. For Molloy's biographical sketch, see Hanaford, *Daughters of America*, 673–76.

20. "A Great Rally for Temperance, Morality and Christianity at the Cherokee Capital," *Cherokee Advocate*, 30 November 1883.

21. "Return of Mrs. Molloy," *Cherokee Advocate*, 11 January 1884.

22. "Mrs. Molloy at Ft. Gibson," *Cherokee Advocate*, 1 February 1884.

23. Emma Hicks to Ann Eliza Worcester Robertson, 31 January 1884. Robertson Papers, Series II, Box 12, Folder 3.

24. IPH, OHS, Elizabeth Ross, Vol. 43, 28.

25. Emma Hicks to Ann Eliza Worcester Robertson, 31 January 1884. Emphasis in original. Robertson Papers.

26. Miss Katie Ellett, "News from the Field, Indian Territory," *Union Signal*, 21 February 1884, p. 11.

27. "Cherokee" to the Editor [D. H. Ross], "From Gibson," *Cherokee Advocate*, 29 February 1884.

28. "Cherokee," "To the Members of the Woman's Christian Temperance Union," *Cherokee Advocate*, 28 March 1884.

29. *Cherokee Advocate*, 9, 16, 23 May 1884.

30. A. Archer, "Ladies of Tahlequah W.C.T.U.," *Cherokee Advocate*, 18 April 1884; "Drops of Water," *Cherokee Advocate*, 6 June 1884; "Drops of Water," *Cherokee Advocate*, 13 June 1884; "Rally Once Again," *Cherokee Advocate*, 5 September 1884.

31. Martha G. Tunstall to [Frances E. Willard], 31 December 1885, in "Work in Indian Territory," *Union Signal*, 25 March 1886, p. 2; *Union Signal*, 16 February 1888, p. 1. Martha G. Tunstall was born in Perry County, Alabama, on December 29, 1838. At her death of April 16, 1911, she was buried in a cemetery in Blue Jacket, Oklahoma. Tunstall believed that she was "one-fourth" Cherokee, and National WCTU workers called her "our Cherokee sister." Between 1906 and 1910 when the U.S. Court of Claims, under the supervision of Special Commissioner Guion Miller, investigated the eligibility of applicants for a one-million-dollar fund appropriated by Congress to members of the Eastern Band of the Cherokees, it rejected her application. "I claim my Indian blood through my mother," she wrote, but none of her statements to the Court proved that she was of Cherokee descent: "My mother did not live with the Indians. . . . My mother's father was the Indian. He came from Georgia. My mother did not speak the Indian language. I never saw an Indian until I was 20 years old. No Indians lived where I was born." IPH, OHS, Cemeteries—Cherokee Bluejacket, Martha Tunstall, Vol. 57, 31; *Minutes of the National Woman's Christian Temperance Union, at*

the Fourteenth Annual Meeting in Nashville, Tenn., November 16 to 21, 1887. With Addresses, Reports and Constitutions. (Chicago: Woman's Temperance Publication Association, 1888), 19. WCTU Historical Files, Roll 2; *Union Signal*, 13 January 1887, p. 3; Jordan, *Cherokee by Blood*, 6:v, 374. Application #16229. See also IPH, OHS, Mrs. R. E. Rogers, vol. 98, 147–48.

32. "Indian Territory, A New Union and Its Work," *Union Signal*, 23 December 1886, p. 11.

33. "Report of the Corresponding Secretary, Indian Territory," *Minutes of the National W.C.T.U. Annual Meeting, 1887*, 116; Mrs. Martha G. Tunstall, "Legislation, Indian Territory," *Minutes of the National W.C.T.U. Annual Meeting, 1887*, ccxxiii; Mrs. J. A. Rogers, "Indian Territory, Interesting Notes," *Union Signal*, 17 March 1887, p. 11.

34. "Report of the Corresponding Secretary, Indian Territory," *Minutes of the National W.C.T.U. Annual Meeting, 1887*, 116.

35. Martha G. Tunstall to the *Union Signal*, 30 November 1887, "Plea from Our Indian Sister," *Union Signal*, 5 January 1888, p. 5; *Union Signal*, 14 October 1886, p. 1.

36. *Union Signal*, 16 February 1888, p. 1.

37. Mrs. J. A. Rogers, "Indian Territory, Interesting Notes," *Union Signal*, 17 March 1887, p. 10. Emphasis in original.

38. Mary E. Griffith to the *Union Signal*, 13 June 1888, "Prohibition in Indian Territory," *Union Signal*, 21 June 1888, p. 5; N. K. Fite and T. M. Fuller, "Temperance," *Cherokee Advocate*, 23 May 1888; T. M. Fuller and N. K. Fite, *Cherokee Advocate*, 6 June 1888.

39. T. M. Fuller, *Cherokee Advocate*, 2 May 1888.

40. Mrs. Julia Rogers, "Proceedings of the Tahlequah W.C.T.U.," *Cherokee Advocate*, 11 April 1888.

41. Mrs. Helen R. Duncan to the *Union Signal*, "Scientific Temperance Instruction in Indian Territory," *Union Signal*, 11 April 1889, p. 5; *Cherokee Advocate*, 26 September 1888.

42. Mrs. Helen R. Duncan to the *Union Signal*, "Scientific Temperance Instruction in Indian Territory," *Union Signal*, 11 April 1889, p. 5; "Letter from Helen R. Duncan," *Cherokee Advocate*, 1 August 1888; *Union Signal*, 20 September 1888, p. 12.

43. See *Compiled Laws of the Cherokee Nation*, 161–62.

44. Cherokee Nation Papers, Roll 31, Folder 2925, Bond for Jesse B.

Mayes, high sheriff, 28 April 1888; Jesse B. Mayes, "Warning Notice!" *Cherokee Advocate*, 26 July; 10 October 1888; *Cherokee Advocate*, 26 July 1888.

45. *Cherokee Advocate*, 14 November 1888.

46. N. K. Fite, "Proceedings of the W.C.T.U.," *Cherokee Advocate*, 16 May 1888; T. M. Fuller, "Temperance Notes," *Cherokee Advocate*, 16 May 1888; T. M. Fuller, "Mrs. Perkins'[s] Lecture," *Cherokee Advocate*, 6 June 1888; Mrs. S. M. Perkins, "Reports of National Organizers," *Minutes of the National Woman's Christian Temperance Union, at the Fifteenth Annual Meeting in New York City, October 19 to 23, 1888. With Addresses, Reports and Constitutions.* (Chicago: Woman's Temperance Publication Association, 1888), 281–83. WCTU Historical Files, Roll 2; Sarah M. Perkins, "Indian Territory," *Union Signal*, 2 August 1888, p. 10.

47. Sarah M. Perkins and others, "Indian Territory, Call for Convention," *Cherokee Advocate*, 11 July 1888; Alice M. Robertson, *Cherokee Advocate*, 11 July 1888; "W.C.T.U.," *Muskogee Phoenix*, 12 July 1888.

48. Mrs. S. M. Perkins, "Reports of National Organizers," *Minutes of the National W.C.T.U. Annual Meeting, 1888*, 283–84; Sarah M. Perkins, "Indian Territory," *Union Signal*, 2 August 1888, p. 10; Annual Convention Program for 1889 with press cutting tipped in. Lindsey Collection, Series III, Box 2, Folder 20; "W.C.T.U. Convention," *Muskogee Phoenix*, 19 July 1888.

49. *Minutes of the Indian Territory Woman's Christian Temperance Union. Held at Tahlequah, Indian Territory, June* [sic] *4, 1889.* (Muskogee, I[ndian] T[erritory]: Our Brother in Red Pub. Co., n.d.), 1–3. Lindsey Collection, Series III, Box 2, Folder 20.

50. "The President's Annual Address," *Minutes of the Indian Territory W.C.T.U., 1889*, 4–6.

51. *Minutes of the Indian Territory W.C.T.U., 1889*, 6

52. Frances E. Willard, "White-Ribboners of Texas and Indian Territory," *Union Signal*, 23 May 1889, p. 10; "Miss Frances Willard," *Cherokee Advocate*, 8 May 1889; *Minutes of the Indian Territory W.C.T.U., 1889*, 10–11.

53. Barbara O'Brian, "Indian Territory, News and Notes," *Union Signal*, 26 December 1889, p. 11.

54. *Minutes of the Indian Territory W.C.T.U., 1889*, 10.

55. *Union Signal*, 4 April 1895, p. 1; Chapin, *Thumb Nail Sketches*, 104. See also "The Watch Tower," *Union Signal*, 9 May 1895, p. 9.

56. According to the *Cherokee Advocate*, these U.S. soldiers were ready customers of alcohol, and such disorderly conditions pleased many whiskey peddlers. "When times became too quiet on the frontier to need the presence of soldiers," in fact, these criminal traders attempted to "draw custom" by hiring gunmen who would commit crimes for them and produce "a general disturbance sufficient to cause the Indian agent to dispatch to Washington—'Indians on the war path—send soldiers immediately.'" *Cherokee Advocate*, 17 June 1899.

57. Mrs. L. Jane Stapler, "Address of President of Indian Territory to National Convention," *Minutes of the National Woman's Christian Temperance Union, at the Seventeenth Annual Meeting in Atlanta, Georgia, November 14th to 18th, 1890. With Addresses, Reports and Constitutions*. (Chicago: Woman's Temperance Publication Association, 1890), 390–92. WCTU Historical Files, Roll 3.

58. *Union Signal*, 27 November 1890, p. 10. See also *Minutes of the National W.C.T.U. Annual Meeting, 1890*, 34–35.

59. *Cherokee Advocate*, 29 June 1892.

60. "Indian Territory," *Minutes of the National Woman's Christian Temperance Union at the Eighteenth Annual Meeting Boston, Mass., November 13th to 18th, 1891 with Addresses, Reports and Constitution*. (Chicago: Woman's Temperance Publishing Association, 1891), 241. WCTU Historical Files, Roll 3.

61. *Minutes of the National W.C.T.U. Annual Meeting, 1891*, 241; Sarah Ford Crosby, "Indian Territory, The W.C.T.U. at the Cherokee Election," *Union Signal*, 10 September 1891, p. 14.

62. IPH, OHS, E. Lee Brown, Vol. 66, 407.

63. Affidavit sworn by Degardunah Judge, 21 October 1891, G. W. Benge Collection, Folder 25, Thomas Gilcrease Institute of American History and Art, Tulsa OK.

64. See *Revised Statutes of the United States*, 18, pt. 1:375.

65. "Intemperance," *Report of the Commissioner of Indian Affairs*, 5 September 1890, *Executive Documents*, 51st Cong., 2nd sess., serial 2841, LV; "Sale of Liquor to Indians," *Report of the Commissioner of*

Indian Affairs, 1 October 1891, *Executive Documents*, 52nd Cong., 1st sess., serial 2934, 74.

66. "Intoxicating Liquors," in Leo E. Bennett to the Commissioner of Indian Affairs [Thomas Jefferson Morgan], 10 September 1890, *Executive Documents*, 51st Cong., 2nd sess., serial 2841, 92; Leo E. Bennett to O. W. Case, 14 April 1890, in "Intoxicating Liquors," *Executive Documents*, 51st Cong., 2nd sess., serial 2841, 92.

67. Leo E. Bennett to O. W. Case, 14 April 1890, in "Intoxicating Liquors," *Executive Documents*, 51st Cong., 2nd sess., serial 2841, 92; IPH, OHS, Arthur Bynum, Vol. 72, 477.

68. John W. Noble to O. W. Case, 14 May 1890, in "Intoxicating Liquors," *Executive Documents*, 51st Cong., 2nd sess., serial 2841, 93.

69. "Intoxicating Liquors," in Leo E. Bennett to the Commissioner of Indian Affairs [Thomas Jefferson Morgan], 10 September 1890, *Executive Documents*, 51st Cong., 2nd sess., serial 2841, 93.

70. H. C. Cross to Mrs. L. J. Stapler, 30 September 1890, in T. M. Fuller, "W.C.T.U. Notes," *Cherokee Advocate*, 15 October 1890.

71. "Sale of Liquor to Indians," *Report of the Commissioner of Indian Affairs*, 1 October 1891, *Executive Documents*, 52nd Cong., 1st sess., serial 2934, 74–75; "Intoxicating Liquors," in Leo E. Bennett to the Commissioner of Indian Affairs [Thomas Jefferson Morgan], 7 September 1891, *Executive Documents*, 52nd Cong., 1st sess., serial 2934, 248–49; "Intoxicating Liquors," in Leo E. Bennett to the Commissioner of Indian Affairs [Thomas Jefferson Morgan], 26 September 1892, *House Executive Documents*, 52nd Cong., 2nd sess., serial 3088, 259–60.

72. *Cherokee Advocate*, 28 August 1891.

73. "Sale of Liquor to Indians," *Report of the Commissioner of Indian Affairs*, 27 August 1892, *House Executive Documents*, 52nd Cong., 2nd sess., serial 3088, 103–4.

74. Tennie M. Fuller, "Indian Territory," *Minutes of the National Woman's Christian Temperance Union at the Nineteenth Annual Meeting Denver, Col., October 28th to November 2d, 1892 with Addresses, Reports and Constitution.* (Chicago: Woman's Temperance Publishing Association, 1892), 222. WCTU Historical Files, Roll 3. See also Sarah Ford Crosby, "Indian Territory, Convention Notes," *Union Signal*, 16 June 1892, p. 12.

75. "Intoxicating Liquors," in Leo E. Bennett to the Commissioner

of Indian Affairs [Thomas Jefferson Morgan], 26 September 1892, *House Executive Documents*, 52nd Cong., 2nd sess., serial 3088, 259.

76. *U.S. Statutes at Large,* 27:260–61.

77. *Union Signal,* 11 August 1892, p. 12.

78. Leo Bennett, Bootlegging, Grant Foreman Collection 83.229, Box 4, Folder 6, Oklahoma Historical Society, Archives and Manuscripts Division, Oklahoma City ok (hereafter cited as Bootlegging, Foreman Collection).

79. *Cherokee Advocate,* 25 September 1889. The Cherokee National Council passed this alcohol regulation law on November 29, 1880. *Compiled Laws of the Cherokee Nation,* 161–62.

80. IPH, OHS, Wallace Thornton, vol. 10, 489. See also Leo Bennett, Bootlegging, Foreman Collection.

81. See *Compiled Laws of the Cherokee Nation,* 305–6.

82. *Purcell Register,* 30 September 1892. C. Johnson Harris Collection, Box H-55, Folder 8, University of Oklahoma Libraries, Western History Collections, University of Oklahoma, Norman ok (here-after cited as Harris Collection); C. J. Harris to the President [of the United States, Benjamin Harrison], 17 September 1892, *Cherokee Advocate,* 14 September 1892, Harris Collection, Box H-55, Folder 4.

83. *Union Signal,* 15 December 1892, p. 12.

84. Leo Bennett, Bootlegging, Foreman Collection.

85. *Union Signal,* 15 December 1892, p. 12; Sarah Ford Crosby, "Indian Territory," *Union Signal,* 12 January 1893, p. 11.

86. T. M. Fuller, "Indian Territory," *Minutes of the National Woman's Christian Temperance Union at the Twentieth Annual Meeting Held in Memorial Art Palace Chicago, Illinois October 18–21, 1893.* (Chicago: Woman's Temperance Publishing Association, 1893), 169. wctu Historical Files, Roll 4.

87. "Sermon by Rev. W. R. King," *Cherokee Advocate,* 14 September 1892. Emphasis in original.

88. Rev. W. R. King, "Lecture on Temperance," 15 January 1893, *Cherokee Advocate,* 28 January 1893.

89. Rev. W. R. King, "Address Before the W.C.T.U. of Tahlequah," *Cherokee Advocate,* 15 July 1893.

90. Prucha, *The Great Father,* 2:659–86, 746–55; *U.S. Statutes at Large,* 30:495–519; "Whiskey Selling Still a Crime in Territory," *Cherokee Advocate,* 22 April 1905.

91. *U.S. Statutes at Large*, 32, pt. 1:716–27. See also "An Act Approved by W. C. Rogers," *Collinsville News*, 24 November 1904. William Charles Rogers Collection, Box R-35, Folder 97, University of Oklahoma Libraries, Western History Collections, University of Oklahoma, Norman OK.

92. "Prohibition for the Indian," *Union Signal*, 1 June 1899, p. 8; "Indian Police," in Leo E. Bennett to the Commissioner of Indian Affairs [Thomas Jefferson Morgan], 21 September 1889, *Executive Documents*, 51st Cong., 1st sess., serial 2725, 210. Emphasis in original; Cherokee Nation Papers, Roll 23, Folder 2504, Correspondence from U.S. District Court Judge I. C. Parker to Principal Chief C. J. Harris regarding the ratio of Indians and U.S. citizens tried in Parker's court, 19 February 1894.

93. "Prohibition for the Indian," *Union Signal*, 1 June 1899, p. 8.

94. Dorothy J. Cleveland, "Work among Indians," *Union Signal*, 28 August 1902, p. 11. Emphasis in original.

95. "National Convention 1901," 19 November 1901, *Union Signal*, 23 November 1901, p. 15.

96. "Convention," *Report of the National Woman's Christian Temperance Union Twenty-eighth Annual Meeting Held in the First Baptist Church Fort Worth, Texas. November 15th to 20th, 1901*, 66–67. WCTU Historical Files, Roll 6.

97. L. M. N. S., "Shall the Government Keep Faith with the Indians," *Union Signal*, 7 April 1904, p. 8; United States Congressional Serial Set, U.S. Senate, *Sale of Intoxicants in Indian and Oklahoma Territories, Etc.*, 58th Cong., 2nd sess., 1904, S. Doc. 194, serial 4591; "Indian Territory and Oklahoma," *Union Signal*, 30 November 1905, p. 8.

98. Mrs. J. M. Escoe, "Indian Territory (Amanda Richey)," *Report of the National Woman's Christian Temperance Union Twenty-ninth Annual Meeting Held in the Jefferson Portland, Maine October 17th to 22d, 1902*, 158. WCTU Historical Files, Roll 6.

99. Lillian M. N. Stevens, "Address of the President," *Report of the National W.C.T.U. Annual Meeting, 1902*, 118.

100. Mrs. J. M. Escoe, "Indian Territory (Amanda Richey)," *Report of the National W.C.T.U. Annual Meeting, 1902*, 158; "Petition President and Congress," *Muskogee Evening Times*, 25 April 1902; Mrs. Belle Brendel, "Indian Territory, Mid Year Conference," *Union Signal*, 12 June 1902, p. 11; *Union Signal*, 14 January 1904, p. 11.

101. "The Liquor Traffic in a New State," *Union Signal,* 10 November 1904, p. 2. Emphasis in original.

102. Cherokee Nation Papers, Roll 24, Folder 2620, Correspondence from Choctaw principal chief Green McCurtain to Principal Chief T. M. Buffington regarding the transmittal of the following, March 27, 1903; and from Mrs. J. S. Morrow [*sic*] to Green McCurtain regarding liquor, March 26, 1903.

103. "For Single Statehood," *Cherokee Advocate,* 30 May 1903.

104. *An Address to the People of Indian Territory on the Question of Independent Statehood for Indian Territory, by the Campaign Committee of the Constitutional Convention. Authorized and Assembled August 21, 1905.* (Muskogee: Phoenix Printing Co., 1905). Thomas Gilcrease Institute of American History and Art, Tulsa OK.

105. "We Want Separate Statehood," *Cherokee Advocate,* 28 October 1905.

106. S. N. to the Editor of *Public Ledger,* 16 January 1906, quoted from *Public Ledger* in "Indians and Prohibition," *Cherokee Advocate,* 10 February 1906.

107. "Constitution of the State of Sequoyah," in United States Congressional Serial Set, U.S. Senate, *Proposed State of Sequoyah,* 59th Cong., 1st sess., 1906, S. Doc. 143, serial 4912, 81–82.

108. Lucy Belle Davis, "Indian Territory Holds Successful Convention," *Union Signal,* 29 September 1904, p. 13.

109. *Report of the National Woman's Christian Temperance Union Thirty-second Annual Meeting Held in First Congregational Church Los Angeles, Cal. October 27–November 1, 1905,* 61. WCTU Historical Files, Roll 6.

110. Mrs. Lucy Belle Davis, "Corresponding Secretary's Report, Indian Territory," *Report of the National W.C.T.U. Annual Meeting, 1905,* 154.

111. *U.S. Statutes at Large,* 34, pt. 1:269–70.

112. Mrs. Cora D. Hammett, "Oklahoma," *Report of the National Woman's Christian Temperance Union Thirty-third Annual Convention Held in Parson's Theater Hartford, Connecticut October 26–31, 1906,* 157–58. WCTU Historical Files, Roll 7; "The Battle Royal Is On In Oklahoma," *Union Signal,* 29 August 1907, p. 2, 15. See also Petition for Statewide Prohibition Signed by Several Individuals. Lindsey Collection, Series III, Box 3, Folder 6.

113. Lillian M. N. Stevens, "Oklahoma and Prohibition," *Report of the National W.C.T.U. Annual Convention, 1906*, 99.

114. Mabel R. Sutherland, *Champion*, August 1906, p. 4.

115. For the Oklahoma statewide prohibition campaign and the birth of the prohibition state of Oklahoma, see Franklin, *Born Sober.*

116. Mary T. Cranston, "Minutes of the Executive Meeting of the Indian Territory W.C.T.U., Held at Tulsa, I. T., April 26 and 27, 1906," *Official Proceedings of the 19th and 20th Annual Meetings of the Women's* [sic] *Christian Temperance Union of Indian Territory Held at Afton, October 26–30, 1906 Tulsa, October 16–20, 1907*, 11. Oklahoma Historical Society, Archives and Manuscripts Division, Oklahoma City OK.

117. Mrs. Lila J. Ross, "Indian Territory," *Report of the National W.C.T.U. Annual Convention, 1906*, 149.

118. Clara Hopson, "Indian Territory's Twentieth Convention," *Union Signal*, 14 November 1907, p. 13; "W.C.T.U. Will Not Merge," *Muskogee Times-Democrat*, 21 October 1907.

119. Abbie B. Hillerman, "President's Letter," *Oklahoma Messenger*, November 1907, p. 3.

120. Lilah D. Lindsey, President's Address, [1908]. Lindsey Collection, Series III, Box 2, Folder 19.

121. Lilah D. Lindsey, President's Address, [1908]. Lindsey Collection, Series III, Box 2, Folder 19; "State W.C.T.U. to Meet Here," *Muskogee Times-Democrat*, 5 September 1908; "The Water Wago[n] Women to Merge," *Muskogee Times-Democrat*, 12 September 1908.

122. "State W.C.T.U. to Meet Here," *Muskogee Times-Democrat*, 5 September 1908; "Oklahoma and Indian Territory Unions are United," *Union Signal*, 8 October 1908, p. 12; Mrs. Harriet D. Heberling, "Oklahoma," *Report of the National Woman's Christian Temperance Union Thirty-fifth Annual Convention Held in the Auditorium Denver, Colorado October 23–28, 1908*, 166–67. WCTU Historical Files, Roll 7; "Mrs. M'Kellop Is Honored," *Muskogee Times-Democrat*, 19 September 1908.

BIBLIOGRAPHY

PRIMARY SOURCES

Archival Manuscript Collections

Frances E. Willard Memorial Library, Evanston IL

Frances E. Willard Journal. Typescript.
Woman's Christian Temperance Union National Headquarters Historical Files. Joint Ohio Historical Society–Michigan Historical Collections–Woman's Christian Temperance Union microfilm edition, Woman's Christian Temperance Union series.

Houghton Library, Department of Manuscripts, Harvard University, Cambridge MA

Papers of the American Board of Commissioners for Foreign Missions. Microcopy.

McFarlin Library, Department of Special Collections, University of Tulsa, Tulsa OK

Lilah D. Lindsey Collection
Alice Mary Robertson Papers

National Archives, Washington DC, U.S. Bureau of Indian Affairs. RG 75.

Letters Received by the Office of Indian Affairs, 1824–1881. Microcopy 234.

Letters Sent by the Office of Indian Affairs, 1824–1881. Microcopy 21.

Letters Sent by the Secretary of War Relating to Indian Affairs, 1800–1824. Microcopy 15.

Records of the Cherokee Indian Agency in Tennessee, 1801–1835. Microcopy 208.

Newberry Library, Chicago IL

Edward E. Ayer Collection. John Howard Payne Papers. Microcopy.

Oklahoma Historical Society, Archives and Manuscripts Division, Oklahoma City OK

Cherokee National Records. Microcopy.

Copies of Manuscripts in the Office of the Commissioner of Indian Affairs, Washington DC (Western Superintendency: Miscellaneous and Schools). Compiled from original records selected by Grant Foreman, 1930. Typescript.

Grant Foreman Collection

Section X. Oversized Box 1. Indian Territory–Organizations–Woman's Christian Temperance Union.

Works Progress Administration, Project S-149, Indian-Pioneer History Collection. Typescript.

Thomas Gilcrease Institute of American History and Art, Tulsa OK

G. W. Benge Collection

University of Oklahoma Libraries, Western History Collections, University of Oklahoma, Norman OK

Papers of Principal Chief D. W. Bushyhead
Cherokee Nation Papers, Microcopy
C. Johnson Harris Collection
James R. Hendricks Papers
William Charles Rogers Collection

Colonial and State Documents

Acts of the General Assembly of the State of Georgia, Passed in Milledgeville at an Annual Session in November and December, 1829. Published by Authority. Milledgeville: Camak & Ragland, Printers, 1830. In *Session Laws of American States and Territories. Georgia. 1787–1899.* Westport CT: Redgrave Information Resources Corporation, Fiche 64–65.

Acts Passed at the Thirteenth Annual Session of the General Assembly of the State of Alabama, Begun and Held in the Town of Tuscaloosa, on the Third Monday in November, One Thousand Eight Hundred and Thirty-One. Tuscaloosa: Wiley, McGuire & Henry, State Printers, 1832. In *Session Laws of American States and Territories. Alabama. State 1819–1899.* Westport CT: Redgrave Information Resources Corporation, Fiche 17.

Cooper, Thomas, ed. *The Statutes at Large of South Carolina.* Vol. 2. Columbia SC: A. S. Johnston, 1837.

———. *The Statutes at Large of South Carolina.* Vol. 3. Columbia SC: A. S. Johnston, 1838.

McDowell, William L., ed. *Colonial Records of South Carolina: Documents Relating to Indian Affairs, May 21, 1750–August 7, 1754.* Columbia: South Carolina Archives Department, 1958.

———. *Colonial Records of South Carolina: Documents Relating to Indian Affairs, 1754–1765.* Columbia: University of South Carolina Press, 1970.

———. *Colonial Records of South Carolina: Journals of the Commissioners of the Indian Trade, September 20, 1710–August 29, 1718.* Columbia: South Carolina Archives Department, 1955.

Rowland, Dunbar, ed. *The Mississippi Territorial Archives, 1798–1803: Executive Journal of Governor Winthrop Sargent and Governor William Charles Cole Claiborne.* Vol. 1. Nashville: Press of Brandon Printing Company, 1905.

United States Government Documents

American State Papers: Indian Affairs. Vol. 1.

American State Papers: Military Affairs. Vol. 7.

Kappler, Charles J., comp. and ed. *Indian Affairs: Laws and Treaties.*

Vol. 2, *Treaties*. Washington DC: U.S. Government Printing Office, 1904.

Report of the Commissioner of Indian Affairs. 1869–1907.

Report of the Secretary of the Interior. 1869–1907.

Report of the Secretary of War. 1836.

Revised Statutes of the United States. Vol. 18, pt. 1.

United States Commission to the Five Civilized Tribes. *The Final Rolls of Citizens and Freedmen of the Five Civilized Tribes in Indian Territory Prepared by the Commission and Commissioner to the Five Civilized Tribes, and Approved by the Secretary of the Interior on or prior to March 4, 1907*. [Washington DC: U.S. Government Printing Office, 1907?].

————. *Index to the Final Rolls of Citizens and Freedmen of the Five Civilized Tribes in Indian Territory Prepared by the Commission and Commissioner to the Five Civilized Tribes, and Approved by the Secretary of the Interior on or prior to March 4, 1907*. Muskogee OK: Phoenix Printing Company, [1907?].

United States Congressional Serial Set

House Document 108. *Intercourse with Indian Tribes*. 1874. 43rd Cong., 1st sess. Serial 1607.

House Document 177. *Penalty for Selling Liquor to Indians*. 1874. 43rd Cong., 1st sess. Serial 1610.

House Report 227. *Removal of Indians*. 1830. 21st Cong., 1st sess. Serial 200.

House Report 448. *The Committee of Claims, to whom was referred the bill from the Senate (No. 192) entitled "An act for the relief of George W. Paschall" report*. 24 April 1840. 26th Cong., 1st sess. Serial 371.

Senate Document 132. *Memorial of the Legislature of Alabama*. 8 February 1836. 24th Cong., 1st sess. Serial 280.

Senate Document 34. *Letter from the Acting Secretary of War*. 1876. 44th Cong., 1st sess. Serial 1664.

Senate Document 194. *Sale of Intoxicants in Indian and Oklahoma Territories, Etc*. 1904. 58th Cong., 2nd sess. Serial 4591.

Senate Document 143. *Proposed State of Sequoyah*. 1906. 59th Cong., 1st sess. Serial 4912.

U.S. Statutes at Large. Vols. 1, 2, 3, 4, 9, 10, 12, 13, 19, 27, 30, 32 pt. 1, 34 pt. 1.

Other Published Primary Sources

Adair, James. *Adair's History of the American Indians*. Edited by Samuel Cole Williams. Johnson City TN: Watauga Press, 1930; reprint, Nashville: Blue and Gray Press, 1971.

An Address to the People of Indian Territory on the Question of Independent Statehood for Indian Territory, by the Campaign Committee of the Constitutional Convention. Authorized and Assembled August 21, 1905. Muskogee, [Indian Territory]: Phoenix Printing Co., 1905.

Bonnefoy, Antoine. "Journal of Antoine Bonnefoy's Captivity among the Cherokee Indians, 1741–1742." In *Travels in the American Colonies*, edited by Newton D. Mereness, 239–55. New York: Macmillan, 1916.

Calhoun, William. "Journal of William Calhoun." Annotated by Alexander S. Salley. *Publications of the Southern History Association* 8 (1904): 179–95.

Cannon, B. B. "An Overland Journey to the West (October–December 1837)." *Journal of Cherokee Studies* 3 (1978): 166–73.

Chicken, George. "Journal of Colonel George Chicken's Mission from Charleston, S.C., to the Cherokees, 1726 [1725]." In *Travels in the American Colonies*, edited by Newton D. Mereness, 95–172. New York: Macmillan Company, 1916.

Compiled Laws of the Cherokee Nation Published by Authority of the National Council. Tahlequah, I[ndian] T[erritory]: National Advocate Print, 1881.

The Constitution and Laws of the Cherokee Nation: Passed at Tahlequah, Cherokee Nation, 1839–1851. Tahlequah, Cherokee Nation, 1852.

Constitution of the State of Sequoyah. Muskogee, [Indian Territory]: Phoenix Printing Co., [1905?]. In *Western Americana: Frontier History of the Trans-Mississippi West, 1550–1900*. New Haven CT: Research Publications, Inc., 1975. Microfilm No. 2781.

Cuming, Alexander. "Journal of Sir Alexander Cuming (1730)." In *Early Travels in the Tennessee Country, 1540–1800*, edited by Samuel Cole Williams, 115–43. Johnson City TN: Watauga Press, 1928.

Deas, Edward. "Emigrating to the West by Boat (April–May 1838)." *Journal of Cherokee Studies* 3 (1978): 158–63.

De Brahm, John Gerar William. "De Brahm's Account (1756)." In

Early Travels in the Tennessee Country, 1540–1800, edited by Samuel Cole Williams, 187–94. Johnson City TN: Watauga Press, 1928.

———. *De Brahm's Report of the General Survey in the Southern District of North America*. Edited by Louis De Vorsey Jr. Columbia: University of South Carolina Press, 1971.

The Evil of Intoxicating Liquor, and the Remedy. Park Hill [Cherokee Nation]: Mission Press, 1844.

Foreman, Grant, ed. "Notes of a Missionary among the Cherokees." *Chronicles of Oklahoma* 16 (1938): 171–89.

Foreman, Grant, ed. and annot. *A Traveler in Indian Territory: The Journal of Ethan Allen Hitchcock, late Major-General in the United States Army*. With a foreword by Michael D. Green. Norman and London: University of Oklahoma Press, 1996.

———. "Notes of a Missionary among the Cherokees." *Chronicles of Oklahoma* 16 (1938): 171–89.

French, Captain Christopher. "Journal of an Expedition to South Carolina." *Journal of Cherokee Studies* 2 (1977): 275–301.

"From *The Indian Chieftain*: History of Vinita." *Chronicles of Oklahoma* 47 (1969): 336–42.

Gifford, Carolyn De Swarte, ed. *Writing Out My Heart: Selections from the Journal of Frances E. Willard, 1855–96*. Urbana and Chicago: University of Illinois Press, 1995.

Gordon, Harry. "Journal of Captain Harry Gordon's Journey from Pittsburgh down to the Ohio and the Mississippi to New Orleans, Mobile, and Pensacola, 1766." In *Travels in the American Colonies*, edited by Newton D. Mereness, 457–89. New York: Macmillan Company, 1916.

[Grant, Ludovick]. "Historical Relation of Facts Delivered by Ludovick Grant, Indian Trader, to His Excellency the Governor of South Carolina." *South Carolina Historical and Genealogical Magazine* 10 (1909): 54–68.

Gunther, Gerald, ed. *John Marshall's Defense of "McCulloch v. Maryland."* Stanford CA: Stanford University Press, 1969.

Herbert, John. *Journal of Colonel John Herbert: Commissioner of Indian Affairs for the Province of South Carolina, October 17, 1727, to March 19, 1727/8*. Edited by A. S. Salley. Columbia SC: The State Company, 1936.

Holway, Hope, annot. "The Cold Water Army." *Chronicles of Oklahoma* 37 (1959): 22–27.

Jacobs, Wilbur R., ed. *Indians of the Southern Colonial Frontier: The Edmond Atkin Report and Plan of 1755.* Columbia: University of South Carolina Press, 1954.

Laws of the Cherokee Nation: Adopted by the Council at Various Periods. Printed for the Benefit of the Nation. Tahlequah, Cherokee Nation: Cherokee Advocate Office, 1852; reprint, Wilmington DE and London: Scholarly Recourses, Inc., 1973.

Laws of the Cherokee Nation, Passed during the Years 1839–1867, Compiled by Authority of the National Council. St. Louis: Missouri Democrat Print, 1868.

Laws and Joint Resolutions of the Cherokee Nation, Enacted during the Regular and Special Sessions of the Years 1881–2–3. Published by Authority of an Act of the National Council. Tahlequah, Cherokee Nation, 1884; reprint, Wilmington DE and London: Scholarly Resources, Inc., 1975.

Lillybridge, C. "Journey of a Party of Cherokee Emigrants." Edited by Grant Foreman. *Mississippi Valley Historical Review* 18 (1931): 232–45.

Lindsey, Lilah Denton. "Memories of the Indian Territory Mission Field." *Chronicles of Oklahoma* 36 (1958): 181–98.

Lipscomb, Andrew A., ed. *The Writings of Thomas Jefferson.* Vol. 12. Washington DC, Issued under the Auspices of the Thomas Jefferson Memorial Association of the United States, 1903.

Longe, Alexander. "A Small Postscript on the ways and manners of the Indians called Cherokees, the contents of the whole so that you may find everything by the pages. (Modern version edited by David H. Corkran)." *Southern Indian Studies* 21 (1969): 3–49.

Louis-Philippe. *Diary of My Travels in America, Louis-Philippe, King of France, 1830–1848.* Translated by Stephen Becker. New York: Delacorte Press, 1977.

———. *Memoirs, 1773–1793.* Translated by John Hardman. New York: Harcourt Brace Joranovich, 1977.

Marsh, John. *Temperance Recollections: Labors, Defeats, Triumphs. An Autobiography.* New York: Charles Scribner & Co., 1866.

Mereness, Newton D., ed. *Travels in the American Colonies.* New York: Macmillan Company, 1916.

Monypenny, Major Alexander. "Diary of March 20–May 31, 1761." *Journal of Cherokee Studies* 2 (1977): 320–31.

Moulton, Gary E., ed. *The Papers of Chief John Ross*. 2 vols. Norman: University of Oklahoma Press, 1985.

Norton, John. *The Journal of Major John Norton, 1816*. Edited by Carl F. Klinck and James J. Talman. Toronto: The Champlain Society, 1970.

Nuttal, Thomas. *A Journal of Travels into the Arkansas Territory during the Year 1819*. Edited by Savoie Lottinville. Norman: University of Oklahoma Press, 1980.

Oliver, Alice W. "Notes on the Carancahua Indians." In *The Karankawa Indians, The Coast People of Texas*, edited by Albert S. Gatschet, 15–20. Archaeology and Ethnological Papers of the Peabody Museum, Harvard University, vol. 1, no. 2. Cambridge MA: Peabody Museum of American Archaeology and Ethnology, 1891.

Perdue, Theda. *Nations Remembered: An Oral History of the Five Civilized Tribes, 1865–1907*. Westport CT: Greenwood Press, 1980.

Perdue, Theda, ed. *Cherokee Editor: The Writings of Elias Boudinot*. Knoxville: University of Tennessee Press, 1983.

Perdue, Theda, and Michael D. Green, eds. *The Cherokee Removal: A Brief History with Documents*. The Bedford Series in History and Culture. Boston and New York: Bedford Books of St. Martin's Press, 1995.

Prucha, Francis Paul, ed. *Cherokee Removal: The "William Penn" Essays and Other Writings*. Knoxville: University of Tennessee Press, 1981.

———. *Documents of United States Indian Policy*. Lincoln: University of Nebraska Press, 1975.

Richardson, James D., comp. *A Compilation of the Messages and Papers of the Presidents, 1789–1897*. Vol. 1. Washington DC: U.S. Government Printing Office, 1899.

Schneider, Martin. "Bro. Martin Schneider's Report of his Journey to the Upper Cherokee Towns (1783–1784)." In *Early Travels in the Tennessee Country, 1540–1800*, edited by Samuel Cole Williams, 245–65. Johnson City TN: Watauga Press, 1928.

Scott, Winfield. "Address." *Journal of Cherokee Studies* 3 (1978): 145.

Steiner, Abraham, and Frederick C. de Schweinitz. "Report of the

Journey of the Brethren Abraham Steiner and Frederick C. De Schweinitz to the Cherokees and the Cumberland Settlements (1799)." In *Early Travels in the Tennessee Country, 1540–1800*, edited by Samuel Cole Williams, 445–525. Johnson City TN: Watauga Press, 1928.

Thoburn, Joseph B., annot. "Letters of Cassandra Sawyer Lockwood: Dwight Mission, 1834." *Chronicles of Oklahoma* 33 (1955): 202–25.

Timberlake, Henry. *Lieut. Henry Timberlake's Memoirs, 1756–1765.* Annotated by Samuel Cole Williams. Johnson City TN: Watauga Press, 1927; reprint, Marietta GA: Continental Book Company, 1948.

Timmons, Boyce D., and Alice Tyner Timmons, eds. and revs. *Authenticated Rolls of 1880: Cherokee Nation–Indian Territory.* N.p.: Chi-ga-u, Inc., 1978.

Waselkov, Gregory A., and Kathryn E. Holland Braund, eds. and annots. *William Bartram on the Southeastern Indians.* Lincoln and London: University of Nebraska Press, 1995.

Webster, Captain L. B. "Letters from a Lonely Soldier." *Journal of Cherokee Studies* 3 (1978): 153–57.

Willard, Frances E. *Glimpses of Fifty Years: The Autobiography of An American Woman.* Chicago: Woman's Temperance Publication Association, 1889.

Periodicals and Newspapers

Arkansas Gazette. Arkansas Post AR. 1819–1836.

Arkansas State Gazette. Little Rock AR. 1836–1866.

Champion. Muskogee, Indian Territory. October, November 1904; June, September 1905; March, May, June, July, August, 1906.

Cherokee Advocate. Tahlequah, Cherokee Nation. 26 September 1844–3 March 1906. Suspended 28 September 1853–April 1870.

Cherokee Almanac. Park Hill, Cherokee Nation. 1838, 1840, 1844, 1846–1853, 1855–1860.

Cherokee Messenger. Breadtown, Cherokee Nation. 1844–1846.

Cherokee Phoenix. New Echota, Cherokee Nation. 21 February 1828–31 May 1834.

Cherokee Rose Buds. [Park Hill], Cherokee Nation. 2 August 1854.

Helper. Tulsa, Indian Territory. January, March, May, July, August,

September 1907.

Helper. Wewoka OK. January, August 1908.

Missionary Herald. Boston MA. 1821–1861.

Muskogee Democrat. Muskogee, Indian Territory. June 1904–October 1905.

Muskogee Evening Times. Muskogee, Indian Territory. 4 September 1900–30 August 1902.

Muskogee Phoenix. Muskogee, Indian Territory. 23 February 1888–13 December 1900.

Muskogee Times-Democrat. Muskogee, Indian Territory. 20 February 1906–12 October 1910.

Oklahoma Messenger. Oklahoma City OK. November 1907; October 1909.

Oklahoma Messenger. Wellston OK. February 1924.

South-Carolina Gazette. Charleston SC. May 1745.

Union Signal. Chicago IL. January 1883–November 1903; Evanston IL. December 1903–December 1908.

A Wreath of Cherokee Rose Buds. [Park Hill], Cherokee Nation. 1 August 1855.

PUBLISHED WORKS

Abel, Annie Heloise. *The American Indian as Slaveholder and Secessionist.* With an introduction by Theda Perdue and Michael D. Green. Cleveland: Arthur H. Clark Co., 1915; reprint, Lincoln and London: University of Nebraska Press, 1992.

———. *The American Indian in the Civil War, 1862–1865.* With an introduction by Theda Perdue and Michael D. Green. Cleveland: A. H. Clark Co., 1919; reprint, Lincoln and London: University of Nebraska Press, 1992.

Agnew, Brad. "A Legacy of Education: The History of the Cherokee Seminaries." *Chronicles of Oklahoma* 63 (1985): 128–47.

Aldrich, Duncan M. "General Stores, Retail Merchants, and Assimilation: Retail Trade in the Cherokee Nation, 1838–1890." *Chronicles of Oklahoma* 57 (1979): 119–36.

Anderson, William A., ed. *Cherokee Removal: Before and After.* Athens and London: University of Georgia Press, 1991.

Andrew, John A., III. *From Revivals to Removal: Jeremiah Evarts, the*

Cherokee Nation, and the Search for the Soul of America. Athens and London: University of Georgia Press, 1992.

Axtell, James. *After Columbus: Essays in the Ethnohistory of Colonial North America.* New York and Oxford: Oxford University Press, 1988.

———. *Beyond 1492: Encounters in Colonial North America.* New York and Oxford: Oxford University Press, 1992.

Baker, Joan M. "Alcoholism and the American Indian." In *Alcoholism: Development, Consequences, and Interventions,* edited by Nada J. Estes and M. Edith Heinemann, 194–203. St. Louis MO: C. V. Mosby, 1977.

Balyeat, Frank A. "Joseph Samuel Murrow, Apostle to the Indians." *Chronicles of Oklahoma* 35 (1957): 297–313.

Bearss, Edwin C. "The Arkansas Whiskey War: A Fort Smith Case Study." *Journal of the West* 7 (1968): 143–72.

Benedict, John Downing. *Muskogee and Northeastern Oklahoma including the Counties of Muskogee, McIntosh, Wagoner, Cherokee, Sequoyah, Adair, Delaware, Mayes, Rogers, Washington, Nowata, Craig and Ottawa.* Vol. 3. Chicago: S. J. Clarke Publishing Company, 1922.

Berkhofer, Robert F., Jr. *Salvation and the Savage: An Analysis of Protestant Missions and American Indian Response.* Lexington: University of Kentucky Press, 1965.

———. *The White Man's Indian: Images of the American Indian from Columbus to the Present.* New York: Alfred A. Knopf, 1978.

Bird, S. Elizabeth, ed. *Dressing in Feathers: The Construction of the Indian in American Popular Culture.* Boulder CO: Westview Press, 1996.

Blochowiak, Mary Ann. "'Woman with a Hatchet': Carry Nation Comes to Oklahoma Territory." *Chronicles of Oklahoma* 59 (1981): 132–51.

Blocker, Jack S., Jr. *"Give to the Winds Thy Fears": The Women's Temperance Crusade, 1873–1874.* Westport CT: Greenwood Press, 1985.

Bloom, Leonard. "The Acculturation of the Eastern Cherokee: Historical Aspect." *North Carolina Historical Review* 19 (1942): 323–58.

Bordin, Ruth. *Frances Willard: A Biography.* Chapel Hill and London: University of North Carolina Press, 1986.

————. *Woman and Temperance: The Quest for Power and Liberty, 1873–1900*. Philadelphia: Temple University Press, 1981.

Bourke, John G. "Distillation by Early American Indians." *American Anthropologist* 7 (1894): 297–99.

Braund, Kathryn E. Holland. *Deerskins and Duffels: The Creek Indian Trade with Anglo-America, 1685–1815*. Lincoln and London: University of Nebraska Press, 1993.

————. "Guardians of Tradition and Handmaidens of Change: Women's Roles in Creek Economic and Social Life during the Eighteenth Century." *American Indian Quarterly* 14 (1990): 239–58.

Brod, Thomas M. "Alcoholism as a Mental Health Problem of Native Americans: A Review of the Literature." *Archives of General Psychiatry* 32 (1975): 1385–91.

Broemeling, Carol B. "Cherokee Indian Agents, 1830–1874." *Chronicles of Oklahoma* 50 (Winter 1972–73): 437–57.

Brown, John P. *Old Frontiers: The Story of the Cherokee Indians from Earliest Times to the Date of Their Removal to the West, 1838*. Kingsport TN: Southern Publishers, Inc., 1938.

Brown, Thomas Elton. "Oklahoma's 'Born-Dry Law' and the Roman Catholic Church." *Chronicles of Oklahoma* 52 (1974): 316–30.

Burton, Jeffrey. *Indian Territory and the United States, 1866–1906: Courts, Government, and the Movement for Oklahoma Statehood*. Norman and London: University of Oklahoma Press, 1995.

Carpenter, Edmund S. "Alcohol in the Iroquois Dream Quest." *American Journal of Psychiatry* 116 (1959): 148–51.

Carson, James Taylor. *Searching for the Bright Path: The Mississippi Choctaws from Prehistory to Removal*. Lincoln and London: University of Nebraska Press, 1999.

Chapin, Clara C. *Thumb Nail Sketches of White Ribbon Women*. Chicago: Woman's Temperance Publishing Association, The Temple, 1895.

Clark, Norman H. *Deliver Us from Evil: An Interpretation of American Prohibition*. New York: Norton, 1976.

Corry, John Pitts. *Indian Affairs in Georgia, 1732–1756*. Philadelphia: George S. Ferguson Co., 1936.

Crockett, Bernice Norman. "Health Conditions in the Indian Territory from the Civil War to 1890." *Chronicles of Oklahoma* 36 (1958): 21–39.

Dailey, R. C. "The Role of Alcohol among North American Indian Tribes as Reported in The Jesuit Relations." *Anthropologica* 10 (1968): 45–57.

Danky, James Philip, ed. *Native American Periodicals and Newspapers, 1828–1982: Bibliography, Publishing Record, and Holdings.* Westport CT: Greenwood Press, 1984.

Dannenbaum, Jed. "The Origins of Temperance Activism and Militancy among American Women." *Journal of Social History* 15 (1981): 235–54.

Debo, Angie. *A History of the Indians of the United States.* Norman: University of Oklahoma Press, 1970.

De Vorsey, Louis, Jr. *The Indian Boundary in the Southern Colonies, 1763–1775.* Chapel Hill: University of North Carolina Press, 1961.

DeWitt, Donald L. *American Indian Resource Materials in the Western History Collections, University of Oklahoma.* Norman and London: University of Oklahoma Press, 1990.

DeWitt, Donald L., comp. and ed. *Guide to Manuscript Collections, Western History Collections, University of Oklahoma.* Bowie MD: Heritage Books, Inc., 1994.

Dorchester, Daniel. *The Liquor Problem in All Ages.* New York: Phillips & Hunt, 1884; reprint, New York: Arno Press, 1981.

Dowd, Gregory Evans. *A Spirited Resistance: The North American Struggle for Unity, 1745–1815.* Baltimore: Johns Hopkins University Press, 1992.

Dozier, Edward P. "Problem Drinking among American Indians: The Role of Sociocultural Deprivation." *Quarterly Journal of Studies on Alcohol* 27 (1966): 72–87.

"Dwight Mission." *Chronicles of Oklahoma* 12 (1934): 42–51.

Edmunds, R. David. *The Shawnee Prophet.* Lincoln: University of Nebraska Press, 1985.

Epstein, Barbara Leslie. *The Politics of Domesticity: Women, Evangelism, and Temperance in Nineteenth-Century America.* Middletown CT: Wesleyan University Press, 1981.

Ezell, John S. "'Demon Rum' and the Five Civilized Tribes 1754–1861." *Mid-America: An Historical Review* 72 (1990): 3–24.

Fairbanks, Charles H. "The Function of Black Drink among the Creeks." In *Black Drink: A Native American Tea,* edited by Charles M. Hudson, 120–149. Athens: University of Georgia Press, 1979.

Finney, Frank F. "The Osage Indians and the Liquor Problem before Oklahoma Statehood." *Chronicles of Oklahoma* 34 (Winter 1956–57): 456–64.

Fischer, LeRoy H. "United States Indian Agents to the Five Civilized Tribes." *Chronicles of Oklahoma* 50 (Winter 1972–73): 410–14.

Fogelson, Raymond D. "Major John Norton as Ethno-ethnologist." *Journal of Cherokee Studies* 3 (1978): 250–55.

Foreman, Carolyn Thomas. "The Armstrongs of Indian Territory." Part 2, "William Armstrong." *Chronicles of Oklahoma* 30 (Winter 1952–53): 420–53.

———. "Augusta Robertson Moore, A Sketch of Her Life and Times." *Chronicles of Oklahoma* 13 (1935): 399–420.

———. "Fairfield Mission." *Chronicles of Oklahoma* 27 (Winter 1949–50): 373–88.

———. "General Benjamin Henry Grierson." *Chronicles of Oklahoma* 24 (1946): 195–218.

———. "General William Babcock Hazen." *Chronicles of Oklahoma* 20 (1942): 322–42.

———. "Gustavus Loomis: Commandant Fort Gibson and Fort Towson." *Chronicles of Oklahoma* 18 (1940): 219–28.

———. "Mrs. Laura E. Harsha." *Chronicles of Oklahoma* 18 (1940): 182–84.

———. "Military Discipline in Early Oklahoma." *Chronicles of Oklahoma* 6 (1928): 140–44.

———. "Notes on the Chickasaw Light-Horsemen." *Chronicles of Oklahoma* 34 (Winter 1956–57): 484–85.

———. *Oklahoma Imprints, 1835–1907; A History of Printing in Oklahoma before Statehood*. Norman: University of Oklahoma Press, 1936.

———. *Park Hill*. Muskogee OK: Star Printery, 1948.

———. "Pierce Mason Butler." *Chronicles of Oklahoma* 30 (1959): 6–28.

———. "Miss Sophia Sawyer and Her School." *Chronicles of Oklahoma* 32 (Winter 1954–55): 395–413.

Foreman, Grant. *Advancing the Frontier, 1830–1860*. Norman: University of Oklahoma Press, 1933.

———. "A Century of Prohibition." *Chronicles of Oklahoma* 12 (1934): 133–41.

———. "Early Trails through Oklahoma." *Chronicles of Oklahoma* 3 (1925): 99–119.

———. *The Five Civilized Tribes: Cherokee, Chickasaw, Choctaw, Creek, Seminole.* Norman: University of Oklahoma Press, 1934.

———. *Indian Removal: The Emigration of the Five Civilized Tribes of Indians.* Norman: University of Oklahoma Press, 1932.

———. "Some New Light on Houston's Life among the Cherokee Indians." *Chronicles of Oklahoma* 9 (1931): 139–52.

Foster, William Omer. "The Career of Montfort Stokes in Oklahoma." *Chronicles of Oklahoma* 18 (1940): 35–52.

Franklin, Jimmie Lewis. *Born Sober: Prohibition in Oklahoma, 1907–1959.* With a foreword by J. Howard Edmondson. Norman: University of Oklahoma Press, 1971.

———. "That Noble Experiment: A Note on Prohibition in Oklahoma." *Chronicles of Oklahoma* 43 (1965): 19–34.

Frederickson, Otto Frovin. *The Liquor Question among the Indian Tribes in Kansas, 1804–1881.* Bulletin of the University of Kansas, Humanistic Studies, vol. 4, no. 4. Lawrence: University of Kansas Department of Journalism Press, 1932.

French, Lawrence A., and Jim Hornbuckle. "Alcoholism among Native Americans: An Analysis." *Social Work* 25 (1980): 275–80.

Fullerton, Eula E. "The Story of the Telephone in Oklahoma." *Chronicles of Oklahoma* 12 (1934): 251–57.

Garrison, Tim Alan. *The Legal Ideology of Removal: The Southern Judiciary and the Sovereignty of Native American Nations.* Athens and London: University of Georgia Press, 2002.

Gordon, Anna A. *The Beautiful Life of Frances E. Willard.* Chicago: Woman's Temperance Publishing Association, 1898.

Green, Michael D. *The Politics of Indian Removal: Creek Government and Society in Crisis.* Lincoln and London: University of Nebraska Press, 1982.

Hagan, William T. *Indian Police and Judges: Experiments in Acculturation and Control.* New Haven CT and London: Yale University Press, 1966.

Hamer, John H. "Acculturation Stress and the Functions of Alcohol among the Forest Potawatomi." *Quarterly Journal of Studies on Alcohol* 26 (1965): 285–302.

Hammond, Sue. "Socioeconomic Reconstruction in the Cherokee Nation, 1865–1870." *Chronicles of Oklahoma* 56 (1978): 158–70.

Hanaford, Phebe A. *Daughters of America; or, Women of the Century.* Boston: B. B. Russell, 1883.

Hargrett, Lester. *A Bibliography of the Constitutions and Laws of the American Indians.* Cambridge MA: Harvard University Press, 1947.

Harman, S. W. *Hell on the Border; He Hanged Eighty-Eight Men. A History of the Great United States Criminal Court at Fort Smith, Arkansas, and of Crime and Criminals in the Indian Territory, and the Trial and Punishment thereof before His Honor Judge Isaac C. Parker, "The Terror of Law-Breakers," and by the Courts of Said Territory, Embracing the Leading Sentences and Changes to Grand and Petit Juries Deliverd [sic] by the World Famous Jurist His Acknowledged Masterpieces. Besides Much Other Legal Lore of Untold Value to Attorneys, and of Interest to Readers in Every Walk of Life a Book for the Millions Illustrated with Over Fifty Fine Half Tones.* Compiled by C. P. Sterns. Fort Smith AR: Phoenix Publishing Company, 1898.

Hatley, Tom. *The Dividing Paths: Cherokees and South Carolinians through the Era of Revolution.* New York and Oxford: Oxford University Press, 1993.

Hayes, Jerry G. "Ardent Spirits among the Chickasaws and Choctaws, 1816–1856." *Chronicles of Oklahoma* 69 (1991): 294–309.

Hertzberg, Hazel W. *The Search for an American Indian Identity: Modern Pan-Indian Movements.* Syracuse: Syracuse University Press, 1971.

Hill, Edward E. *The Office of Indian Affairs, 1824–1880: Historical Sketches.* New York: Clearwater Publishing Company, Inc., 1974.

Hill, Thomas W. "Ethnohistory and Alcohol Studies." In *Recent Developments in Alcoholism*, edited by Marc Galanter. Vol. 2, *Learning and Social Models, Alcohol and the Liver, Aging and Alcoholism, Anthropology*, 313–37. New York and London: Plenum Press, 1984.

Hillerman, Abbie B., comp. *1888–1925 History of the Woman's Christian Temperance Union of Indian Territory, Oklahoma Territory, State of Oklahoma.* Sapulpa OK: Jennings Printing & Stationery Co., [1925?].

"The Hon. Alice M. Robertson." *Chronicles of Oklahoma* 10 (1932): 13–17.

Hudson, Charles. *The Southeastern Indians.* Knoxville: University of Tennessee Press, 1976.

Hudson, Charles M., ed. *Black Drink: A Native American Tea.* Athens: University of Georgia Press, 1979.

Hudson, Peter J. "Temperance Meetings Among the Choctaws." *Chronicles of Oklahoma* 12 (1934): 130–32.

Hunter, Charles E. "The Delaware Nativist Revival of the Mid-Eighteenth Century." *Ethnohistory* 18 (1971): 39–49.

Ishii, Izumi. "Alcohol and Politics in the Cherokee Nation before Removal." *Ethnohistory* 50 (2003): 671–95.

———. "'Not A Wigwam Nor Blanket Nor Warwhoop': Cherokees and the Woman's Christian Temperance Union." *Journal of American and Canadian Studies* 18 (2000): 1–15.

Jacob, Wilbur R. *Dispossessing the American Indian: Indians and Whites on the Colonial Frontier.* New York: Scribner, 1972.

———. *Wilderness Politics and Indian Gifts: The Northern Colonial Frontier, 1748–1763.* Lincoln: University of Nebraska Press, 1950.

James, Louise Boyd. "The Woman Suffrage Issue in the Oklahoma Constitutional Convention." *Chronicles of Oklahoma* 56 (Winter 1978–79): 379–92.

Jimerson, Randall C., Francis X. Blouin, and Charles A. Isetts, eds. *Guide to the Microfilm Edition of the Temperance and Prohibition Papers.* Ann Arbor: University of Michigan, 1977.

Johnson, Steven L. *Guide to American Indian Documents in the Congressional Serial Set: 1817–1899.* New York and Paris: Clearwater Publishing Company, Inc., 1977.

Jordan, Jerry Wright, comp. *Cherokee by Blood: Records of Eastern Cherokee Ancestry in the U.S. Court of Claims 1906–1910.* Vol. 6, *Applications 13261 to 16745.* Bowie MD: Heritage Books, Inc., 1990.

King, Duane H., ed. *The Cherokee Indian Nation: A Troubled History.* Knoxville: University of Tennessee Press, 1979.

Kunitz, Stephen J., and Jerrold E. Levy with Tracy Andrews, Chena DuPuy, K. Ruben Gabriel, and Scott Russell. *Drinking Careers: A Twenty-five-year Study of Three Navajo Populations.* New Haven CT and London: Yale University Press, 1994.

Kunitz, Stephen J., and Jerrold E. Levy with K. Ruben Gabriel, Gilbert Quintero, Eric Henderson, Joanne McCloskey, and Scott Russell. *Drinking, Conduct Disorder, and Social Change: Navajo Experiences*. Oxford: Oxford University Press, 2000.

Kupferer, Harriet J., and John A. Humphrey. "Fatal Indian Violence in North Carolina." *Anthropological Quarterly* 48 (1975): 236–44.

Kutsche, Paul. *A Guide to Cherokee Documents in the Northeastern United States*. Native American Bibliography Series, no. 7. Metuchen NJ and London: Scarecrow Press, Inc., 1986.

Kvasnicka, Robert M., and Herman H. Viola, eds. *The Commissioners of Indian Affairs, 1824–1977*. With a foreword by Philleo Nash. Lincoln and London: University of Nebraska Press, 1979.

Leland, Joy. *Firewater Myths: North American Indian Drinking and Alcohol Addiction*. Monographs of the Rutgers Center of Alcohol Studies, no. 11. New Brunswick NJ: Publications Division, Rutgers Center of Alcohol Studies, 1976.

———. "Women and Alcohol in an Indian Settlement." *Medical Anthropology* 2 (1978): 85–119.

Lemert, Edwin M. *Alcohol and the Northwest Coast Indians*. University of California Publications in Culture and Society, vol. 2, no. 6. Berkeley and Los Angeles: University of California Press, 1954.

Levy, Jerrold E., and Stephen J. Kunitz. *Indian Drinking: Navajo Practices and Anglo-American Theories*. New York: John Wiley & Sons, Inc.,1974.

Logan, John Henry. *A History of the Upper Country of South Carolina, from the Earliest Periods to the Close of the War of Independence*. Charleston: S. G. Courtenay & Co., 1859; reprint, Spartanburg SC: Reprint Co., 1960.

Lurie, Nancy Oestreich. "The World's Oldest On-Going Protest Demonstration: North American Indian Drinking Patterns." *Pacific Historical Review* 40 (1971): 311–32.

MacAndrew, Craig, and Robert B. Edgerton. *Drunken Comportment: A Social Explanation*. Chicago: Aldine Publishing Company, 1969.

Mail, Patricia D., and David R. McDonald, comps. *Tulapai to Tokay: A Bibliography of Alcohol Use and Abuse among Native Americans of North America*. With a foreword and literature review by Joy

H. Leland and indexes by Sandra Norris. New Haven CT: Hraf Press, 1980.

Mancall, Peter C. "'The Bewitching Tyranny of Custom': The Social Costs of Indian Drinking in Colonial America." *American Indian Culture and Research Journal* 17 (1993): 15–42.

———. *Deadly Medicine: Indians and Alcohol in Early America.* Ithaca NY and London: Cornell University Press, 1995.

———. "Men, Women, and Alcohol in Indian Villages in the Great Lakes Region in the Early Republic." *Journal of the Early Republic* 15 (1995): 425–48.

Maxwell, Amos. "The Sequoyah Convention." *Chronicles of Oklahoma* 28 (1950): 161–92.

May, Philip A. "The Epidemiology of Alcohol Abuse among American Indians: The Mythical and Real Properties." *American Indian Culture and Research Journal* 18 (1994): 121–43.

McLoughlin, William G. *After the Trail of Tears: The Cherokees' Struggle for Sovereignty, 1839–1880.* Chapel Hill and London: University of North Carolina Press, 1993.

———. *Champions of the Cherokees: Evan and John B. Jones.* Princeton NJ: Princeton University Press, 1990.

———. *Cherokee Renascence in the New Republic.* Princeton NJ: Princeton University Press, 1986.

———. *The Cherokees and Christianity, 1794–1870: Essays on Acculturation and Cultural Persistence.* Edited by Walter H. Conser Jr. Athens and London: University of Georgia Press, 1994.

———. *Cherokees and Missionaries, 1789–1839.* New Haven CT and London: Yale University Press, 1984.

———. "Parson Blackburn's Whiskey and the Cherokee Indian Schools, 1809–1810." *Journal of Presbyterian History* 57 (1979): 427–45.

McLoughlin, William G., with Walter J. Conser Jr. and Virginia Duffy McLoughlin. *The Cherokee Ghost Dance: Essays on the Southeastern Indians 1789–1861.* [Macon GA]: Mercer University Press, 1984.

Meriwether, Robert L. *The Expansion of South Carolina, 1729–1765.* Kingsport TN: Southern Publishers, Inc., 1940.

Merrell, James H. *The Indians' New World: Catawbas and Their*

Neighbors from European Contact through the Era of Removal. Chapel Hill: University of North Carolina Press, 1989.

Merrill, William L. "The Beloved Tree: *Ilex vomitoria* among the Indians of the Southeastern and Adjacent Regions." In *Black Drink: A Native American Tea*, edited by Charles M. Hudson, 40–82. Athens: University of Georgia Press, 1979.

Merton, Robert K. "Social Structure and Anomie." *American Sociological Review* 3 (1938): 672–82.

Mihesuah, Devon A. *Cultivating the Rosebuds: The Education of Women at the Cherokee Female Seminary, 1851–1909*. Urbana and Chicago: University of Illinois Press, 1993.

———. "Too Dark to Be Angels: The Class System among the Cherokees at the Female Seminary." *American Indian Culture and Research Journal* 15 (1991): 29–52.

Miller, Christopher, and George R. Hammell. "A New Perspective on Indian-White Contact: Cultural Symbols and Colonial Trade." *Journal of American History* 73 (1986): 311–28.

Milling, Chapman J. *Red Carolinians*. Chapel Hill: University of North Carolina Press, 1940.

Miner, H. Craig. "Cherokee Sovereignty in the Gilded Age: The Outlet Question." *Chronicles of Oklahoma* 71 (1993): 118–37.

Misch, Mrs. J. O. "Lilah D. Lindsey." *Chronicles of Oklahoma* 33 (1955): 193–201.

Mohatt, Gerald. "The Sacred Water: The Quest for Personal Power through Drinking among the Teton Sioux." In *The Drinking Man*, edited by David C. McClelland, William N. Davis, Rudolf Kalin, and Eric Wanner, 261–75. New York: The Free Press, 1972.

Mooney, James. "The Cherokee Ball Play." *American Anthropologist* 3 (1890): 105–32.

———. *James Mooney's History, Myths, and Sacred Formulas of the Cherokees: Containing the full texts of "Myths of the Cherokee" (1900) and "The Sacred Formulas of the Cherokees" (1891) as published by the Bureau of American Ethnology*. With a new biographical introduction, "James Mooney and the Eastern Cherokees," by George Ellison. Asheville NC: Historical Images, 1992.

Mooney, Thomas G. *Exploring Your Cherokee Ancestry: A Basic Genealogical Research Guide*. Tahlequah OK: Cherokee National Historical Society, Inc., 1987.

Morris, John Wesley. *Historical Atlas of Oklahoma*. Norman: University of Oklahoma Press, 1986.

Morrison, James D. "The Union Pacific, Southern Branch." *Chronicles of Oklahoma* 14 (1936): 173–88.

Moulton, Gary E. *John Ross: Cherokee Chief*. Athens and London: University of Georgia Press, 1978.

Norgren, Jill. *The Cherokee Case: The Confrontation of Law and Politics*. New York: McGraw-Hill, 1996.

Norgren, Jill L., and Petra T. Shattuck. "Limits of Legal Action: The Cherokee Cases." *American Indian Culture and Research Journal* 2 (1978): 14–25.

O'Beirne, H. F., and E. S. O'Beirne. *The Indian Territory: Its Chiefs, Legislators and Leading Men*. St. Louis MO: C. B. Woodward Company, 1892.

Park, Hugh. *Reminiscences of the Indians by Cephas Washburn*. Van Buren AR: The Press-Argus, 1955.

Perdue, Theda. *Cherokee Women: Gender and Culture Change, 1700–1835*. Lincoln and London: University of Nebraska Press, 1998.

———. "Cherokee Women and the Trail of Tears." *Journal of Women's History* 1 (1989): 14–30.

———. "The Conflict Within: Cherokees and Removal." In *Cherokee Removal: Before and After*, edited by William A. Anderson, 55–74. Athens and London: University of Georgia Press, 1991.

———. "Rising from the Ashes: The *Cherokee Phoenix* as an Ethnohistorical Source." *Ethnohistory* 24 (1977): 207–18.

———. *Slavery and the Evolution of Cherokee Society, 1540–1866*. Knoxville: University of Tennessee Press, 1979.

Peters, Bernard C. "Hypocrisy on the Great Lakes Frontier: The Use of Whiskey by the Michigan Department of Indian Affairs." *Michigan Historical Review* 18 (1992): 1–13.

Price, John A. "An Applied Analysis of North American Indian Drinking Patterns." *Human Organization* 34 (1975): 17–26.

Prucha, Francis Paul. *American Indian Policy in the Formative Years: The Indian Trade and Intercourse Acts, 1790–1834*. Cambridge MA: Harvard University Press, 1962; reprint, Lincoln: University of Nebraska Press, 1970.

———. *The Great Father: The United States Government and the Am-*

erican Indians. 2 vols. Lincoln and London: University of Nebraska Press, 1984.

Reese, Linda Williams. *Women of Oklahoma, 1890–1920.* Norman and London: University of Oklahoma Press, 1997.

Reid, John Phillip. *A Better Kind of Hatchet: Law, Trade, and Diplomacy in the Cherokee Nation during the Early Years of European Contact.* University Park and London: Pennsylvania State University Press, 1976.

Rights, Douglas L. "The Trading Path to the Indians." *Southern Indian Studies* 38 (1989): 49–73.

Romans, Bernard. *A Concise Natural History of East and West Florida.* Gainesville: University of Florida Press, 1962.

Room, Robin. "Alcohol and Ethnography: A Case of Problem Deflation?" *Current Anthropology* 25 (1984): 169–91.

Rorabaugh, W. J. *The Alcoholic Republic: An American Tradition.* Oxford: Oxford University Press, 1979.

———. "Estimated U.S. Alcoholic Beverage Consumption, 1790–1860." *Journal of Studies on Alcohol* 37 (1976): 357–64.

Rothrock, Mary W. "Carolina Traders among the Overhill Cherokees, 1690–1760." *East Tennessee Historical Society's Publications* 1 (1929): 3–18.

Routh, E. C. "Early Missionaries to the Cherokees." *Chronicles of Oklahoma* 15 (1937): 449–65.

Sanders, J. G., comp. *Who's Who among Oklahoma Indians.* Oklahoma City: Trave Company, 1928.

Satz, Ronald N. *American Indian Policy in the Jacksonian Era.* Lincoln: University of Nebraska Press, 1975.

Saunt, Claudio. *A New Order of Things: Property, Power, and the Transformation of the Creek Indians, 1733–1816.* Cambridge: Cambridge University Press, 1999.

Schwarze, Edmund. *History of the Moravian Mission among the Southern Indian Tribes of the United States.* Bethlehem PA: Times Publishing Co., 1923.

Self, Nancy Hope. "The Building of the Railroads in the Cherokee Nation." *Chronicles of Oklahoma* 49 (1971): 180–205.

Sheehan, Bernard W. *Seeds of Extinction: Jeffersonian Philanthropy and the American Indian.* Chapel Hill: University of North Carolina Press, 1973; reprint, New York: W. W. Norton & Company, Inc., 1974.

Shirk, George H. "Some Letters from the Reverend Samuel A. Worcester at Park Hill." *Chronicles of Oklahoma* 26 (Winter 1948–49): 468–78.

Smith, Betty Anderson. "Distribution of Eighteenth-Century Cherokee Settlements." In *The Cherokee Indian Nation: A Troubled History*, edited by Duane H. King, 46–60. Knoxville: University of Tennessee Press, 1979.

Smith, William Roy. *South Carolina as a Royal Province 1719–1776.* [New York: Macmillan,] 1903; reprint, Freeport NY: Books for Libraries Press, 1970.

Southwell, Kristina L., rev. and ed. *Cherokee Nation Papers: Inventory and Index.* Norman OK: Associates of the Western History Collections, 1996.

Starr, Emmet. *History of the Cherokee Indians and Their Legends and Folk Lore.* Oklahoma City: The Warden Company, 1921; reprint, Millwood NY: Kraus Reprint Co., 1977.

Stein, Gary C. "A Fearful Drunkenness: The Liquor Trade to the Western Indians as Seen by European Travelers in America, 1800–1860." *Red River Valley Historical Review* 1 (1974): 109–21.

Stratton, Ray. "Variations in Alcohol Problems within the Oklahoma Indian Population." *Alcohol Technical Reports* 6 (1977): 5–12.

Stratton, Ray, Arthur Zeiner, and Alfonso Paredes. "Tribal Affiliation and Prevalence of Alcohol Problems." *Journal of Studies on Alcohol* 39 (1978): 1166–77.

Stewart, Omer C. "Contemporary Document on Wavoka (Jack Wilson) Prophet on the Ghost Dance in 1890." *Ethnohistory* 24 (1977): 219–22.

Swanton, John R. *The Indians of the Southeastern United States.* Washington DC: U.S. Government Printing Office, 1946; reprint, Washington and London: Smithsonian Institution Press, 1979.

Taylor, William B. *Drinking, Homicide and Rebellion in Colonial Mexican Villages.* Stanford CA: Stanford University Press, 1979.

Topper, Martin D. "Navajo 'Alcoholism': Drinking, Alcohol Abuse, and Treatment in a Changing Cultural Environment." In *The American Experience with Alcohol: Contrasting Cultural Perspec-*

tives, edited by Linda A. Bennett and Genevieve M. Ames, 227–51. New York and London: Plenum Press, 1985.

Travis, V. A. "Life in the Cherokee Nation a Decade after the Civil War." *Chronicles of Oklahoma* 4 (1926): 16–30.

Tyler, Alice Felt. *Freedom's Ferment: Phases of American Social History to 1860*. Minneapolis: University of Minnesota Press, 1944.

Tyrrell, Ian R. *Sobering Up: From Temperance to Prohibition in Antebellum America, 1800–1860*. Westport CT: Greenwood Press, 1979.

———. *Woman's World Woman's Empire: The Woman's Christian Temperance Union in International Perspective, 1880–1930*. Chapel Hill and London: University of North Carolina Press, 1991.

Unrau, William E. "Indian Prohibition and Tribal Disorganization in the Trans-Missouri West, 1802–1862." *Contemporary Drug Problems* 21 (1994): 519–33.

———. *White Mans' Wicked Water: The Alcohol Trade and Prohibition in Indian Country, 1802–1892*. Lawrence: University Press of Kansas, 1996.

Usner, Daniel H., Jr. *American Indians in the Lower Mississippi Valley: Social and Economic Histories*. Lincoln: University of Nebraska Press, 1998.

———. *Indians, Settlers, & Slaves in a Frontier Exchange Economy: The Lower Mississippi Valley before 1783*. Chapel Hill: University of North Carolina Press, 1992.

Waddell, Jack O. "Malhiot's Journal: An Ethnohistoric Assessment of Chippewa Alcohol Behavior in the Early Nineteenth Century." *Ethnohistory* 32 (1985): 246–68.

Waddell, Jack O., and Michael W. Everett, eds. *Drinking Behavior Among Southwestern Indians: An Anthropological Perspective*. Tucson: University of Arizona Press, 1980.

Wallace, Anthony F. C. *The Death and Rebirth of the Seneca*. New York: Alfred A. Knopf, 1970.

———. "Revitalization Movements: Some Theoretical Consideration for Their Comparative Study." *American Anthropologist* 58 (1956): 264–81.

Wardell, Morris L. *A Political History of the Cherokee Nation, 1838–1907*. Norman: University of Oklahoma Press, 1938.

Warren, Hanna R. "Reconstruction in the Cherokee Nation." *Chronicles of Oklahoma* 45 (1967): 180–89.

Weibel-Orlando, Joan. "Indians, Ethnicity, and Alcohol: Contrasting Perceptions of the Ethnic Self and Alcohol Use." In *The American Experience with Alcohol: Contrasting Cultural Perspectives*, edited by Linda A. Bennett and Genevieve M. Ames, 201–26. New York and London: Plenum Press, 1985.

Westermeyer, Joseph. "'The Drunken Indian': Myths and Realities." *Psychiatric Annals* 4 (1974): 29–36.

White, Richard. *The Roots of Dependency: Subsistence, Environment, and Social Change among the Choctaws, Pawnees, and Navajos.* Lincoln and London: University of Nebraska Press, 1983.

Wilkins, Thurman. *Cherokee Tragedy: The Story of the Ridge Family and the Decimation of a People.* New York: Macmillan, 1970.

Willard, Frances E. *Woman and Temperance or the Work and Workers of the Woman's Christian Temperance Union.* 6th ed. Chicago: The Temple, 1897.

Williams, Sam'l C. "Christian Missions to the Overhill Cherokees." *Chronicles of Oklahoma* 12 (1934): 66–73.

Winkler, A. M. "Drinking on the American Frontier." *Quarterly Journal of Studies on Alcohol* 29 (1968): 413–45.

Wissler, Clark. *Indians of the United States: Four Centuries of Their History and Culture.* Garden City NY: Doubleday & Company, Inc., 1940.

Witthoft, John. "The Cherokee Green Corn Medicine and the Green Corn Festival." *Journal of the Washington Academy of Sciences* 36, no. 7 (1946): 213–19.

Wright, James R., Jr. "The Assiduous Wedge: Woman Suffrage and the Oklahoma Constitutional Convention." *Chronicles of Oklahoma* 51 (Winter 1973–74): 421–43.

Wright, Muriel H. "Samuel Austin Worcester: A Dedication." *Chronicles of Oklahoma* 37 (1959): 2–21.

Young, Mary E. "The Exercise of Sovereignty in Cherokee Georgia." *Journal of the Early Republic* 10 (1990): 43–64.

Dissertations and Theses

Flanagan, Johnny Tyrone, Jr. "Drink of a Cup Filled with Anger: The Interaction of Indians, Spirituous Liquors, Europeans, and Americans on the Southeastern Frontier." Master's thesis, University of Kentucky, 1994.

Ishii, Izumi. "The Cherokee Temperance Movement: An Internal Struggle for a Sober Nation before the 'Trail of Tears.'" Master's thesis, University of Kentucky, 1996.

Ivie, Mattie Louise. "Woman Suffrage in Oklahoma 1890–1918." Master's thesis, Oklahoma State University, 1971.

Wickham, Wendy Marie. "Tea Which Grows Here: Cassina Tea in Colonial Georgia." Master's thesis, University of Georgia, 1994.

Zwick, Gwen W. "Prohibition in the Cherokee Nation, 1820–1907." Master's thesis, University of Oklahoma, 1940.

INDEX

abstinence: missionaries on, 63;
pledge of western Cherokees
for, 65–66, 76, 101–5, 107, 138,
141; resolutions for, 63, 64
Adair, James, 16, 21
Adair, John Lafeyette, 197n61
Adair, Walter S., 102, 187n19
agriculture. *See* farming
Alabama, 57, 74–75, 78, 80, 84
alcohol: ceremonial uses of,
13–15, 32–34, 36, 44, 45, 173n14,
180n16; Cherokee terms for,
15–16; as commodity, 7, 21; as
gift, 16; history of in Cherokee Nation, 2, 7–8, 165–68;
medicinal uses of, 14–15, 33,
64, 65, 74, 112–14, 152–53, 160,
165–66, 172n7; significance of
Cherokee regulation of, 39,
50, 57–58, 165; for solace, 81,
83. *See also specific types*
alcohol addiction, 170n17;
occurrence of among Native
Americans, 5, 6
alcoholism: of Coody, 197n61;
diagnosis of, 4, 170n17;

occurrence of among Native
Americans, 5, 6, 36
ale. *See* malt liquors
American Board of Commis-
sioners for Foreign Missions,
59, 61–63, 73, 101
Americans: and business partnerships with Cherokees,
42–44; and Cherokee land,
57; and Cherokee tax law, 49;
and citizenship, 89, 95, 111,
117, 119–21, 131, 155, 193n26,
196n47, 203n35, 203n36,
209n31; drinking behavior
of, 61, 67–70, 73; as laborers
in Cherokee country, 116–17;
and prohibition, 130; and
punishment by Cherokees,
56; and responsibility for
alcohol problems, 47, 63,
67–81, 131, 147–48, 156, 166–68;
and temperance movement,
60–61, 69
American Temperance Society
(ATS), 61
annuity payments, 52, 56, 185n53

245

Butterfly (interpreter), 149

Caddo, 144
caffeinated beverages, 14, 171n4
Calhoun, John C., 50, 184n44
Calhoun TN, 78
Campaign Committee of the
Constitutional Convention,
159
Candy's Creek TN, 63–64, 66
Cannon, B. B., 85
Carnes, Peter A., 88, 193n19
Carthage TN, 46
Cary, James, 89–90
Cass, Lewis, 89, 90
Catabawa Indians, 17, 23
Chamberlain, Rev. William, 74
Charlestown TN, 17, 21–23, 27
Chatuga, 31
Cherokee Advocate: on alcohol
and weapons, 129, 130; on
alcohol as medicine, 113–14,
152; on enforcement of law,
107; on malt liquors, 151–52;
and reports of violence,
95–97, 99–100; on sovereign-
ty, 159–60; on temperance
activities, 101, 104, 136, 137–40,
146, 148; on U.S. soldiers,
212n56
Cherokee Cold Water Army, 10,
102–4, 109
Cherokee Constitution (1827),
66, 67, 187nn17–18
Cherokee Female Seminary, 133
Cherokee Female Society for
Doing Good, 66, 91

Cherokee Indians, western: and
abstinence pledge, 65–66,
76, 101–5, 107, 138, 141; and
Brown, 187n21; citizenship
of, 190n40; intemperance
among, 64–65, 87–88; and political disunity, 93–95, 100–111;
and sovereignty, 86–87, 108–9
Cherokee Nation: citizenship
of, 89, 95, 111, 117, 119–21,
131, 190n40, 193n26, 196n47,
203n35, 203n36, 209n31;
demise of, 11, 57–58, 75–76,
155–56, 167; disunity in, 93–95,
100–101; failure to enforce
laws of, 134; incarceration and
trials of, 126–28; jurisdiction
of, 56, 117–19, 121, 129–31, 155;
laws passed by, 45–47, 53–54;
petition to Arkansas by,
105–6; revitalization of, 9–10,
39, 58, 166–67; and war of
independence, 35
Cherokee National Committee,
53, 55, 101–2, 107
Cherokee National Council,
129–30; authority of, 50, 51;
on deputy marshals, 118;
Georgia's disregard of, 57,
75–76; on intermarriage, 95,
196n47; and permits, 92, 116;
on prohibition, 53, 89, 94–97;
and tax law, 49; and temperance activities, 70, 101, 108,
136, 138, 141, 146, 148–49; and
Trade and Intercourse Act,
42–44

temperance activities, 136, 144; uses of alcohol by, 34

crime: alcohol as cause of, 156; punishment for, 117–19, 129–30; and U.S. soldiers, 212n56

cultural identity, 4–6, 13, 35–36. *See also* anomie

Cumberland Road, 42–43, 46

Curtis Act (1898), 155

Cuthbertson, Robert, 119–20

dances, 53

Davis, Lucy Belle, 160–63

Dawes Commission, 155

Dawes General Allotment Act (1887), 155. *See also* land

Dearborn, Henry, 41

Deas, Edward, 85

De Brahm, John Gerar William, 13

debts, 21

deerskin trade: alcohol as commodity in, 7, 8, 13–14, 21, 26–27, 36; demise of, 166; effect of war on, 17, 35

Demere, Raymond, 27–34

Denver, James W., 111–12

Department of the Missouri, 112

Detroit MI, 127–28

diplomacy, 13–14, 17–19, 27–33

doctors, 153

Doublehead (Cherokee), 43

Dowey, David, 21

Downing, Lewis (Cherokee), 118, 121–24, 149, 204n41

Downingville, 114

Dozier, Edward P., 3

Drew, John, 89

drinking behavior: of Americans, 61, 67–70; Anglo perceptions of Cherokee, 35–36, 41, 45; and Cherokee anomie, 8–9, 35; of Native Americans, 3–5, 166; of traders, 19–21. *See also* drunkenness

drugstores, 153

Drunken Comportment (MacAndrew and Edgerton), 3

drunkenness: American opinions on, 179n4; excuses for, 34, 179n102; punishment for, 129, 141. *See also* drinking behavior

Duncan, DeWitt Clinton (Cherokee), 141, 143

Duncan, Helen R., 143

Duncan, Rev. W. A., 138

"Dupleix" (Arkansan), 97

DuVal, William, 88, 193n19

Eastern Oklahoma Woman's Christian Temperance Union, 161–62

Eaton, John H., 88

Edgerton, Robert B., 3, 5

education, 9, 62, 146, 154–55

Ellett, Katie, 140

Elliott, James, 28–30

Eufaula, 144, 159

European contact, 1–4, 7, 13, 16, 168. *See also* France; Great Britain

Evans, J. P., 45

Great Warrior of Chota, 29, 30
Green Corn Ceremony, 15, 45,
    172n7
Griffith, Mary E., 142
Gunter, Edward, 187n19
Gunter's Island, 84
Gunter's Landing, 84

Hagey, Charitey, 16
Hamer, John H., 3
Handsome Lake, 9
Harper, Peter, 89, 194n26
Harris, C. J., 153
Harris, Elbert, 92–93
Harrison, Benjamin, 152
Hastings, Theophilus, 18
Hatley, Tom, 7, 178n99
Hatton, William, 19
Henry, Samuel, 54
Herring, Elbert, 75, 90, 91
Hicks, Charles, 55, 56
Hicks, Elijah, 137
Hicks, Emma, 139–40
Hillerman, Abbie B., 161–62
Hillsboro OH, 135
Hitchcock, Ethan Allen, 94–95
Hitchcock, I. B., 146
Hiwassee Old Town, 31
Holland, William, 63–64
Holston River Valley, 33
Hopi Indians, 4, 5
horse stealing, 35
House Committee on Indian
    Affairs, 70
Huckleberry, James H., 120
Hudson, Charles, 172n6
Huffacre, Michael, 183n35

Hughs, Bernard, 22
Huss, John, 187n19

Indian Journal, 136
Indian police, 149n50
Indian Removal Bill (1830),
    57–58, 72–73. *See also* removal
Indian superintendency system:
    26–27, 176n72, 179n1
Indian Territory Woman's Chris-
    tian Temperance Union: an-
    nual conventions, 144–45; on
    beer sales, 151–52; and Indian
    statehood, 158, 160–64; Stapler
    as president of, 144–48, 153
    See also Tahlequah Woman's
    Christian Temperance Union
International Temperance
    Convention, 136

Jackson, Andrew, 44, 57, 59, 73,
    183n34
Jamaica ginger, 153
James, William M. (Cherokee),
    125–26
Jefferson, Thomas, 40, 41–42
Jones, John B., 113, 115–16, 123,
    203n35
Jore, 172n5
Journal of Communication, 71–72
Judge, Degardunah, 149

Kansas and Arkansas Valley
    Railway, 149
Karankawa Indians, 173n14
the "Katy" (Missouri, Kansas, and
    Texas Railway Co.), 115, 149, 151

social class, 61

South Carolina: deerskin trade in, 7; embargo in, 22–27, 36; and licensing of traders, 19–20; prohibition of alcohol sales in, 16–17; rum smuggling in, 28–33

Southern District of North America, 20

sovereignty: and Cherokee sovereignty (*cont.*) alcohol regulation, 9–10, 36–37, 39, 50, 52, 56–58, 70, 83, 111, 130–31, 165, 168; Marshall's recognition of Cherokee, 75; missionaries on, 59; and prohibition, 156–64; and railroads, 134; and temperance movement, 133; and Trade and Intercourse Acts, 92, 122–23; U.S. government on, 51–52, 56–58, 157–58, 166, 183n37; of western Cherokees, 86–87, 108–9

Spaniard, Polly, 99

spirituality, 8–9, 13–15, 36

Stapler, John W., 137, 139

Stapler, L. Jane, 137, 139, 143–47, 151–53

state laws, 10. *See also specific states*

St. Augustine FL, 178n99

Stevens, Lillian M. N., 161

Sticoe SC, 22

Stinson (American), 46–47

St. Johns River, 178n99

Stokes, Montfort, 92–93

Stuart, John, 20, 90–91, 93

Supreme Court of Georgia, 78

Sutherland, Mabel R., 160, 161

Sweet, Miss, 141

Swiney, Jeremiah, 22

Tacit (Cherokee), 23

Tahlequah: enforcement of law at, 107, 125; Hitchcock at, 95; meeting on Fort Gibson at, 100; temperance activities at, 101–3, 136, 138, 139, 140, 145, 148–9. *See also* Tahlequah Woman's Christian Temperance Union; Woman's Christian Temperance Union (WCTU)

Tahlequah Baptist Church, 138, 139

Tahlequah Christian Temperance Union, 134, 138–40.

Tahlequah Presbyterian Church, 141, 146

Tahlequah Telephone, 142

Tahlequah Woman's Christian Temperance Union: on alcohol as medicine, 153; at Cherokee National Council meetings, 141, 146, 148–49; formation of, 137–38; Griffith before, 142; Perkins before, 143–45; praise of, 154–55; reinvigorating activities of, 140–41. Stapler as president of, 143–44.

Tannehill, Ninnian, 126

Tanner, George, 126

tuberculosis, 128
Tuckasegee NC, 25
Tulsa OK, 144
Tunstall, Martha G., 141–42, 209n31
Tuscumbia AL, 86
Tuttle, Emeline H., 136
typhoid fever, 113
Tyrrell, Ian R., 60–61
Union Signal, 140, 142, 146, 156
Unrau, William E., 169n2
U.S. Army: and alcohol as medicine, 112–13; and Cherokee temperance activities, 103; confinement by, 78; purchase of alcohol by, 97–100, 212n56; and right to inspect for alcohol, 53
U.S. Congress: and annuity deductions, 185n53; and Cherokee tax law, 52; failure of, 147; on Indian statehood, 157, 158; Jefferson's address to, 40; on judicial districts, 122; on land allotments, 155; and malt liquors, 152; power of to regulate alcohol trade, 179n1; and railroads, 114; and removal, 57–58, 73; and Trade and Intercourse Acts, 41–42, 123–24; and Treaty of New Echota, 77; and Tunstall, 209n31
U.S. Constitution, 40, 55, 179n1
U.S. Court for the Eastern District of Texas, 151, 152
U.S. Court for the Western District of Arkansas: abuse at, 127–28, 131; authority of, 117–31; and Going Snake Tragedy, 203n36; location of, 202n24; and Trade and Intercourse Act, 122, 124–25; trips to, 126–28
U.S. Court of Claims, 209n31
U.S. deputy marshals, 117–26, 131, 151–52, 203n36
U.S. District Courts, 117–31; on alcohol-related crimes, 156; on beer sales, 151–52; promise by to establish in Indian territory, 117, 131. *See also* U.S. Court for the Eastern District of Texas; U.S. Court for the Western District of Arkansas
U.S. government: Archer on laws of, 133–34; attempts by to regulate alcohol, 10, 21–22, 39–42, 45, 53, 88–91, 147, 168; and bootleggers, 152; on Cherokee jurisdiction, 117–19; on Cherokee revitalization, 166; and Cherokee sovereignty, 51–52, 56–58, 157–58, 166, 183n37; and "civilization" program, 39–41, 56–57, 71–73, 155–56, 167; and "drunken Indian" image, 1; on removal, 71–75, 86. *See also* U.S. District Courts
U.S. Supreme Court, 166

Van Buren, Martin, 79
Van Buren AR, 202n24

Vann, Andrew (Cherokee), 94
Vann, James (Cherokee), 43, 46
Vann, Joseph, 182n30
Vashon, George, 88–90
"Veritas" (letter writer), 98–99
Vinita, 113–16, 140, 144
violence: on Arkansas border, 96–97; in Cherokee Nation, 45–48, 129–30; in families, 83–84; at Fort Gibson, 99–100; at U.S. District Court in Arkansas, 127–28, 131. *See also* murders
Virginia, 23

Waddell, Jack O., 6
Walker, John, Jr., 54
Wallace, Zerelda G., 148
Wardell, Morris L., 10
War Department, 51, 52, 90, 114
war preparation, 8, 15, 32–33, 44, 165–66, 178n99
Washburn, Cephas, 86–87
Waters, George M., 187n19
WCTU. *See* Woman's Christian Temperance Union (WCTU)
weapons, 129–30, 165
Webber, Walter, 89–90
Webbers Falls, 118, 144, 153
Webster, L. B., 78
Wells-Fargo Express Company, 149
whiskey: Americans' sale of to Cherokees, 44, 54, 57, 74, 78, 88–90, 125; availability of to western Cherokees, 93, 96, 131, 136, 156; at ball game, 45;

ceremonial uses of, 173n14; Cherokee courts on, 129; Cherokee destruction of, 95, 107; at Fort Gibson, 97–99; at Fort Smith, 88, 96, 119, 127; as medicine, 113; and "planting," 125; and railroads, 115–16; on removal journeys, 83–87; Rogers's sale of, 89, 193n24; and violence, 46–48; vote buying with, 148–49
White, Hugh Lawson, 50–51, 182n34
White, James B., 125
White, Richard, 9, 36
White Mankiller, 33
White Mountain Apache Indians, 4
Wicket, Jack, 62–63
Willard, Frances E., 135–38, 141, 145–46, 149
"William Penn" essays, 73
Williams (man from Estatoe), 27–28
Williamsburg VA, 23
Willstown Mission, 33, 74
wine, 91, 122, 124, 150, 152
Wirt, William, 51–52, 183n37
Woman's Christian Temperance Union (WCTU): on alcohol-related crimes, 156; and Cherokee women, 167; convention in Atlanta, 147–48; and Indian statehood, 156–58, 160–64; origins of, 134–36; on Tunstall, 209n31; visits to Indian territory by, 136–46.